Contents at a Glance

Table of Contents

Windows 8

ABSOLUTE
BEGINNER'S
GUIDE

Paul Sanna

800 East 96th Street,
Indianapolis, Indiana 46240

Windows 8 Absolute Beginner's Guide

ISBN-13: 978-0-7897-4993-2
ISBN-10: 0-7897-4993-9

Second Printing December 2012

Trademarks

All terms mentioned in this book that are known to be trademarks or service marks have been appropriately capitalized. Que Publishing cannot attest to the accuracy of this information. Use of a term in this book should not be regarded as affecting the validity of any trademark or service mark.

Warning and Disclaimer

Every effort has been made to make this book as complete and as accurate as possible, but no warranty or fitness is implied. The information provided is on an "as is" basis. The author and the publisher shall have neither liability nor responsibility to any person or entity with respect to any loss or damages arising from the information contained in this book.

Bulk Sales

Que Publishing offers excellent discounts on this book when ordered in quantity for bulk purchases or special sales. For more information, please contact

U.S. Corporate and Government Sales
1-800-382-3419
corpsales@pearsontechgroup.com

For sales outside of the U.S., please contact

International Sales
international@pearsoned.com

Editor-in-Chief
Greg Wiegand

Executive Editor
Loretta Yates

Development Editor
Todd Brakke

Managing Editor
Sandra Schroeder

Project Editor
Seth Kerney

Copy Editor
Apostrophe Editing Services

Indexer
Brad Herriman

Proofreader
Sheri Cain

Technical Editor
J. Boyd Nolan

Publishing Coordinator
Cindy Teeters

Cover Designer
Anne Jones

Compositor
Trina Wurst

About the Author

Paul Sanna is a software professional, and he is the author or co-author of two dozen computer books on topics such as Windows 2000, Internet Explorer, VBA, Windows security, and more. He has been writing about computers since his first literary agent said to him many years ago, "I didn't know Boston University had an English program," and "Have you heard of this Windows 95 thing?" Mr. Sanna has worked in the IT field his entire career, building software, selling high tech, helping customers understand how to be successful with technology, and helping to market breakthrough analytics technology. His home with his family is in Charlotte, NC. Go Gamecocks!

Dedication

To Andrea—my beautiful bride of almost 25 years.

Acknowledgments

No one deserves more credit for helping this project cross the finish line than Loretta Yates, my editor. Thanks for having faith in me, for working with my strengths and interest to come up with a project, for the support and great ideas, and for gently whacking me every time I looked for more time. Todd Brakke, the development editor, hereby known as "The Architect," is the man for keeping the book cohesive, smart, focused, and organized. J. Boyd Nolan, the technical editor, kept me honest and accurate, and thanks to San Dee Phillips who deserves a big raise after editing my work!

The unnamed co-captain of this project is my wife, who kept me happy, well-fed, focused, and in clean clothes throughout. This could not have been done without her. Thanks also to the three absolute beginners whom I channeled, namely Andrea, Mom, and Bob—thanks for the ideas and perspectives. Please stay novices forever (or as long as I write beginner books).

I have to acknowledge my precious daughters, Rachel, Allison, and Tori, checking on me and bringing me smoothies, snacks, candy, and sandwiches (and imploring me to get sleep!). Thanks to Karsyn and Camryn for their regular visits to Mr. Paul. Finally, no list of acknowledgments would be complete without mentioning Abby, my 15-pound cocker spaniel/golden retriever mix who never left my side, from proposal to last chapter.

We Want to Hear from You!

As the reader of this book, *you* are our most important critic and commentator. We value your opinion and want to know what we're doing right, what we could do better, what areas you'd like to see us publish in, and any other words of wisdom you're willing to pass our way.

We welcome your comments. You can email or write us directly to let us know what you did or didn't like about this book—as well as what we can do to make our books better.

Please note that we cannot help you with technical problems related to the topic of this book.

When you write, please be sure to include this book's title and author as well as your name, email address, and phone number. We will carefully review your comments and share them with the author and editors who worked on the book.

Email: feedback@quepublishing.com

Mail: Que Publishing
         ATTN: Reader Feedback
         800 East 96th Street
         Indianapolis, IN 46240 USA

Reader Services

Visit our website and register this book at www.informit.com/title/9780789749932 for convenient access to any updates, downloads, or errata that might be available for this book.

IN THIS INTRODUCTION

- What this book covers
- How this book is organized
- Conventions for menu commands, keyboard short-cuts, and mouse and trackpad actions used in this book
- Special elements used to call your attention to notes, tips, and cautions
- How to send the author your feedback

INTRODUCTION

I am delighted you are reading this introduction, whether you're considering buying this book or because you already own it. I'm sure you'll find value reading it and using it while you wrestle with this beast called Windows 8.

Windows 8 is just a few years removed from Windows 7, but it's incredibly different from its predecessors. Microsoft easily could have called this release "Windows 2020" or "Not Your Parents' Windows." The user interface, which is the near-technical term that describes the part of the software you see and touch and control, is quite different. Gone is our old friend, the Start menu, and in its place is an exciting layout of tiles, each representing a piece of software installed on your system.

The new style of applications you use in Windows 8 (known as Windows 8-style apps) are attractive, engaging, and fast. They run full screen; sit flat on your monitor with no raised buttons or widgets; take advantage of video and animation better than any prior Windows release; and behave quite nicely in the sandbox with other apps—seldom crashing or locking up Windows. The Windows 8 start-up process is so quick, you'll wonder whether you really clicked Restart or you just imagined doing so. And if you're pining for the old Windows Desktop to run all your existing Windows 7 applications, it's just a touch, click, or swipe away.

Yep, for you beginners, that means there's basically two wholly different Windows environments to learn. Good thing there's a book out there for the absolute beginner; am I right?

This book is intended to help you, whether you're new to Windows or just new to Windows 8 to accomplish whatever it is you need or want to do during your personal or professional day. If you walk into the office and find your computer has been upgraded to Windows 8, you can read how to run (and where to find) your old programs. You can learn how to move around the system, and how to work with your old files. You can also learn how to do those seemingly difficult administrative functions such as setting up a printer or a second monitor.

If Windows 8 is loaded on a new computer you acquire for use at home, you can learn how to connect in all those social media networks, such as Facebook and Twitter. You can see how to have fun with all those photos you take and those that are shared with you. You can read how to buy and enjoy movies, music, and games. And for those times when work follows you home, or your personal time is overrun by home business tasks, such as homework or creating a budget, you can learn how to be productive and efficient.

For the hardware you use to run Windows 8, Microsoft has made a big deal about how Windows 8 can run on laptops, workstations, servers, and tablets. Allowing for form factor differences, the user interface is identical on all devices with the exception of how you interact with it: mouse, keyboard, stylus, speech, or touch. This book works for you regardless of the hardware you use. Although this book doesn't cover the unique capabilities of certain models, such as the Samsung Series 7, you can follow along with the lessons, how-to's, and explanations using whatever hardware you have. The screenshots shown in this book come from a wide range of devices, some from small laptops, others from gigantic servers, and a few from tablets. Odds are you won't see a difference between them.

What Is an Absolute Beginner?

The book is respectful of your level of expertise. You are probably either new to Windows or, especially, new to Windows 8. You probably can handle a mouse and a keyboard, but the book guides you the moment your computer or tablet starts on through all the most common functions you're likely to demand from it.

If, in looking this book over, you feel your expertise is just short of what may be needed for this book—if you aren't comfortable using a mouse and keyboard, for example—you should consider reading *Computer Basics Absolute Beginner's Guide* by Michael Miller (Pearson Education, 2012).

How This Book Is Organized

The book is divided into five parts. All the chapters in a part are related. For example, Part 2, "Getting Connected," contains chapters that help you connect to the Internet, as well as help you stay connected with your family, friends, and work associates. The chapters are grouped into parts to make it easy for you to find information related to what you're reading. You can read chapters and parts in any order you like with one exception:

- Chapter 1, "Starting and Stopping Windows 8," and Chapter 3, "Learning Windows 8 Basics," covers the new Windows 8-style bells, buttons, windows, and whistles in some detail. Chapter 1 presents the basics, whereas Chapter 3 focuses on the Start screen. If you are new to Windows 8, and only folks who have used Windows Phone 7 or worked with the Windows 8 Preview releases can say they're not, you should probably give these chapters a close read.

- If you are brand new to Windows, you'll also want to spend some time with Chapter 10, "Sharing Your Windows 8 Computer with Others." This chapter explains how to navigate and take action in the smaller Windows 7-like environment.

Each chapter in this book follows a standard format; although, there are diversions from the format here and there. The first section in each chapter is a short list describing the things you can learn and do in the chapter, along with a brief description of the chapter and why it's important to you. This short section in each chapter closes with important information that alerts you to any particularly important techniques or gestures you need to know to complete the tasks described in the chapter, as well as where in the book to find that guidance. Here is an example:

The Mail app is a new Windows 8-style app. As such, it relies on many of the techniques covered in Chapter 3. Refer to that chapter if you need help, or perhaps review the entire chapter if you need a refresher. Pay particular attention to these features, which play an important role in this chapter:

- Displaying the App bar, which reveals several formatting commands you can use to dress up your email.
- Opening the Setting charm, where you specify the various email accounts you can consolidate in the Mail app.

From that point, the chapter gets underway. You can find a number of elements to help you understand the topic of the chapter.

That's it. So now that you've got that down, here is the list of parts that organize all the chapters:

- **Part I, "Getting Started,"** is a great introduction to Windows 8. You learn how to navigate through the screens and applications, how to sign-in and sign-out, and, most important, how to spruce up Windows 8 so it feels just like home. You learn how to adjust the colors, how to add photos as a background to some screens, how to change the resolution of your display, and how to set the keyboard and certain screens to match your language and culture.

- **Part II, "Getting Connected,"** gets you connected! Every Windows user needs to access the Internet, so the first chapter in this part helps you do so, regardless of whether you use a cable modem, DSL, or dial-up, and whether you connect from home, the gym, a café, or wherever. When connected, you can send emails, see what your friends are up to through all the new social media channels, send instant messages, launch a video chat conversation, and last-but-not-least, browse the web. Microsoft has built several new Windows 8-style apps to help you with these tasks. The chapters in this part help you set up these apps, including loading up the names of all your contacts in Facebook, Twitter, Hotmail, Exchange, Google, and LinkedIn, and you can learn how to use them to keep connected.

- **Part III, "Punching the Clock,"** covers the parts of Windows 8 that you'll probably use doing your job or executing a task. You learn how to work in the Desktop environment, and in that environment, how to manage files and folders. The part also includes a chapter designed to help you manage all the files and data in your system, stored in external drives and in the Cloud. The chapters in this part don't show off the most exciting or charming elements of Windows 8, but the chapters can help you take advantage of a number of important features.

- **Part IV, "Configuring and Protecting,"** helps you complete some tasks that you might consider advanced, such as setting up new hardware, deleting some unused files to create more disk space, protecting your computer from viruses, and backing up your data. The information is presented at a pace and in a tone that you can understand and learn from. You must understand how to troubleshoot and prevent problems and how to solve problems that are slightly more complicated.

- **Part V, "After Hours with Windows,"** is the fun section of this book. You learn how to set up Windows 8 to play movies, music, videos, and games. Not only can you learn how to bring in your collections, but also, you can learn how to shop through the massive marketplaces Windows 8 accesses for you. Because Xbox 360, the game and entertainment console from Microsoft, is so integrated into Windows, you learn how to connect to it and take advantage of its features, such as controlling Xbox from your computer and even buying games from your computer. Although this part is referred to as "After Hours," you might use it 24/7.

Conventions Used in This Book

This book is easy to understand. Even though Windows 8 might be hard to learn, to help make your task of learning Windows simpler, certain types of instructions are formatted or written in a specific way to keep them consistent. Some decisions were made as to how to handle all the interfaces to Windows 8: keyboard, mouse, and touch. You can read about how to handle the keyboard instructions, as well as all these conventions, in the next few short sections.

Selects and Selecting

Windows asks you to do lots of things. You're asked to click here, choose that, press this, and enter these. Given that you might use a touch-driven tablet or a mouse and keyboard, some of the instructions in the book are streamlined to reduce confusion by settling, as often as possible, on using the word "select." When you see Select, you complete the most natural action for the thing you are asked to select, whether that's a click of the mouse or a finger tap of the screen.

That established, this book loves and features the mouse. Every how-to, detailed explanation, or quick tip or timesaver leads with use of the mouse. You'll have no trouble following instructions such as, "With your mouse, click here," or "Double-click the smiley face picture."

Touchscreen users can find countless sets of specific instructions to interact with Windows 8 via touch whenever the gesture for doing so with a touchscreen device is not obvious or is notably different than doing so with a mouse.

Finally, although you can accomplish most tasks in Windows 8 with a mouse or via touch, there's still a lot you can do with a keyboard that enables you to work faster than with a mouse or touch. With that in mind, you'll find plenty of keyboard shortcuts throughout the book.

Special Elements

A few special tools emphasize certain points and concepts that might not be directly related to the topic discussed but are important enough to mention. These elements come in the form of Tips, Cautions, and Notes, examples of which you can find here.

 NOTE   A note is a useful piece of information that is not quite part of the core topic of the chapter or the section of the chapter where the note appears.

 TIP   A tip is a useful piece of information that should help you get your work done a bit faster or a bit better in Windows 8.

 CAUTION   A caution appears if there is a particular pitfall you must avoid or if there's a chance of losing your data executing one of the procedures in the book.

1

STARTING AND STOPPING WINDOWS 8

If you have just brought home a new computer with Windows 8 preinstalled, or if your computer has just been upgraded to Windows 8, maybe you're thinking, "Now what?" The obvious answer is to power up your computer and sign in to Windows 8. Like everything else in Windows 8, though, the power-up and sign-in phases are quite different than those in prior versions of Windows, especially Windows 7. And if you haven't used Windows before, the start-up process appears unique. For these reasons, this chapter walks you through the steps necessary to start your computer and then sign in to Windows. You also learn how to put your computer to sleep if you won't be using it for a while, plus you learn how to exit Windows 8. First to cover, though, is powering up your Windows 8 hardware and then signing in to Windows 8.

Starting Up Windows 8

Before you can start up Windows 8, there are a couple of steps to take first. After these few steps of preparation, you can read next in this section how to power-up Windows and how manage if more than one operating system is stored on your computer. Think about these issues first:

- If someone other than you installed Windows 8, check with him for the user ID and password you should use. Be sure to ask if he used a *local account* or *a Windows account*. You'll learn more about these two different account types in Chapter 10, "Sharing Your Windows 8 Computer with Others" in the "Windows 8 Users and Account Basics" section.

- If you sign into Windows 8 for the first time at your place of business, check with a person from your IT or Support organization for your user ID and password, and, if required, your domain. The domain identifies what part of the corporate network you log into. If your computer has been upgraded to Windows 8, your user ID, password, and domain are probably the same as you used previously.

- If you couldn't connect to the Internet for some reason when Windows 8 was installed, it would be helpful to be able to connect now. Try to address your connection issues before starting Windows 8.

Powering Up Your Computer

If your computer is off, or *powered down*, you need to power it up to start your Windows 8 experience. If you are turning the computer on for the first time after installing Windows 8, be sure the DVD has been removed from the DVD drive or else your system could restart the installation program.

 NOTE   When a computer starts, a number of internal programs run to prepare the computer for operation. You will likely see a flurry of messages run up your screen in white text over a black background. These messages aren't required, though, so don't call the hotline if you don't see anything happen initially. Depending on your type of your computer, this initial startup process might run for just a second or two or for a few minutes,

When the computer start-up process is complete, Windows takes over control of your computer, launching its own start-up process. You can tell Windows has started by the appearance of the Windows logo, as shown in Figure 1.1.

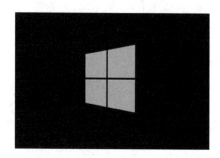

FIGURE 1.1

The appearance of this Windows 8 logo indicates Windows has taken over control of your device.

Shortly after Windows starts, the sign-in screen appears, enabling you to finally sign in. Before that sign-in screen appears, however, you may have one more step to take, as covered in the next section.

Choosing an Operating System

If another version of Windows were installed and running properly on your computer when Windows 8 was installed, whomever installed Windows 8 may have chosen to create a *dual-boot* setup. This setup enables you to choose the operating system to use when the computer is turned on—yes, this is possible. You may be wondering, "Why wouldn't I want to use Windows 8 if it were installed?" Here are a few reasons:

- You have a number of older Windows programs, and you rely on these programs. As much as Microsoft expresses confidence that your programs will run in Windows 8, you might not want to commit to Windows 8 until you are sure your programs run properly.

- You are not sure you have time to learn Windows 8.

You can find more information about dual-booting in the "Understanding Dual-Booting" section. For now, learn how to respond if Windows prompts you to choose an operating system.

If a screen like the one shown in Figure 1.2 appears, you must choose which operating system you want to work with. Presumably, Windows 8 is the choice. If, instead of a screen like the one in Figure 1.2, you see a screen with either a single sign-in portrait or multiple sign-in portraits, as shown in Figure 1.3 (with your own name and email address, of course), you don't need to worry about dual-booting for now, and you can skip to the "Signing In to Windows 8" section.

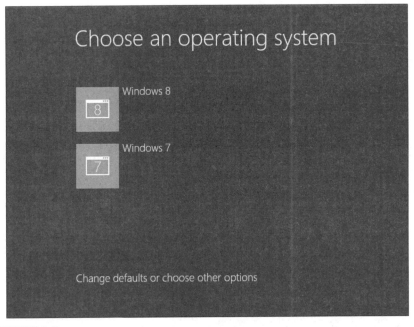

FIGURE 1.2

You can use Windows 8 or your old operating system (Windows 7 in this case).

FIGURE 1.3

If a screen with one or more sign-in portraits appears, dual-booting has not been enabled.

NOTE The screen shown in Figure 1.2 depicts a system in which Windows 8 is installed on a computer running Windows 7. A computer might have more than two operating systems, in which case there are three or more choices shown on the menu. Your computer might also show an older operating system, such as Windows XP or Windows Vista, as a choice.

Signing In to Windows 8

With your computer running and Windows 8 booted up, the next step is to sign in to Windows. You'll find a helpful step-by-step list to help you sign in successfully in a page or so. Before starting down the list, there are a few new alternatives to the venerable password in Windows 8 to talk about.

TIP If you wonder if "signing in" is the same as "logging in," you are correct. Microsoft has adopted the term, "signing in" to describe that process to identify one's self to Windows 8.

You probably are accustomed to entering a password to access secured content on websites, as well as to sign in to computers, tablets, and some software programs. The passwords you use might be a randomly-generated string of numbers and letters or they might be the names of members of your family or perhaps the name of your favorite sports hero.

Windows 8 provides an alternative to the password for use when signing-in. When you create your new account in Windows 8, you need to supply a password, but you can also specify use one of two new sign-in options, replacing the use of the password after you initially supply it. These two options are **PIN** and **Picture Password**. Besides saving you the repetitive stress of entering your password often, these two new options offer a lot of flexibility to determine how to access your user account. Plus, using them will certainly impress your friends and family!

- **PIN**—A PIN is a 4-digit number you use to identify yourself when you sign in to Windows. A PIN is particularly useful to tablet users who normally don't have a physical keyboard. On a tablet, a virtual keyboard appears on the screen as you sign in to Windows, enabling you to enter just your PIN to access Windows.

- **Picture Password**—If you have enjoyed drawing mustaches and other funny shapes on pictures of your friends and family, this is the password replacement for you. A picture password is a combination of a picture and touch gestures. To define a picture password, you choose a picture from your Pictures folder and then make three gestures, which can be your choice to tap or draw a line or circle. Windows records the position of the gestures, their length and the order in which you make them.

If you did not set up Windows, be sure to ask the person that did set up Windows if a PIN or Picture Password is used. For information on setting up one of these two options, refer to Chapter 10.

With all the preparation and explanations behind you, follow these steps to sign in to Windows 8:

1. You can sign in to Windows if the Welcome screen, also known as the Lock screen, appears, as shown in Figure 1.4. The picture in your Welcome/Lock screen might be different than the one shown here, but you can tell you're in the right place if you see the time and date superimposed on your picture.

FIGURE 1.4

The Windows Welcome screen appears when Windows 8 is locked, such as occurs if you do not enter your user ID and password promptly, or if you enter the command to lock Windows.

2. From the Welcome screen, swipe up, tap the spacebar, or click once on the screen. Any of these three gestures reveals the sign-in screen.

3. Select your portrait if more than one portrait appears (see Figure 1.5). If your portrait is the only portrait on the screen, skip this step and continue with step 4.

FIGURE 1.5

Select your portrait to sign in to Windows 8.

4. Your portrait should appear alone on the screen. From there, how you sign in depends on the type of password protection you have. Use the directions in the set of following sections that matches how your log in account is set up.

Signing In with Your Password

To sign in with your password, select your account from the sign in screen, as described in the previous section, and then follow these steps:

1. The cursor will be flashing inside the **Password** box, as shown in Figure 1.6. If it is not flashing, tap or click once in the **Password** box.

FIGURE 1.6

The flashing vertical line indicates you should enter your password.

2. Type your password. If you want to verify you entered your password correctly, tap-and-hold or click-and-hold the eye-shaped icon near the end of the Password box, as shown in Figure 1.7.

FIGURE 1.7

You can check that you entered your password accurately.

3. Select the arrow tile at the end of the Password box, or press **Enter**.

Signing In with Your PIN

To sign in with your PIN, follow these steps:

1. If the last time you signed in you used your PIN, a screen like the one shown in Figure 1.8 appears.

If you signed in last with your password or picture password, tap or click **Sign-in options**. The three sign-in tiles appear. Next, tap or click the PIN tile.

2. The cursor should be flashing inside the **PIN** box. If it is not flashing, tap or click once in the PIN box.

FIGURE 1.8

Windows "remembers" if you last signed-in with a PIN.

3. Enter your PIN. Note that you will be signed in immediately after correctly entering the last digit of your PIN.

Signing In with Your Picture Password

To sign in with your picture password, follow these steps:

1. If the last time you signed in, you used your picture password, a screen like the one shown in Figure 1.9 appears. (Your picture will be different than the one shown here.)

   If you signed in last with your password or PIN, tap or click **Sign-in options**. The three sign-in tiles appear. Next, tap or click the picture password tile. The Picture Password screen appears.

2. Make your three gestures on the picture.

FIGURE 1.9

The Picture Password screen appears if you last signed in using your picture password.

3. If you made a mistake, Windows 8 prompts you to try again. Select **OK** and (more accurately) make your three touch gestures on the picture. To redo the gestures before Windows prompts you, select **Start Over**. If you successfully make the three gestures, you are signed in and the Start screen appears.

Handling Special Windows 8 Startup Situations

As pointed earlier in this chapter, powering up your computer and then starting Windows 8 are easy, usually predictable tasks. Every once in a while, though, the unpredictable happens, and sometimes, you do things that are out of the norm. The next three sections look at some special situations that could occur during startup.

Restarting Windows After a Problem

The Microsoft engineers built Windows 8 to handle many problems, but there is always a chance that something can go wrong. Some software programs might interfere with others; hardware you add to your computer might interfere with Windows 8; and programs you download from the Internet can cause issues. As a result, Windows 8 can freeze, become sluggish, or shut down unexpectedly, and sometimes you may need to force your computer to power down. If Windows shuts down while experiencing problems, you might see the screen shown in Figure 1.10 when your computer restarts.

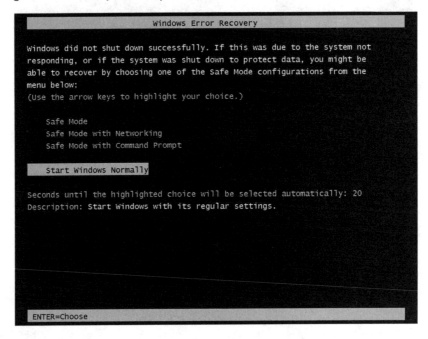

FIGURE 1.10

Windows guides you when it restarts if it crashes or shuts down unexpectedly.

If you have experience running Windows in one of the diagnostic modes listed, such as Safe Mode or Safe Mode with Networking, you can use one of those options. If you are like most users, select **Start Windows Normally** and press **Enter**. Ideally everything should run just like normal at this point. If it doesn't, refer to Chapter 21, "Troubleshooting and Problem Solving," for assistance troubleshooting Windows 8 problems.

Waking Up Windows

If, instead of powering off your system, you place Windows in sleep mode, eventually you need to wake up Windows to resume using your computer. Although some computers might use a different button for waking from sleep, it's most likely that you use the Power button on your computer. (Sometimes just moving or clicking your mouse works, too.) This doesn't mean you should press and hold the Power button until you see something happen. Rather, press the Power button once and then release it to wake up Windows. It's best to check the documentation that came with your computer or to check the computer manufacturer's website to confirm how to wake your computer.

 TIP   Be sure you do not hold the Power button too long. Doing so typically restarts the computer, which can cause problems with programs that were running when you put Windows 8 to sleep. Plus, you would lose any unsaved work.

Handling Messages You Might Receive While Signing In

Passwords are the one area of your account that requires regular maintenance (unless you regularly change your name). Windows 8 sends messages to you, reminding you what needs to be done with your password.

Expiring and Expired Passwords

You might see a message when you sign in informing you that your password will soon expire. Unless you have extremely tight controls over computer use at home, you will see this message only at work. If you see this message at work, it means your company has established a policy requiring you to change your password on a regular, scheduled basis.

If you see the message shown in Figure 1.11, your password has expired and you need to create a new one before you can use Windows 8. Seeing this message tells you that your company has established a policy requiring you change your password on a regular, scheduled basis.

FIGURE 1.11

This message appears if your password has expired.

Password Not Complex

If you see the message shown in Figure 1.12, your company has established a policy that passwords must be complex, and your password is too simple and easy to figure out. This message appears when you try to change your password, such as when it expires or when you change it on your own. Also, you need to follow the complexity rules when you create your password for the first time.

FIGURE 1.12

The password entered did not meet the minimum complexity requirements.

Here are the complexity requirements:

- The password cannot contain the user's account name or any more than two consecutive characters from the user's full name.

- The password must be at least six characters long.

- Of the four categories that follow, the password must match three of these characteristics:

  - Contains at least one English uppercase character (A through Z)

  - Contains at least one English lowercase character (a through z)

  - Contains at least one digit, 0–9)

  - Contains at least one non-alphabetic character (for example, !, $, #, %)

Exiting Windows

When you need to take a break from your computer and Windows 8, perhaps to shop for computer books, you should consider how long you will be away and in what state you should leave your computer. For example, if you are going to be away from your computer for a short period of time but you are working on sensitive information, you should lock your computer. Locking your computer immediately displays the Lock screen without affecting the programs running or the files that are open. This enables you to get back to work quickly as soon as you sign back in. With the sleep option, there are four choices available to manage your computer while you take a break.

Signing Out of Windows 8

You leave no trail behind when you sign out of Windows. Any programs running when you signed out are shut down, and any connections you had open are closed. If you attempted to sign out with unsaved work in either a Desktop or Windows 8 app, Windows 8 prompts you to save the work, as shown in Figure 1.13.

Closing 1 app and signing out

Letter to Maria and Jeff - WordPad
This app is preventing you from signing out.

FIGURE 1.13

You see a warning on the Start screen if you try to sign out with unsaved work.

To log out of Windows, use one of these methods:

- On the Start screen, select your portrait, and then select **Sign Out**.
- From the Desktop, press **Alt+F4**. Then, select **Sign Out** and tap or click **OK**.

Locking Windows 8

Locking Windows 8 is useful if you are going to be away from your computer but you want to resume your work or play when you return. Locking also prevents strangers from accessing the information on your computer.

To lock Windows 8, use one of these methods:

- Select your portrait on the Start screen and then select **Lock**.

- Press **Windows+L**.

Putting Windows 8 to Sleep

Windows 8 does not have a sleep command. You cannot put your computer into sleep mode with Windows 8. Instead, you must press the Power button on your computer to put it to sleep. However, your computer must be set up to put itself to sleep when the Power button is pressed, as shown in Figure 1.14. If your computer is instead set up to power down when the Power button is pressed, you could lose important unsaved data. You can put your computer to sleep with a few other options, but the Power button option seems like a good one to standardize on and that most computers support.

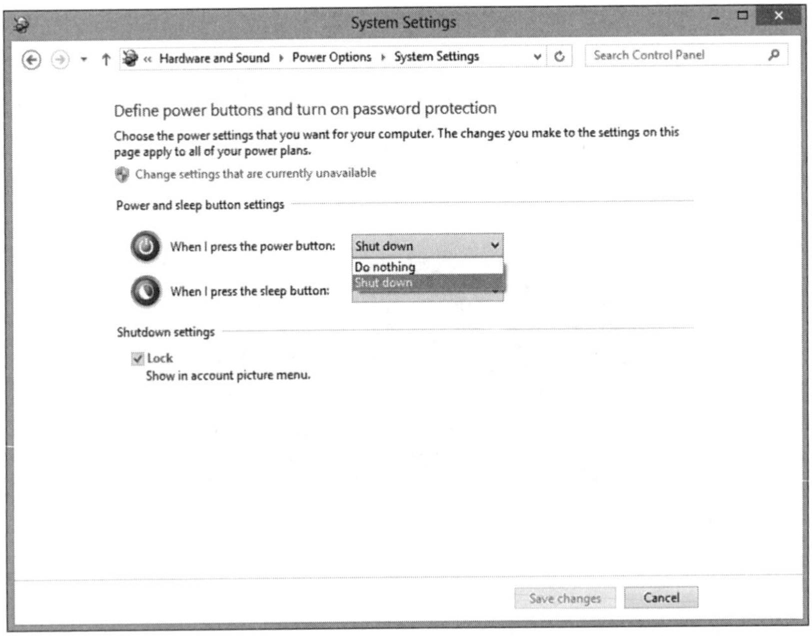

FIGURE 1.14

Two options are available to configure what happens when your computer sleeps and wakes up.

NOTE If you will not use your computer for a few days, it makes sense to put the computer to sleep. When a computer is asleep, it is still running, though in a low-power mode. Because you can leave your applications and documents open when you put your computer to sleep, it usually takes far less time to start work again by awakening a computer than to restart it and open the program you were working on.

Shutting Down Your Windows 8 Computer

You have a number of options available to shut down Windows 8. Regardless of the option you use, when you shut down Windows 8, your computer powers down. You don't need to close any running programs or apps, but you must save any unsaved work or you will lose your changes since the last time you saved.

To shut down Windows 8 if you use a Windows 8 application or are at the Start screen, do the following:

- From the **Settings** charm, choose **Power**, and then select **Shut Down**.

To shut down Windows 8 from the Desktop,

- Press Alt+F4. Then, select **Shut Down** and select **OK**, as shown in Figure 1.15.

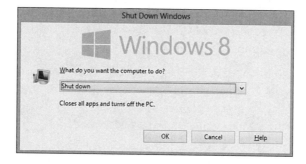

FIGURE 1.15

You may also issue the Shut Down command from the Desktop.

Restarting Windows 8 to Install Updates

A program as large and complicated as Windows is bound to have some unexpected problems, such as features that do not work as promised, programs that don't work at all, and conditions that cause Windows or your compute to shut down suddenly. In the software world, these problems are known as *bugs*. Don't worry. Microsoft, like most software companies, anticipates bugs. Short of an infestation, the engineers at Microsoft squash bugs and release small software programs that automatically update your computer with fixes to the bugs. Your computer must be restarted for the updates to take effect. You receive a notification that you must restart your computer, as shown in Figure 1.16. If you do not restart your computer soon enough, you are alerted again, this time being informed that Windows will automatically restart shortly.

Your PC will restart in 14 minutes, 52 seconds

Your PC needs to restart to finish installing updates. If you've already saved your work, you can restart now. Otherwise, you should close this message and use the remaining time to save anything you don't want to lose.

Restart   Close

FIGURE 1.16

Windows alerts you that you must restart your computer for updates to be applied.

THE ABSOLUTE MINIMUM

Here are the key points to remember from this chapter:

- You don't need to give up your old operating system before you are comfortable with Windows 8. Using a dual-boot setup, you can fall back on your old operating system when you need to.

- You can use a PIN or a picture password instead of a password to sign in to Windows 8. You know what a PIN is. The picture password requires you to draw with your finger or mouse three simple shapes or lines (in order) on a familiar picture to let you sign in to Windows 8.

- You have a wide choice of options with which to pause your work and protect your files in Windows 8. Be sure to make the right choice—sleep, sign-out, lock, or shut down—based on how long you will be away from your computer and where your computer is located.

2

INTERACTING WITH WINDOWS 8

It's unusual for a book about a single software program, such as Windows 8, to devote an entire chapter to helping you learn how to interact with the software, specifically, how to use the various switches, dials, knobs, buttons, and pulleys that enable you to control what the program does. But it's not often a program as mature as Windows gets an update that so drastically changes its user experience. Microsoft referred to the effort in designing Windows 8 as "reimagining of Windows." So you can bet there is significant change throughout Windows 8 for all Windows users. The newness of Windows 8, though, is not the only challenge in learning to work with it.

One of the more notable new features in Windows 8 is the support for mobile devices, such as tablets. Microsoft planned to simultaneously release versions of Windows 8 that run on laptops, desktop, servers, and tablets. Allowing for form factor differences, the user interface (the part of the software that you touch, look at, and respond to) is identical on all devices, but how you interact with each is different. There are some things the mouse can't do that the finger or stylus can, and the keyboard can bring 100 keys to the party, whereas the mouse brings just 2.

So when you take into account the new Windows 8 user interface, plus the various ways to interact with Windows based on the devices you use, and add to that the Windows Desktop app you learned about in Chapter 1, "Starting and Stopping Windows 8," perhaps one chapter is not enough to present how you get your message across to Windows 8. In this chapter, you learn how to use touch, the mouse, and the keyboard with Windows 8, and then you can read a review of the screens, buttons, and other standard parts of the pre-Windows 8 environment of the Desktop app.

Getting to Know the Windows 8 Interfaces

In 2011, Microsoft announced Windows 8 would support tablets and other full touchscreen devices. This new support would be added to the continued support for hundreds of different models of desktops, servers, and laptops. Immediately after the announcement, a number of manufacturers announced their plans to build Windows 8 tablets. Fortunately, Microsoft dictated specific guidelines as to how these new hardware devices should work with Windows 8. These guidelines also apply to the traditional personal computers mentioned before. So the product of all this consistency is a batch of techniques (for example, "Click like this," "Swipe like that") that work across all kinds of different devices. In this section of the chapter, you review how to interact with these Windows 8 computers using the four main interfaces: touch, the mouse, the keyboard, and the virtual keyboard. Some of the combinations are natural, such as touch and a tablet, and some combos aren't as obvious. You can read about both and everything in between in this section. The mouse is discussed first.

Using the Mouse in Windows 8

The first interface to cover is the ubiquitous mouse. The mouse is a great choice for any device, although touch is probably more efficient and easy to use with a tablet. Following are the commands you see associated with use of the mouse:

- **Point**—Unless you have a special version of Windows that can read your mind, using a mouse with Windows means pointing to an item on the screen that you want to work with. The mouse pointer is usually in the shape of an arrow, but you can always change it to another shape, as explained in Chapter 17, "Setting Up Common Hardware." You can also download Windows *themes* that bring together a new color scheme and fun graphics, including cool, new mouse pointers, to give Windows a new look and feel.

- **Click**—Besides picking up dust, the most common action you take with the mouse is to click. You click to select items, to start and stop actions in Windows, to indicate where text you write should be inserted, and more. To click with your mouse, just tap the primary mouse button.

- **Double-click**—The double-click mouse action traditionally has been used in Windows to start a program or launch a task. In Windows 8, though, most of those double-clicks have been changed over to single-clicks, mainly to make things more consistent for users. Any of the programs you ran in previous versions of Windows that required a double-click have the same requirements if you run the same programs in the Desktop app.

- **Right-click**—The right-click traditionally is used to display a menu of commands related to the item you click. For example, right-clicking a photo might present commands to open your photo editing application and to add the picture to a slide show. This convention does not work any longer in Windows 8; although it does work in the Desktop app. On the Start screen, right-clicking displays the Apps bar, and in Windows 8 apps, right-clicking displays the Command bar. The App bar and Command bar are described in Chapter 3, "Doing Windows the Windows 8 Way."

 NOTE When you see the command to select or click, this always refers to use of the primary mouse button, as described in this section. Any task that requires the secondary mouse button to be clicked calls out clearly that the *secondary* or *right* mouse button should be clicked. You can specify which button on your mouse is the primary button. Refer to Chapter 17 for help with configuring the mouse.

- **Click-and-drag**—The click-and-drag action is used to move files, folders, icons, and so on from one place to another in Windows 8. You can always use the cut-and-paste menu convention (when available) to move things, but you can save time and look smarter by using click-and-drag. Click-and-drag is also known as drag-and-drop. One of the most prominent areas in which you can employ click-and-drag on the Windows 8 Start screen is where you can drag a tile to a new location on the Start screen.

TIP   Windows always treats click-and-drag as a move action. This means the item you were dragging will no longer be in the location from which you dragged it. To use click-and-drag as a copy action, just press and hold down the Ctrl key before you release the mouse key to drop the file in its new location. Windows will copy the file rather than move it.

- **Right-click-and-drag**—A cousin to the click-and-drag is the right-click-and-drag. Just as the right-click displays a menu with commands specific to the item you click, so does the right-click-and-drag. Windows recognizes the item you are dragging and pops up a menu relevant to the item and the destination of your drag.

Using the Keyboard in Windows 8

Windows 8 includes an on-screen keyboard that appears when you need it. This section is dedicated to the physical keyboard. You can read about the virtual keyboard in a bit.

The keyboard is an important tool for interacting with Windows 8, but its role is for more than entering text and punctuation. You can use a large number of quick key combinations to issue commands to Windows 8. A quick key combination refers to two keys pressed simultaneously to issue a specific command, such as to j the Search charm. The quick key combinations in Windows 8 use the Windows key as the first key in the combination. Keep in mind when using quick key combinations that you should always press the Windows key slightly before pressing the second key.

Table 2.1 lists some useful quick key combinations you can use with Windows 8.

TABLE 2.1   Quick Key Combinations

Press This	To Do This
Windows (alone)	Switch to the Start screen
Windows+B	Opens the Desktop app
Windows+C	Displays the Charms bar; also displays time/date tile
Windows+D	Opens the Desktop app
Windows+E	Starts Windows Explorer
Windows+F	Opens the Search Files charm
Windows+Ctrl+F	Searches for computers on the network

Press This	To Do This
Windows+G	Cycles through Desktop gadgets (you must be in the Desktop app for this to work)
Windows+H	Opens the Share charm
Windows+I	Opens the Settings charm
Windows+J	Switches between two snapped apps
zWindows+K	Opens the Devices charm
Windows+M	Minimizes all windows on the Desktop
Windows+O	Locks screen orientation
Windows+P	Configures a projector or second display device
Windows+Q	Opens the Search charm
Windows+T	Goes to Taskbar on the Desktop and cycle through running apps
Windows+U	Opens Ease of Access Center
Windows+V	Cycles through notifications
Windows+W	Opens the Search Settings charm
Windows+Z	Opens the App bar (you must be at the Start screen for this to work)
Windows+Comma	Peeks at the Desktop
Windows+Period	Cycles through the three docked app positions: snapped left, docked right, and snapped right.
Windows+Shift+Period	Cycles backward through the three docked app positions: snapped right, docked left, and snapped left.
Windows+Tab	Cycles through the list of apps you most recently used; doesn't include programs you run in the Desktop app
Windows+PrtScn	Takes a picture of a screen and places the picture in the Photos folder in Screenshots
Windows+PgUp	Using multiple monitors, moves Start screen to the left monitor
Windows+PgDn	Using multiple monitors, moves the Start screen to right monitor

Using Touch in Windows 8

The touch interface is new to Windows 8. In previous versions of Windows, you could use a stylus, a mouse, and the keyboard to work with Windows, such as to sketch and trace. With Windows 8, you can now use your finger or another touch device as if it were a mouse to completely interact with Windows and issue command to Windows. Before Windows 8 was available for consumers to purchase, many hardware manufacturers were preparing to bring mobile devices to market to take advantage of the new Windows' touch interfaces. Here are some of the devices available that would leverage the new touch capabilities:

- Tablets
- Touch-sensitive displays
- Phones

The word *gesture* describes just about any action you take with your touch device. Here is a list of the gestures used with Windows 8, including some tidbits on how the gesture works:

- **Swipe**—The swipe is a short movement with your finger or fingers across the screen of the device. The fingers are only on the screen for a short period of time. A direction is usually given when you are instructed to swipe, such as Swipe Down from the top of the screen.

- **Tap**—It doesn't get any easier than this gesture. To tap, just touch your finger to the screen.

- **Press-and-hold**—The press-and-hold action is the touch equivalent of the right-mouse-click. You usually press-and-hold on a specific item, such as a file or folder. This action is used predominantly to display a special menu that contains commands relevant to the item on which you pressed-and-held. You can tell you pressed long enough by the appearance of small circular symbol at the point on the screen where you held.

- **Rotate**—Windows 8 supports a *rotate* gesture , which enables you to turn an image or document clockwise or counterclockwise. You might not see regular use for this gesture on a computer or laptop, but a tablet user should take advantage of the capability to pivot an image to better see it on a device with limited screen real estate.

  To pivot a document or an image with the rotate gesture, place two or more fingers on the display. Turn your fingers and wrist in a circular motion while keeping the display stationary.

- **Pinch and stretch**—Use the pinch gesture and the stretch gesture to expand an image (stretch) or to shrink an image (pinch).To pinch, place two fingers on the display separated a bit over the image you want to change. While keeping contact with the screen, slowly draw both fingers together as if you were softly pinching a baby's cheek. You can stop drawing your fingers together when you are happy with the results of the pinch, such as reducing the size of an image.

To stretch, place two fingers on the display slightly touching one another over the image you want to affect. While keeping contact with the screen, slowly draw both fingers apart. You can stop drawing your fingers apart when you are happy with the new size of the image.

Using the Virtual Keyboard

Windows 8 displays an on-screen keyboard when it believes you need one, as shown in Figure 2.1. Here are the two conditions that, together, let Windows 8 know that a virtual keyboard is needed.

- You use a touch device. (Windows 8 can detect it.)

- You are on a screen requiring text input.

FIGURE 2.1

Windows displays a keyboard automatically when it believes you need one.

You can choose between three different keyboard modes. To choose the keyboard mode, tap the main keyboard key at the bottom-right corner of the virtual keyboard, and then tap the tile for the keyboard mode you need:

- Split Keyboard , as shown in Figure 2.2

- Regular Keyboard
- Handwriting Recognition, as shown in Figure 2.3

FIGURE 2.2
You can split the virtual keyboard to see a bit more of the screen.

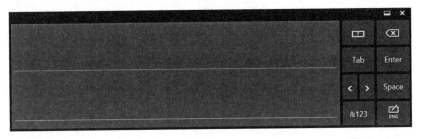

FIGURE 2.3
The virtual keyboard also is used for the handwriting palette.

Although the keyboard automatically appears when you use a Windows 8 app, you must make a few clicks for the keyboard to display on the Desktop. To display the virtual keyboard on the Desktop, follow these steps:

1. Press-and-hold on the Taskbar.

2. Tap **Toolbars** and then **Touch Keyboard**. A keyboard icon appears on the Taskbar.

3. Tap the keyboard icon on the Taskbar.

Using Windows Controls in the Desktop App

If you have experience with Windows 7 or an even earlier version of Windows, you can skip this section unless you would like a refresher. If you are a beginner to Windows or are new to computers in general, this section of the chapter can make you comfortable with the tools and objects you use in the Desktop app.

Remember, the Desktop app is an environment for pre-Windows 8 applications and programs. It's Windows 7 running in Windows 8!

Window

The window is the big cheese of controls. A window is the control that organizes and stores other controls. It is the main organization unit in all Windows software—that's right, all Windows software. The window is so important Microsoft named its operating system after it. Software programs present their options and settings in a window, you supply information to those programs in a window, and the messages the program reports back to you are organized in a window.

So, with all that buildup about Windows, they have much less prominence in Windows 8 than in the previous version of Windows. Actually, the only area of Windows 8 in which windows are used is in the Desktop app, which is the environment where older pre-Windows 8 programs run.

Figure 2.4 shows a window and points out a few key parts of a window. You can find a lot of information about windows in Chapter 13, "Working at the Desktop."

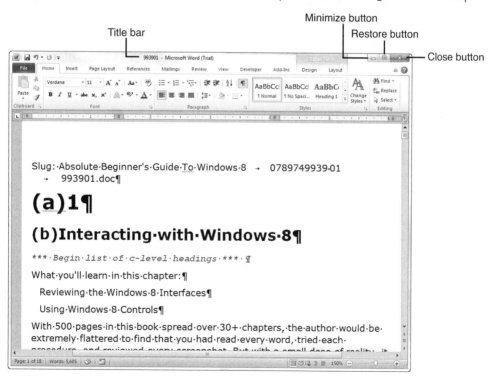

FIGURE 2.4

A typical window found on the Desktop.

Button

A button's use is fairly obvious. You click a button to execute the command indicated by the text on the button. In many cases, a button that is labeled OK means, when clicked, *Proceed as Planned* or *I Am Through Making Choices—Go Ahead and Finish the Job*. A button with the label Cancel usually indicates, when clicked, *Forget It, I Changed My Mind* or *Don't Finish What You Started*. Sometimes a picture or an image is used as a button. You click the picture to execute the command portrayed by the picture. Figure 2.5 shows examples of different buttons, including both traditional buttons and new tile buttons used in Windows 8.

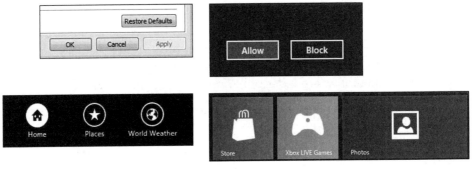

FIGURE 2.5

Most buttons in Windows look the same; though buttons can appears as pictures on your screen.

Option Button or Group

You use an option group collect a single choice from a group of possible options. A border with a label usually is used to organize the group of option buttons on the screen, as shown in Figure 2.6. Option buttons are also known as *radio buttons*.

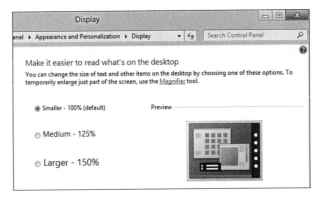

FIGURE 2.6

Option, or radio, buttons are organized for you to choose only one from the group.

Text Box

Use a text box to enter words or descriptions. If you have ever entered your name or address to register a new program or to identify yourself to a web site, you have used a text box. If the program you use requires more information from you than just your name or address, you can use a much larger text box that can collect multiple lines of text.

 TIP Most text boxes work properly with Windows' cut/copy/ paste mechanism. This means you can copy information from a document or email and then paste it into a text box. Sometimes you can't access a menu when entering information into a text box, and can't choose paste. In these cases you can usually still use the keyboard command to Paste by pressing Ctrl+V.

Check Box

Use a check box to select whether some state or condition is ON or OFF. The label determines whether checking the box indicates on or off. In most uses, a check box actually isn't checked. Rather, an "x" symbol fills the box part of the control. Figure 2.7 shows examples of check boxes.

To check or uncheck a check box

Click in the check box or on the caption to change it.

Tap in the check box or on the caption to change it.

Turn messages on or off

For each selected item, Windows will check for problems and send you a message if problems are found. How does Action Center check for problems?

Security messages

☑ Windows Update   ☑ Spyware and related protection

☑ Internet security settings   ☑ User Account Control

☑ Network firewall   ☑ Virus protection

☑ Microsoft account   ☑ SmartScreen

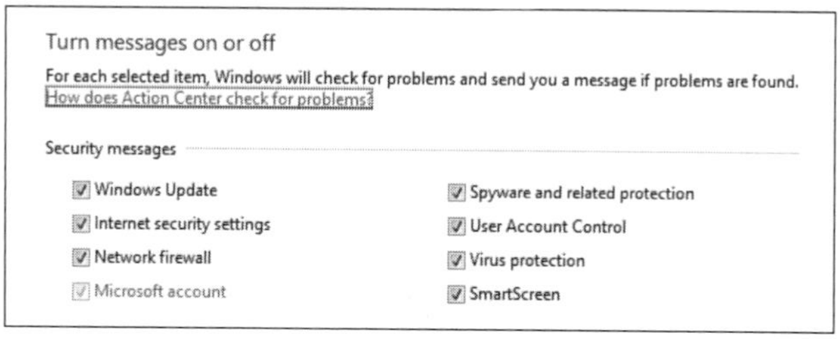

FIGURE 2.7

A check box indicates an ON or OFF condition.

Windows 8 Toggle

Like the check box control, the toggle presents an on or off condition. The label next to toggle tells you what setting is controlled. It's easy to slide the toggle to on or off with the mouse or touch, as shown in Figure 2.8.

To switch a Windows 8 toggle

🖱 Click-and-drag the bar to the other end of the toggle.

👆 Press-and-hold on the bar, and then drag it to the far end of the toggle.

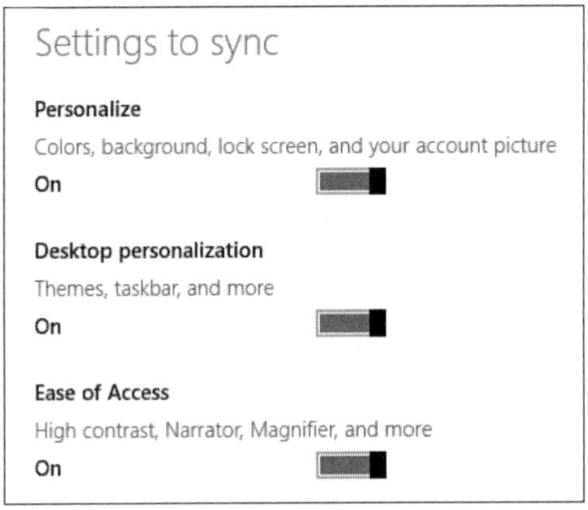

FIGURE 2.8

The toggle is used to turn some setting on or off.

List Box

The list box appears when you must select an item from a list of options. Sometimes you need to select one item from the list; other times you may be asked to select multiple items. Figure 2.9 shows an example of a list box.

To select one item in a list

- With your mouse or touch, scroll through the list to locate the item you're looking for. Tap or click once on the item.

To select multiple contiguous (next to one another) items in the list

- With a mouse, click and drag the mouse pointer over all the items. Windows 8 highlights the area of the screen selected, making it easy to see the files and folders selected.

- Also with a mouse, click once on the first item. Next, press and hold Shift while you click once on the last item.

- With your finger or a stylus, tap once on the first item. Next, press and hold Shift while you tap on the last item.

To select multiple noncontiguous (not next to one another) items in the list

- With a mouse, click once on the first item. Next, press and hold Ctrl while you click each remaining item. Do not release Ctrl until you have clicked each of the items you intend to select.

- With your finger or a stylus, tap once on the first item. Next, press and hold Ctrl while you tap each remaining item. Do not release Ctrl until you have tapped each of the items you intend to select.

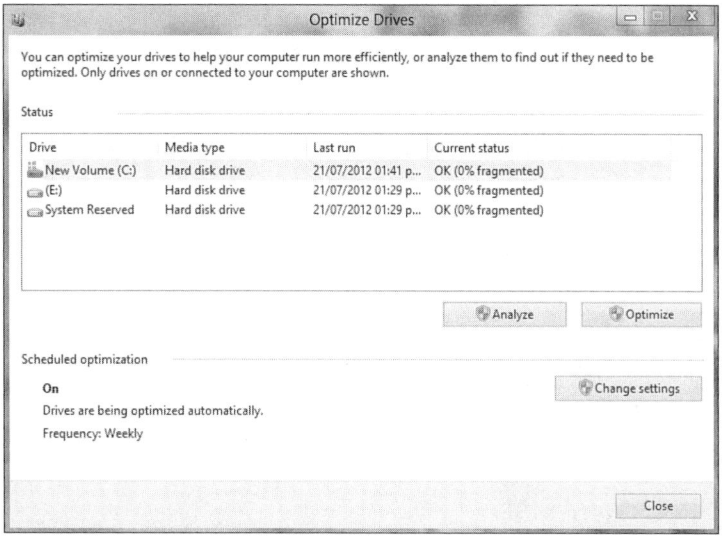

FIGURE 2.9

A list box is used for you to review and select items from a list.

Drop-Down List

A drop-down list, such as the list box, presents a list of items. The items in the list appear to drop down beneath the control when you select the arrow button found on the right side of the control, as shown in Figure 2.10. The selected item in the list is always shown in the visible portion of the drop-down list, even after you close the dialog box or window where the drop-down list is located.

To select an item from a list in a drop-down control

- Click the arrow at the end of the control. Then scroll through the list to find your item. Click your item when you find it.

- Tap the arrow beside the control to drop down the list of choices. Scroll through the list until you find your item. When you do, tap it.

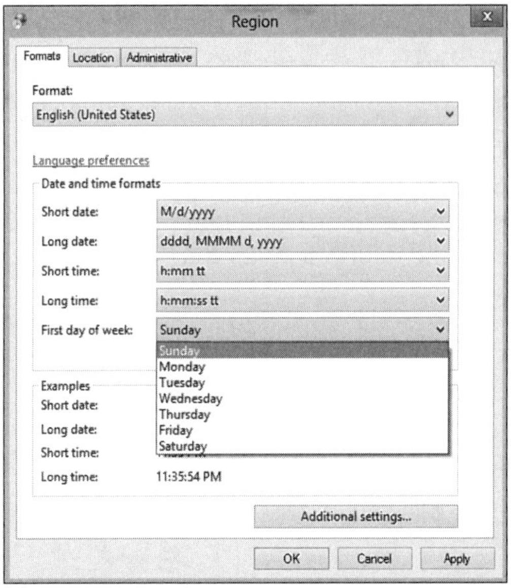

FIGURE 2.10

A drop-down list takes up less room than the list box, but it's harder to find the item you are looking for.

Combo Drop-Down List

A combo drop-down list is similar to the drop-down list control described earlier. The only difference is you can enter the name of the item you want to select in the part of the control that displays the selected item with the combo drop-down list.

The list automatically selects the first item in the list whose name matches the text you type. This control is used when it is believed you might not know if the item you're interested in is actually in the list. It's quicker to verify the item you want is listed by entering its name rather than scrolling through the list.

THE ABSOLUTE MINIMUM

- There are four interfaces with which to interact with Windows 8: mouse, keyboard, virtual keyboard, and touch.

- Windows 8 appears and operates almost identically on the different devices that it runs on.

- Provided you set up your Windows 8 credentials properly, your personal settings and preferences are used on any Windows 8 device you sign-in to.

- Although the keyboard alone does not have the capability to access all the buttons, lists, and switches that a mouse or your finger does, approximately 30 quick key combinations are available that automate many of the tasks.

LEARNING WINDOWS 8 BASICS

If you take a few minutes and poke around Windows 8, looking at various screens, windows, and apps, you'll notice that things look fairly consistent. Nothing looks to be out of place or seems like it doesn't belong. This is not an accident. Microsoft uses a set of designs, conventions, rules, and themes to govern the look and feel of Windows 8. Not only do the folks at Microsoft building Windows follow these guidelines, but the programmers who work for other software companies also are expected to follow these rules. This way, if you learn one Windows 8 program, including Windows, you can learn another very quickly. This look and feel that you observed as you poked around in Windows is known as the *user interface* (UI). The Windows 8 UI is on the current generation Windows Phone models. It's rare for a product as widely used and as established in the market as Windows to go through as radical a change as moving to Windows 8 represents. So this chapter covers this new Windows 8 UI style, helping you understand how to accomplish everyday tasks—tasks applicable to topics covered in all the other chapters in this book. This chapter is required reading for working the Windows 8 way.

WORKING WITH DIFFERENT INTERFACES

Before getting into the meat of this chapter, there's some important info to share with you as to how the chapter is formatted. Windows 8 supports a number of interfaces, including the mouse, keyboard, and touch. Windows 8 was designed for touch as the first priority. To help you master the Windows 8 UI regardless of the device, you'll learn how to complete many of the tasks in this chapter using each of these interfaces:

🖱 Mouse

⌨ Keyboard

👆 Touch, like your finger or stylus

Look for instructions formatted like the preceding list so you can easily pick out the interface you want to learn. As you learn the various techniques and procedures, you should try out any interface you have access to. For example, you can switch between the use of the mouse and the use of the keyboard. If you have a Windows 8 tablet, you can also work with the on-screen keyboard.

Working at the Start Screen

Fitting to its name, the Start screen is where you begin your work and play in Windows 8. After signing-in to Windows 8, you are dropped off at the Start screen. In fact, it is difficult to get anything done in Windows 8 without passing through the Start screen first. For a component of Windows that has so much responsibility, perhaps you expect to see more widgets and gadgets on the screen than shown in Figure 3.1, the example Start screen. But in this new Windows, you don't see the tools unless you need them. You'll learn more about these tools throughout this book, but for now take a look at how to organize and customize the Start screen so that you have an efficient and useful workplace with which to use Windows.

To start, here's a short review of the items you can see on the Start screen. These are called out in Figure 3.1:

- **Tiles**—A tile is the representation of an app or program. Tiles can be live, displaying updated information from the app, such as a new email alert, weather details, or a recent social life status changes. This chapter and Chapter 4, "Personalizing Windows 8," provide plenty of information about using, organizing, and manipulating tiles. To activate a tile you need merely click or tap it.

- **App bar**—This area always shows the settings available for the app you're using.

Tiles

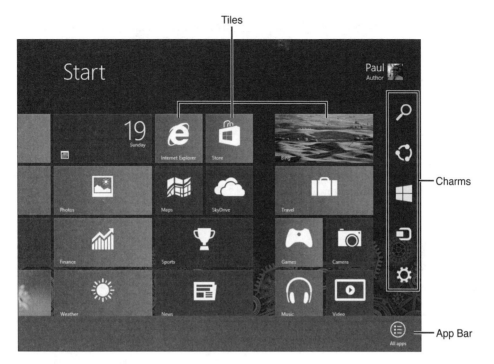

FIGURE 3.1

The Start screen.

- **Charms bar**—The Charms bar is a special toolbar that contains a set of five buttons, known as *charms*. Each charm represents an important, very-useful feature or tool in Windows, such as search, work with devices, like printers, change Windows settings, and a few more. These charms are available everywhere in Windows. There are a few different methods available to display the Charms bar. You can find details about charms later in this chapter in the "Using Charms" section.

Returning to the Start Screen

Although most of your work in Windows initiates from the Start screen, when you're in an app, all of which run in full screen mode, you need to know how to return to the Start screen. Based on the device you use, follow one of these methods to return to the Start screen.

 Swipe in from the middle of the left border and then tap the Start button that appears.

Press the Windows key.

Point to the bottom-left corner of the screen, and click the Start screen portrait when it appears, as shown in Figure 3.2.

FIGURE 3.2

It's a bit tricky without practice, but point to the bottom left of the screen to show the Start portrait, and then select it to reach the Start screen.

Seeing Tiles off the Screen

It doesn't take long for new tiles to start to appear on the Start screen. When you install new software in Windows 8 and when you pin apps, pictures, and documents to Start, your display of tiles starts to grow. The collection of tiles grows from the right side out. This means you must scroll to the right to see tiles off the screen, and then you must scroll back to the left to see the tiles you passed.

To see tiles off the screen, follow these steps based on the device you use:

Pan to the right by placing your finger or stylus on the screen and then swiping it to the left. You can reverse the direction by swiping to the right. Try to swipe on an empty spot on the Start screen, avoiding tiles.

Use your left and right arrow keys to move across the Start screen. If pressing the left or right arrow key has no effect, either you are already at the edge of the Start screen, or the pointer is not on the Start screen. Press Tab once or twice to move the pointer to the Start screen.

Use the horizontal scroll bars at the bottom of the screen to move left and right. Click the dark colored areas of the scroll bar to scroll in that direction.

Displaying All Tiles

Certain types of apps do not appear on the Start screen automatically. These apps include Windows accessories, such as the Calculator and Notepad; Windows Ease of Access tools, such as the Magnifying Glass tool; Windows System tools, such as the Control Panel and the virus protection tool, and many more.

If you want easy access to these apps (you can always run a search for them), you can show their tiles on the Start screen. Displaying these tiles also gives you an opportunity to pin one to the default Start screen, making it easy to select the app the next time. When you pin an app to the Start screen, the tile always appears on the Start screen. Pinning an app is covered later in this chapter.

To show all the tiles in Windows 8, as shown in Figure 3.3, do one of the following based on the device you use:

👆 Swipe up from the bottom of the Start screen, which reveals the App bar. Select **All Apps**.

⌨ Press Windows+Z to reveal the App bar. Press the down arrow key once to select **All Apps** on the App bar. Press Enter.

🖱 Right-click any empty location on the Start screen. The App bar appears. Select **All Apps**.

FIGURE 3.3

You can easily see all the apps installed in Windows 8 by selecting All Apps from the App bar.

NOTE There is a group of applications known as administrative tools. These are special programs that are used to configure and tune Windows 8. While you control many aspects of Windows 8 with the tools and programs available to every user, the administrative tools are very specialized. Making an error with the some of these tools can render Windows 8 non-functional, even though the tools are designed to make Windows 8 perform . These tools are hidden by default. To display the administrative tools, open the Charms bar from the Start screen and select Settings. Select **Tiles**, and then move the **Show administrative tools** slider to the Yes position. Note that these tools are not discussed in the book; refer to an advanced-level book for help with these programs.

Selecting a Tile

An option for personalizing the Start screen, which is discussed both in this chapter and the next one, Chapter 4, "Personalizing Windows 8," is setting how the tiles look and behave. Before you change any tile's appearance or function, of course, you need to indicate to Windows 8 which tile you want to work with. This is known as selecting, and in this case, you are selecting a tile.

When a tile is selected, a check mark appears in the top-right corner of the tile, as shown in Figure 3.4. To select a tile, do one of the following based on the device you use:

- Swipe down on the tile. Be sure not to press too hard on the tile when you start to swipe or else Windows 8 interprets your swipe as a tap. Also be sure you don't swipe onto an adjacent tile. Think of this gesture as a flick on the tile you're interested in.

- Use your left and right arrow keys to move across the Start screen. As you do so, a colored border appears around tiles as you pass over them. Press the spacebar when you have moved to the tile you want to select.

- Right-click the tile.

TIP To deselect a tile, just repeat what you did to select the tile.

FIGURE 3.4

A check mark appears in the top-right corner of a selected tile.

Moving a Tile

You can reorganize the tiles on the Start screen as you like. There are no rules dictating where certain tiles should appear, so you can move a tile to whatever position you like on the Start screen.

To move a tile, do one of the following based on the device you use:

- Tap and hold on the tile to be moved, and immediately drag it to its new location.

- Click and drag the tile to its new location. Notice when you click and hold the tile, it seems to tip backward slightly. Also notice how the other tiles on the Start screen seem to move out of the way and open an empty spot as you drag a tile across the screen.

Making a Tile Bigger or Smaller

You can select the size for any tile. There are just two sizes: large and small. You can see an example of each size in Figure 3.5. You might prefer smaller tiles to fit more tiles on the screen. You might also use the size of a tile to distinguish certain types of tiles from another. For example, apps you use online, such as Messaging and Email, might be represented by large tiles, and apps you use on your computer or tablet, such as the Photo app, might be represented with small tiles.

FIGURE 3.5

These images show the Mail tile in the different sizes available.

To change a tile's size, do one of the following based on the device you use:

- Select the tile (see previous section "Selecting a Tile"). Tap **Smaller** or **Larger** on the App bar.

- Select the tile (see previous section "Selecting a Tile"). Then press the down arrow to highlight the App bar. Use the arrow keys again to highlight either **Smaller** or **Larger**. Press the spacebar one more time.

- Select the tile (see previous section "Selecting a Tile") and then click **Larger** or **Smaller** on the App bar.

Adding a Tile to the Start Screen

Adding a tile to the Start screen is less challenging probably than you might expect. You can add a tile for an installed application only, so you first must install any program you'd like to show on the Start screen. Most of the Windows programs (those components of Windows not delivered as Windows 8 apps) do not appear on the Start screen. You can access them in one click by adding a tile for the ones you expect to use often.

To add a tile to the Start screen, do one of the following based on the device you use:

- Show all tiles on the Start screen (see previous section "Displaying All Tiles") and then select the tile to be added (see previous section "Selecting a Tile"). Tap **Pin to Start** at the bottom of the screen.

Show all tiles on the Start screen (see previous section "Displaying All Tiles") and then select the tile to be added (see previous section "Selecting a Tile"). Press the down arrow key, which moves the selector down to the App bar. Press the right arrow key to select **Pin to Start**. Press the spacebar.

Show all tiles on the Start screen (see previous section "Displaying All Tiles") and then select the tile to be added (see previous section "Selecting a Tile"). Click **Pin to Start.**

Opening the App Bar

Most apps in Windows 8 have at least one or two settings that you can tweak to determine how the app works. This applies to the big parts of Windows 8, such as the Start screen, where you can determine if all apps display, rather than just Windows 8 apps, as well as to the smallest apps, such as the Map app, where you can specify whether traffic jams appear on the map you're looking at. These settings for Windows 8 apps all appear in one place: the App bar. The App bar appears at the bottom of the screen (refer to Figure 3.1).

To open the App bar, follow these instructions based on the device you use:

Swipe up from the bottom middle of the screen.

Press Windows + Z.

Right-click.

When the App bar opens, click or tap on the command you want to issue to the app.

Using the Charms Bar

Charms are one of the cool, new features in Windows 8. Each charm (there are five in Windows 8) represents a tool, capability, or way to do things in Windows 8.

Now you might think that search and sharing functions aren't new to Windows, right? You are correct, but here's the difference: Before Windows 8, changing a program's settings, including how the program prints or how you can share your information from the program with other users, would differ with each program you use. For example, the printer that worked perfectly with your word processing, a moment later, might not work with your greeting card software. These scenarios change with Windows 8 charms.

In Windows 8, charms are the responsibility of Windows, so, whatever app is open when you open the charm, and whatever you do with that app, the feature that the charm represents still works the same way.

Here's how it works inside of Windows. When smart developers create a program to run in Windows 8, they decide to *contract* with Windows for certain functionality, such as printing, sharing, or using a device such as a second monitor. By entering into that contract, your program says, "Windows, I grant you responsibility for printing/sharing/devices. Thanks for letting me pay attention to the important stuff that I want to do!"

The five charms in Windows 8 are:

- **Search charm**—Search for files, apps, programs, and settings, as well as content from the Internet.

- **Devices charm**—Access the devices and hardware attached to your computer, such as a printer or second monitor.

- **Share charm**—Share what you are looking at with another app.

- **Settings charm**—Change settings for whatever part of Windows 8 you're working with.

- **Start charm**—Go to the Start screen.

These capabilities are available from a handy pop-up menu available at all times. That menu is known as the *Charms bar*. You can display the Charms bar, which gives you access to the capabilities previously described, or you can use some handy shortcuts that bring you directly to those capabilities.

To open the Charms bar, do one of the following based on the device you use. The Charms bar appears, as shown in Figure 3.6.

🖐 Swipe in from the right edge of the screen.

⌨ Press Windows+C.

🖱 Point to the top-right corner of the screen.

To open any of the individual charms, open the Charms bar as instructed here, and then select the charm you're interested in. There are a series of keyboard shortcuts that each open an individual charm directly (see Table 3.1). There's also a list of all keyboard shortcuts, including those listed here, in Table 2.1 of Chapter 2, "Interacting with Windows 8."

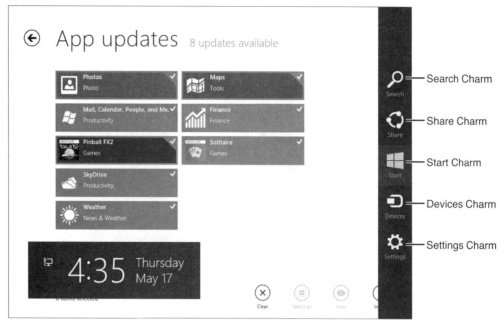

FIGURE 3.6

The Charms bar gives you access to important tools across Windows 8.

TABLE 3.1   Charms and Charms Bar Quick Key Combinations

Press This	To Do This
Windows+C	Display the Charms bar. Also displays time/date tile.
Windows+F	Open the Search Files charm.
Windows+H	Open the Share charm.
Windows+I	Open the Settings charm.
Windows+K	Open the Devices charm.
Windows+Q	Open the Search charm.
Windows+W	Open the Search Settings charm.

Using the Search Charm

In Windows 8, you use the Search charm to search for anything in Windows, such as a file or folder, a setting, or an app. The Search charm also is used to search the web.

NOTE You can use any search tool you can find on the web, such as Google. To search with a web-based search tool, you must open Internet Explorer and navigate to a page where you can launch the search. Of course, a search tool you open in your web browser cannot find apps or files in Windows 8.

Like the other charms, the Search charm provides a capability across Windows 8 regardless of what you are doing, what apps are running, and what device you're using. You can search for files, apps, or programs, and even for specific settings, such as "volume" or "email address." Figure 3.7 shows the screen after the Search charm is opened.

FIGURE 3.7

Use the Search charm to search for apps, settings, or files, as well as to search the web.

Here's what you need to know about the Search charm:

- When the Search charm appears, you can select Apps, Settings, Files, or Internet Explorer to narrow the focus for what you want to search for.

 NOTE Windows sorts the results of your search by popularity.

- From the Start screen, you can type the search terms without opening the Search charm first. Windows interprets your action as searching for apps, so it opens the Search charm and selects Apps for you.

- How many times have you hunted through menus, looking for some option or feature you just know exists? With Windows 8, you can search for the setting. When found, you can open the area of the software where the setting is located. Cool! For example, if you receive so much email that you would like to mute the sound that plays when an email arrives, you can enter the word "sound" to search for a setting where you change the mail notification setting. Figure 3.8 shows how to search for apps whose name starts with the letter "m."

- After finding a file you searched for with the Search charm, the results show you information about each file found, such as the time/date the file was last modified and its size. If you point to the file in the list of found results, the location of the file displays as well (see Figure 3.9).

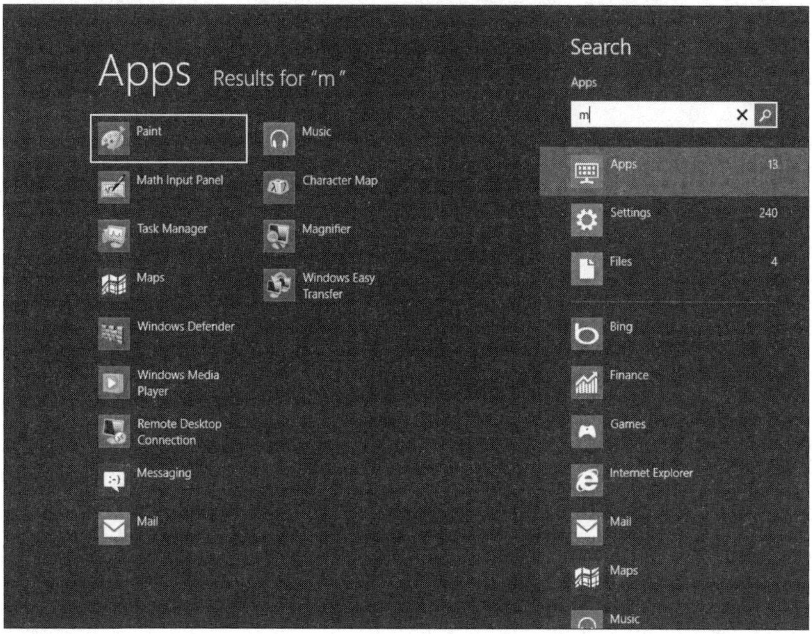

FIGURE 3.8

This image shows the results of a search for apps whose name starts with the letter "m," including the part of the name that does not appear on the screen (such as Microsoft Paint).

FIGURE 3.9

You can review information about any file you've located with the Search charm.

Using the Share Charm

The Share charm provides a simple way to pass information from one app to another. The app you're working with is the one doing the sharing. Not every app is capable of receiving shared information, so Windows 8 filters the list of apps shown when you open the Share charm. Examples of apps you can share with are Email, People, and Messaging, but apps can be configured by the teams that build them to share with just about any other program.

When you summon Share, Windows prepares a link or some other capsule of the page you're looking at. Windows then creates a message containing the link or capsule for the app doing the sharing.

The most obvious example of using the Share charm is with Internet Explorer. When you open the Share charm from Internet Explorer, you'll see Email as an option. If you select Mail, Windows creates a message containing an image plus a summary of the page, as shown in Figure 3.10. It can do so for any page on any website!

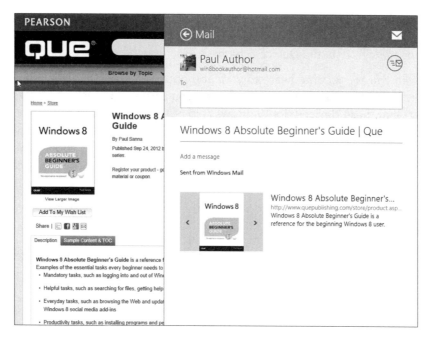

FIGURE 3.10

You can use the Share charm to pass along information from the page you are looking at via email.

To open the Share charm, do one of the following based on the device you use:

- Swipe in from the right and then tap the Share charm.
- Press Windows+H.
- Point to the top-right corner of the screen. When the Charms bar appears, click the Share charm.

Using the Devices Charm

When you think about the stuff that makes computer users a bit nervous, especially beginning users, working with hardware, such as printers, scanners, projectors, and other gear, is near the top of the list. Now if you don't' routinely think about these things, it's okay—this book has done the work for you.

It's not a surprise that hardware causes confusion. Think about it: When you print, you usually select File and then Print from a menu. But when you scan a document, you need to figure out if you should use the software on your computer or the controls on the scanner. Who knows? But if you need to project from your computer, do you work with the display settings in the software you're using or maybe turn the projector on and off? There is no such thing as consistency...until the Devices charm.

When you connect hardware to your computer or when Windows notices the hardware attached to your system when you upgraded to Windows 8, it figures out what these devices do. Windows also notes what kind of hardware typically is used with each of your apps and programs. When you open the Devices charm, Windows 8 shows you just the devices that would work (and should work) with your app. And from the Devices charm, you can carry out your job, such as print or project or scan.

To open the Devices charm, do one of the following based on the device you use:

🖐 Swipe in from the right and then tap the Devices charm.

⌨ Press Windows+K.

🖱 Point to the top -right corner of the screen. When the Charms bar appears, click the Devices charm.

When the Devices charm appears, just click the device you want to use and follow the on-screen instructions. Yes, it's as easy as that.

Using the Settings Charm

Most apps you run have various options that you tweak to control how the app works. Well, Windows 8 also has some control over how apps run. There are a few settings for each app that control how the app works with Windows 8. The Settings charm also enables you to reach some common Windows settings that have nothing to do with an app, such as volume, network connection, screen brightness, and more. Figure 3.11 shows the settings for the Photo app.

To open the Settings charm, do one of the following based on the device you use:

🖐 Swipe in from the right and then tap the Settings charm.

⌨ Press Windows+I.

🖱 Point to the top-right corner of the screen. When the Charms bar appears, click the Settings charm.

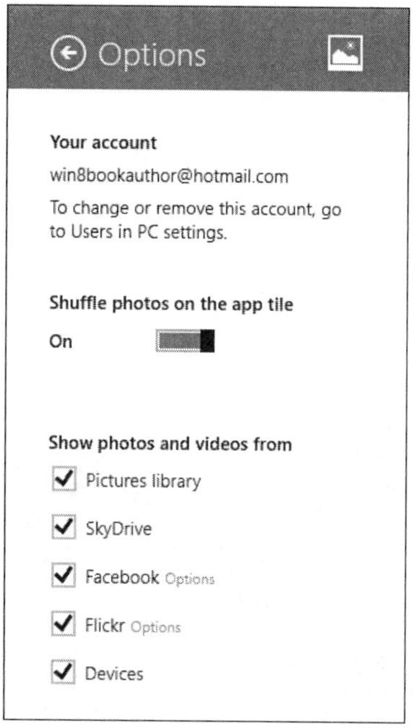

FIGURE 3.11

The Photo settings (which has a menu of commands under the heading "Options") enable you to set up how Photos accesses your pictures on various sites.

Selecting Files in Windows 8

You are sometimes required in Windows to select one or more files for different purposes. Here are a few such situations:

- You may need to pick out files from a DVD loaded with pictures to import into your photo library.

- You might need to select and then pull a number of documents from a removable drive someone provided to you.

- You plan to work on a project over the weekend at home, so you must select the project files to load to your SkyDrive account.

Windows has a File Picker tool you use to select files. This tool is used throughout Windows, so once you use the tool once (and learn how to use it), you'll be ready to select files anywhere else in Windows. The files you select with the File

Picker might be stored on your computer's hard drive, a removable drive you just connected to your computer, a drive on a computer that you can reach over your home network, or on SkyDrive.

Using the File Picker, you can select one file or many at one time. If you select multiples files at once, they can be located in different places.

You needn't do anything special to use the File Picker. Windows displays the tool whenever you need to choose files. Figure 3.12 shows the File Picker when you initially open it.

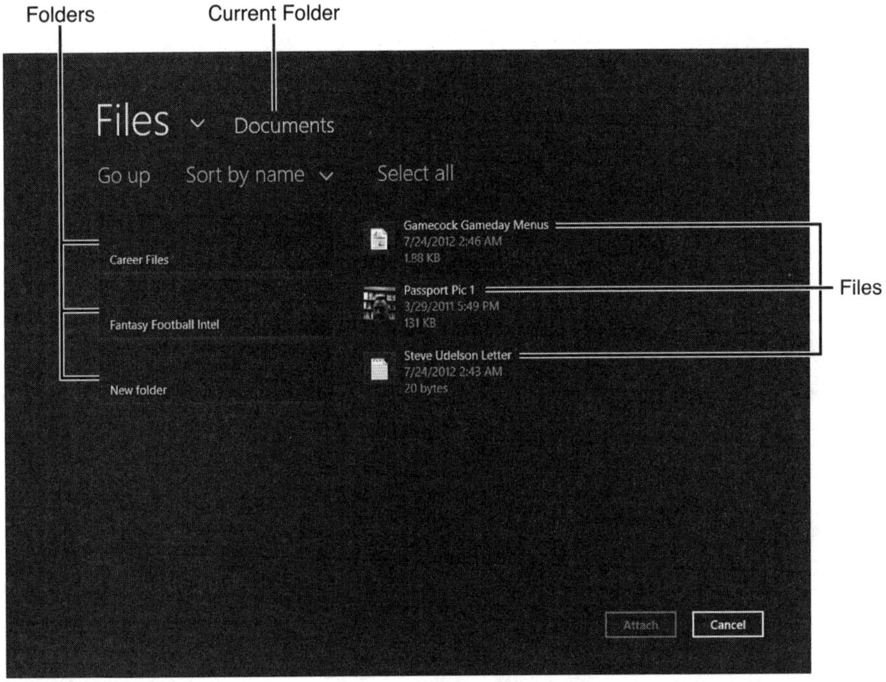

FIGURE 3.12

The File Picker enables you to easily navigate your file system to select one or more files.

Here's how to use the File Picker:

- Select a **Folder** box to open the folder to see its contents.

- Select **Go Up** to move to the parent folder of the folder displayed.

- Select **Files** to see libraries and other special locations where files are stored and organized, as shown in Figure 3.13. Click or tap a file to select it. Depending on the use of the File Picker, you may select multiple files.

- Select the button beside the Cancel button to close the File Picker. The name of the button (it's Attach in Figure 3.13) is different based on the app that uses the File Picker.

To learn more about how files and folders are organized on your computer, check out Chapter 15, "Organizing Files and Folders with Windows Explorer."

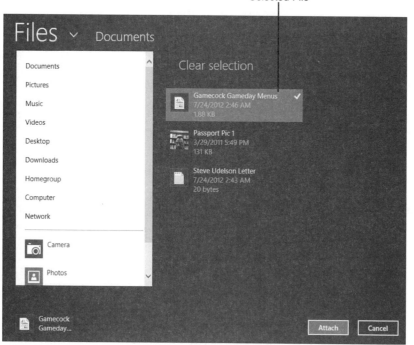

FIGURE 3.13

Select **Files** *to reveal all the folders and other containers you can use to select files.*

Finding and Using the Control Panel

The Control Panel is a special program that houses several smaller programs that each has a role in configuring Windows. These smaller programs are known as applets. These Control Panel applets are used to control everything from changing the color of your Windows background to setting up a printer. Each applet has a name, such as "Personalization" and "Power Options." Also, applets are organized into categories, as shown in Figure 3.14. Each category you see in Control Panel has many more applets than what you see initially in Control Panel.

NOTE If you are a stickler for details, you might complain that, Control Panel is not part of Windows 8, as suggested by the title of this chapter, as it has been around since Windows 3.0. Well, you are right. But Control Panel is important to almost every part of Windows 8, and it's referred to throughout this book. So, you should get used to working with the Control Panel early in your learning about Windows 8.

Applets   Categories

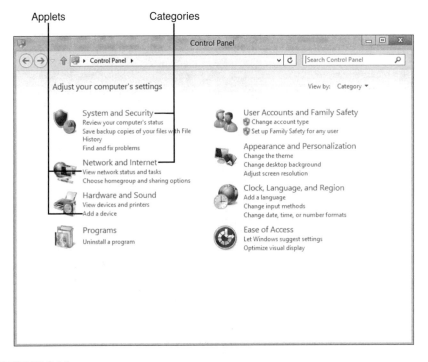

FIGURE 3.14

The Control Panel enables you to configure most features and functions of Windows 8.

Control Panel is one of those programs that does not appear automatically on the Windows 8 Start screen. And most Control Panel applets don't appear on the Start screen when you reveal All Apps, as described earlier, in the section, "Displaying All Tiles." It makes sense to pin Control Panel or an app you plan to use often to the Start screen the next time you access either. You can read how to do so here:

To open Control Panel, follow these steps:

1. From the Start screen, open the App bar, as instructed in the previous "Open the App Bar" section.

2. Select **All Apps**.

3. Select **Control Panel** from the Windows System group. The Control Panel should open.

To open a Control Panel applet, follow these steps:

1. Open Control Panel.

2. Select a category to reveal the applets it contains. Or if you can see the applet you are interested in, select it.

 TIP   Considering how often you're likely use Control Panel, it's probably a good idea to create a tile for Control Panel on the Start screen. To do so, follow the instructions to open Control Panel. After you reveal all apps, right-click Control Panel, and then select Pin to Start from the App bar at the bottom of the screen. (The App bar opens automatically when you right-click a tile.)

THE ABSOLUTE MINIMUM

You can access the Charms bar from anywhere in Windows 8. The Charms bar, in turn, gives you access to the Search, Share, Devices, Settings, and Start charms. Each of these charms gives you consistent, reliable support for basic Windows functions.

The File Picker is a special tool you use to select files. Windows 8 automatically opens the File Picker when you need to select files.

You can customize the appearance of the tiles on the Start screen. You can change their size and move them around. You can also add new tiles to the Start screen.

You can use Control Panel to configure many aspects of Windows 8. It's a good idea to pin the Control Panel to the Start screen, making it easy to access many Windows 8 tools.

Open the App bar to access many of the settings for the apps you use. In contrast, open the Settings charm to manipulate how Windows 8 looks and behaves.

PERSONALIZING WINDOWS 8

Short of playing games and keeping up with Twitter and Facebook, there probably is no greater distraction from real work than tweaking and adjusting all those preferences that make Windows 8 your own. You wouldn't be the first person to spend more time picking colors and pictures for your Windows 8 background than actually working. Although this version of Windows may seem like it has fewer options with which to personalize Windows than previous versions, there certainly are enough options to help you make Windows 8 unique and just yours. This chapter takes you through the various personalization settings, including providing you some before and after examples.

Personalizing Windows 8 to your liking requires you to work with a number of different areas of Windows. Many of the procedures and skills necessary to set these personal options are described in Chapter 2, "Interacting with Windows 8." If you run into difficulty with this chapter, refer to the two previous chapters. In addition, review "Returning to the Start Screen" and "Using Charms" in Chapter 3, "Learning Windows 8 Basics."

Personalizing Language, Keyboard, and Number Settings

One of the most personal aspects of Windows 8 you can set up is your language and other locale settings. You can customize the number, currency, time, and date formats to match your nationality and cultural preferences. You might find the step-by-step procedure provided here to be a bit long, but there are lots of options to cover. Don't worry, the steps are easy to understand.

The first phase is to set your language in Windows:

1. Open the Settings charm, and select **Change PC settings**.

2. Select **General** from the list on the left side of the screen. Then under the Language heading, which appears about halfway down the page, select **Language Preferences**. The Language dialog box appears, as shown in Figure 4.1.

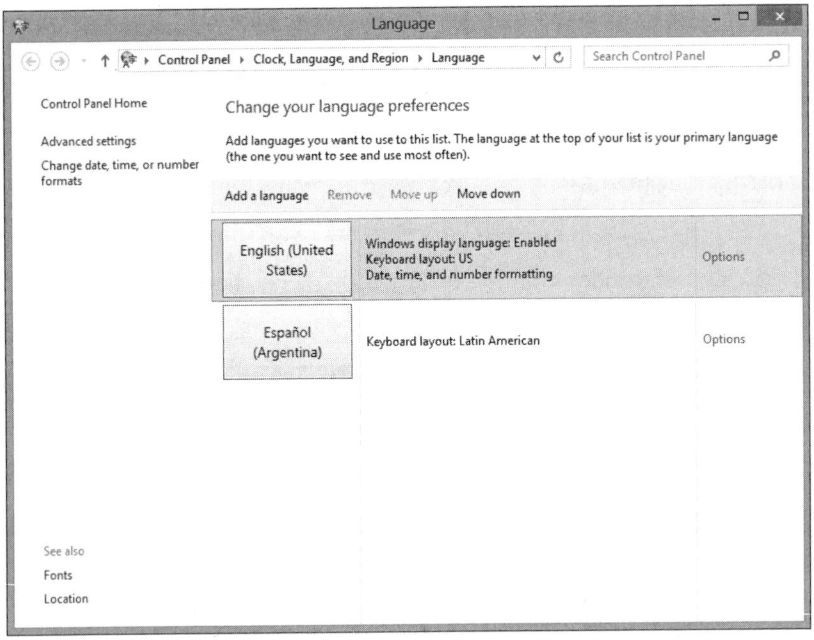

FIGURE 4.1

You can select language and other aspects of your locale from the Language dialog box.

3. If the language you want to switch to is shown, skip to step 6. If not, select **Add a language**. A dialog box like the one shown in Figure 4.2 should appear displaying a list of languages.

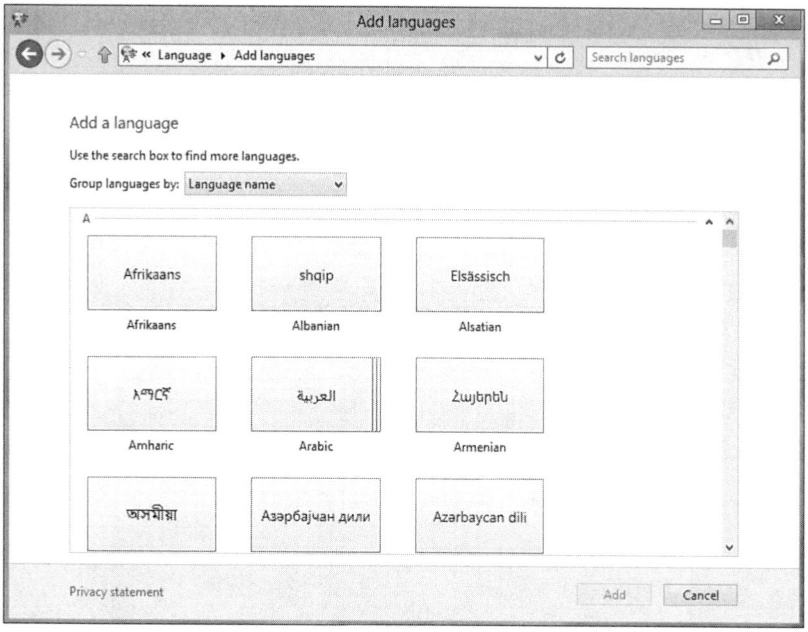

FIGURE 4.2

You can select from a long list of base languages, as well as select a dialect.

4. Scroll down the list and locate the base language you want to select. For example, if you want to select Mexican Spanish, for now, locate Spanish. When you find the language, select it, and then select **Open**. If you cannot locate the Open button, it means there are no regional variants of the language you selected. Select **Add** and skip to step 6.

5. A list of the regional variants of the language you chose should be on the screen. Select the dialect you want; then select **Add**.

6. You should be back to the Language dialog box, shown in Figure 4.1. If there is more than one language in the list, the first language in the list is the one used. Select the language to use; then select **Move Up** a few times until the language is at the top of the list.

Next set up your locale's time, date, and number formats, picking up where you left off in step 6:

1. Select **Change date, time, or number formats** (refer to Figure 4.1). The Region dialog box appears, as shown in Figure 4.3.

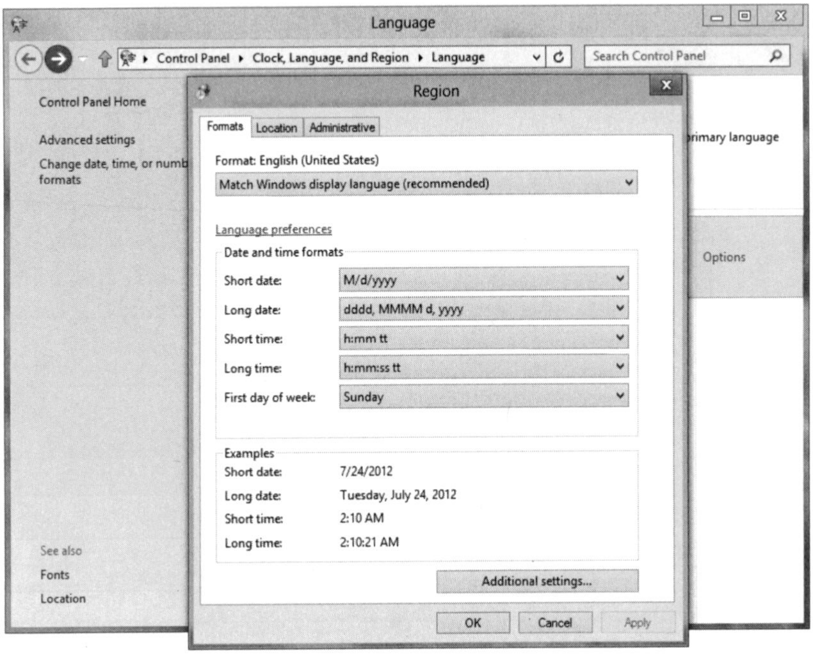

FIGURE 4.3

You can customize how dates appear based on your language of choice.

2. If the language you want to work with is not shown in the box at the top of the screen, select your language from the **Format** list.

3. The examples in this dialog box show you how the different date fields, such as long date, short date, and so on will appear throughout Windows (based on the language you selected). If you want to change any of the fields, select the down arrow button for any of the dates you want to customize; then select the format from the list. If after adjusting some formats, or if you are happy with the automatic selections for your language, select **Additional Settings**. The Customize Format dialog box should appear.

4. From the Customize Format dialog box, select the **Number**, **Currency**, **Time**, and **Date** tabs to change any of the information under each tab.

5. As in step 3, select the down arrow button for any symbol, field, separator or any other aspect of a number, currency, date or time display, then select the format from the list that appears. As you switch from tab to tab, you <u>do not</u> have to select **OK** in between.

6. When you finish setting up the locale formats, select **OK**. You should be at the Region dialog box. Select **OK** again.

7. Close the Language window by clicking the red **X** at the top-right corner of the window. You should be back at the Desktop.

Personalizing Colors and Pictures

You can use colors and photos to personalize Windows 8. You can personalize Windows 8 by using one of your own photos as the background of the lock screen, plus you can use any photo you like for your account picture. You also can select from a palette of eight color themes plus from a selection of five background patterns to personalize Windows. The color and photo selections appear in several places in Windows, including the Start screen, which is discussed in the next section.

Personalizing the Start Screen

The color you choose for the Start screen applies not only to Start, but also to any Windows 8 app you have installed. The color selection finds its way to the banner where certain apps display their name, as well as a few other places.

To change the color of your Start screen, follow these steps:

1. Open the Charms bar and select **Settings**.

2. Select **Change PC settings**.

3. Select **Personalize** from the list on the left side of the screen.

4. On the top right of the screen, select **Start Screen**. The sample Start screen appears, along with background and color pallets, as shown in Figure 4.4. Note that the color on your screen reflects what was selected when Windows was installed, or what was selected since then. It might not match the colors shown in Figure 4.4.

5. To change the background pattern of the Start screen, select the pattern you like from the two rows of patterns beneath the Start screen example. The sample Start screen changes with the background you selected.

6. To change the main color used throughout Windows 8, select the color you like from the pallet at the bottom of the screen. The sample Start screen changes with the color you selected, as shown in Figure 4.5.

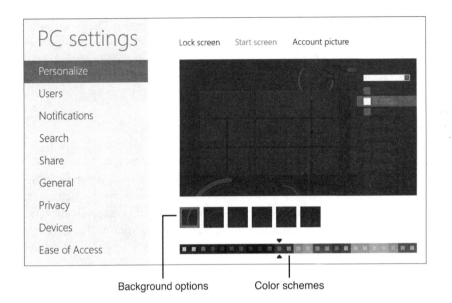

Background options   Color schemes

FIGURE 4.4

You can personalize the color used throughout Windows 8, as well as the background of the Start screen.

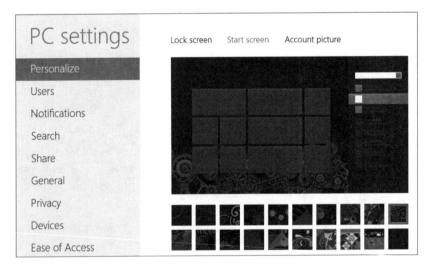

FIGURE 4.5

You can sample different Start screen backgrounds and color patterns.

Personalizing Your Account Picture

You can select one of your personal photos to use as your account picture. Your account picture appears not only on the screen where you sign in, but also on the Start screen.

To change your account picture, follow these steps:

1. Open the Settings charm, and select **Change PC settings**.

2. Select **Personalize** from the list on the left side of the screen.

3. Select **Account Picture**. The Account Picture screen appears, as shown in Figure 4.6.

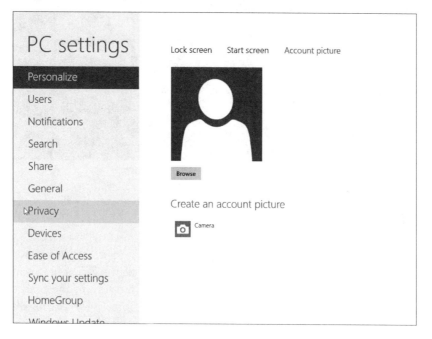

FIGURE 4.6

You can select a photo to use as your account picture or shoot a new photo to use.

4. To shoot a picture using a camera connected to your computer, select **Camera**. When the Camera app starts, snap the photo, set the crop marks, and select **OK**.

    To choose a photo stored on your computer, select **Browse**. The File picker window appears. Select the photo to use as your account picture, and select **Choose image**. For information on navigating your folder system, refer to Chapter 2.

5. The image you chose will appear in the portrait back on the account picture screen, as shown in Figure 4.7.

FIGURE 4.7

Choose your account picture from any photo on your computer. Or shoot a new photo to use easily to update your account picture.

6. You are returned to the Account picture screen. Your account picture now reflects the photo you selected, as shown in Figure 4.7. There is no Close or Exit button on the Account picture screen, so to return to the Start screen, press the Windows key, or slowly move to the bottom-left corner with your finger or mouse to display the Start portrait. Select the portrait.

Personalizing the Lock Screen

The Lock screen appears when you have signed out of Windows 8 or you haven't used Windows 8 for a period of time and it kicks you out.

To change the picture that appears on your lock screen, follow these steps:

1. Open the Settings charm, and select **Change PC Settings**.

2. Select **Personalize** and **then Lock Screen**. Your current Lock screen picture appears in the right pane, as shown in Figure 4.7.

FIGURE 4.7

The Lock screen can fill up the space of your display, so you can certainly choose a large image to personalize the screen.

3. Under **Change Your Picture**, review the five pictures that come with Windows 8. Do one of the following:

   - To use one of the pictures that ships with Windows 8, select the picture you like. The picture you chose replaces the current Lock screen picture on the screen.

   - If you want to use one of your pictures as the Lock screen background, select **Browse**.

4. Your screen displays the photos in your Picture folders. Look through the photos to find one to use as your Lock screen. Select the photo to use and then select **Choose Image**. For help navigating through the selection of Files, refer to "Using the File Picker" in Chapter 3.

Personalizing Tile Groups

Your collection of tiles is bound to grow as you install new programs and Windows 8 apps. You can also pin documents and web pages to the Start screen, so it's likely you will add many, many tiles to the Start screen in a short period of time. To help keep track of tiles and to easily locate them, you can organize tiles into groups of your own design. For example, you might create a group of tiles of all your photo-related applications. The groups are organized into columns on the Start screen. A wider margin separates one group from another. You can move your tile groups when you like, and you also can place a name above each group.

An example of a number of tile groups appears in Figure 4.8.

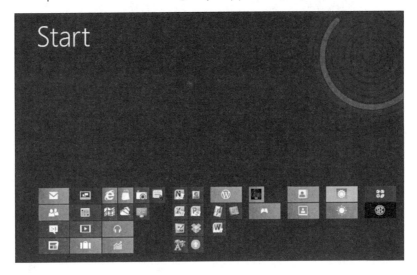

FIGURE 4.8

You can organize the tiles on the Start screen into groups.

Creating a Tile Group

To create a tile group, do one of the following based on the device you use:

- Touch and then drag the first tile in the group to the right beyond the last tile until a vertical bar appears on the screen. Be sure the first tile is to the right of the bar. Release your finger or the stylus from the tile. Drag other tiles in the group the same way either to the right or below any other tile in the group.

- Click and drag the first tile in the group to the right beyond the last tile until a vertical bar appears on the screen. Be sure the first tile is to the right of the bar. Release the mouse. Drag other tiles in the group either to the right or below any other tile in the group.

Moving Tile Groups

To move a tile group, follow these directions based on the device you use:

🖱 From the Start screen, press Ctrl+Mouse-Wheel-Scroll-Forward. This creates an effect of zooming out from the Start screen, as shown in Figure 4.9. With your mouse, click the group to move, and then drag the group to the new location.

👆 Touch the zoom button at the bottom-right corner of the screen, as shown in Figure 4.9. This creates an effect of zooming out from the Start screen (see Figure 4.10). Touch the group you want to move, and then drag it to a new location.

FIGURE 4.9

The small zoom button enables you to move tile groups.

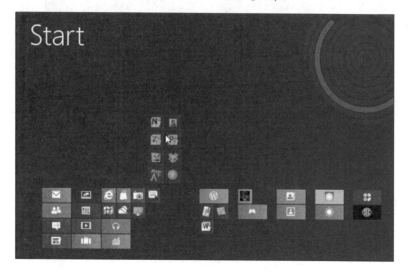

FIGURE 4.10

By zooming out from the Start screen, you can easily rearrange tile groups.

Naming a Tile Group

If you have more than two groups, it makes sense to label the groups. To label a tile group, follow the following advice based on the device you use:

From the Start screen, press Ctrl+scroll the mouse wheel forward. Follow the instructions after the instructions for touch users.

From the Start screen, press Ctrl+scroll the mouse wheel forward. Follow the instructions after the instructions for touch users.

Touch the zoom button at the bottom-right corner of the screen. Tap-and-hold on the group you want to name.

Now whether you use touch or mouse, select the **Name Group** button, and then enter the name of the group in the box that appears, as shown in Figure 4.11. You can repeat these steps for another group, or click or tap anywhere on the screen to return the tiles back to the normal size.

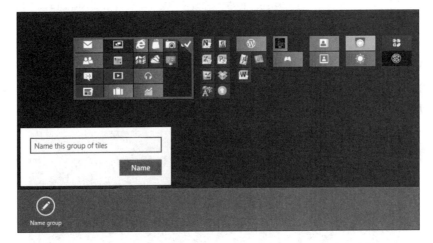

FIGURE 4.11

You enter the name of the tile group in the small box that appears when you select the Name group button.

Setting Up Accessibility Options

The accessibility options in Windows 8, known as Ease of Access, are of use to both folks with disabilities and folks without. You might find it easier to work with the display configured in a high-contrast format, and hearing a voice confirmation of commands also can be helpful.

Figure 4.12 shows the screen where you set up the Ease of Access settings with the High Contrast option on, and you can also see the same screen with the option turned off. Figure 4.13 shows the Ease of Access setting screen with the Make Everything Bigger on Your Screen setting turned on.

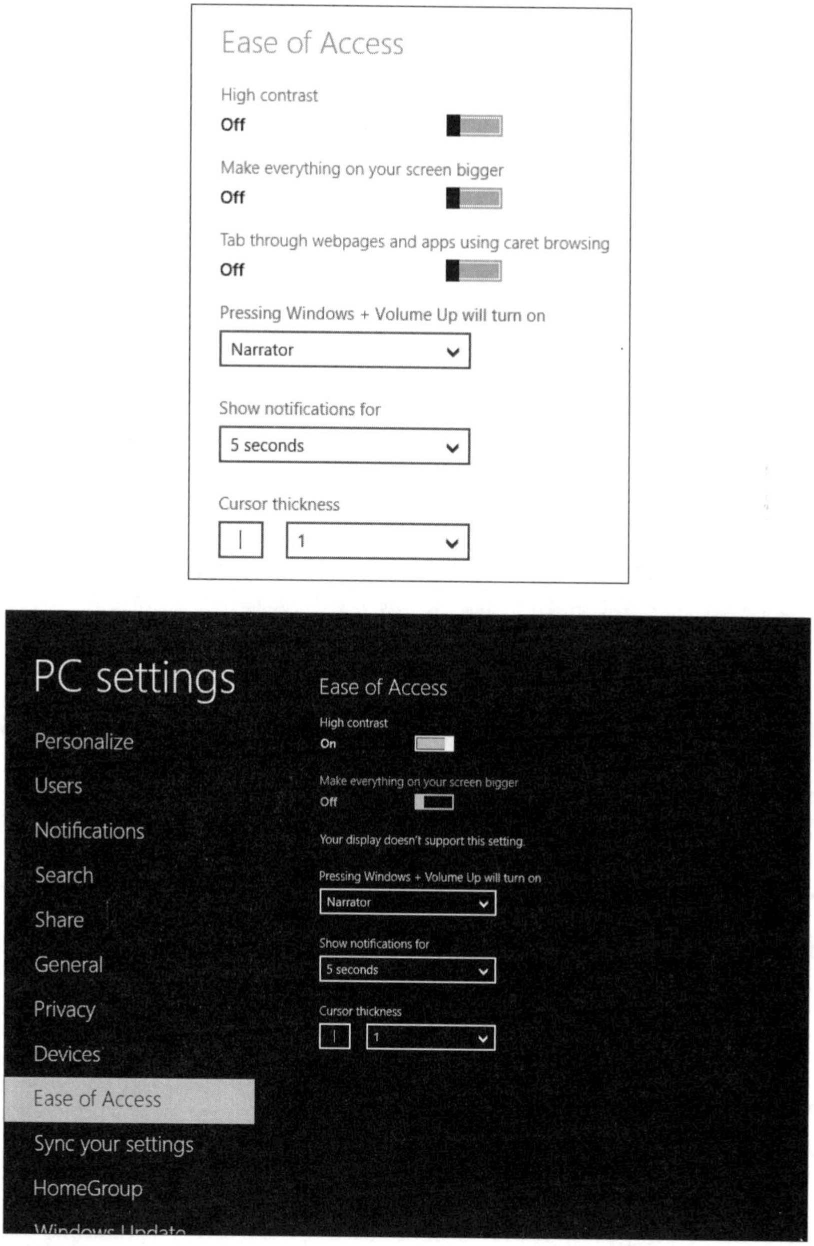

FIGURE 4.12

The top image shows the Ease of Access screen with the High Contrast setting turned off, and the image on the bottom shows the same screen with the High Contrast setting turned on.

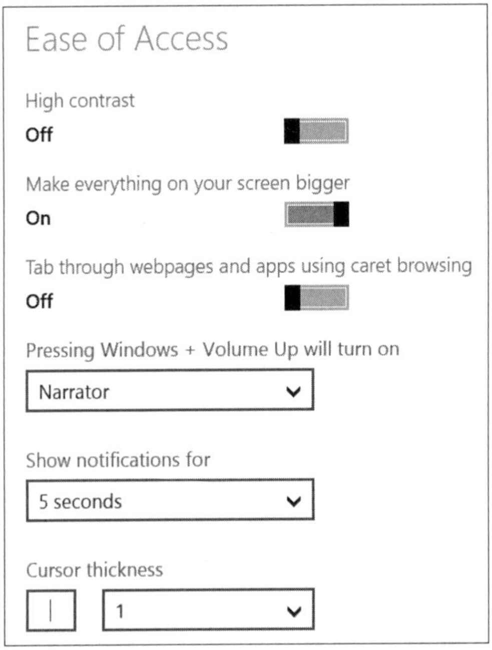

Ease of Access

High contrast
Off

Make everything on your screen bigger
On

Tab through webpages and apps using caret browsing
Off

Pressing Windows + Volume Up will turn on
| Narrator ▾ |

Show notifications for
| 5 seconds ▾ |

Cursor thickness
| | | | 1 ▾ |

FIGURE 4.13

This image shows the Ease of Access settings screen enlarged with the Make Everything on Your Screen Bigger option turned on.

To use the Ease of Access settings, follow these steps:

1. Open the Settings charm and select **Change PC Settings**.

2. Select **Ease of Access.**

3. To use one or more of the following options, move the slider to the right to the On position for the appropriate option:

- High Contrast
- Make Everything on the Screen Bigger
- Tab Through Webpages

4. To use one of the options to enhance the Windows 8 readability and usability, choose Magnifier, Narrator, or On-Screen Keyboard from the **Pressing Windows+Volume Up Will Turn On** list (see Figure 4.14). Select on the down arrow on the right side of the list; then click or tap on the option you want.

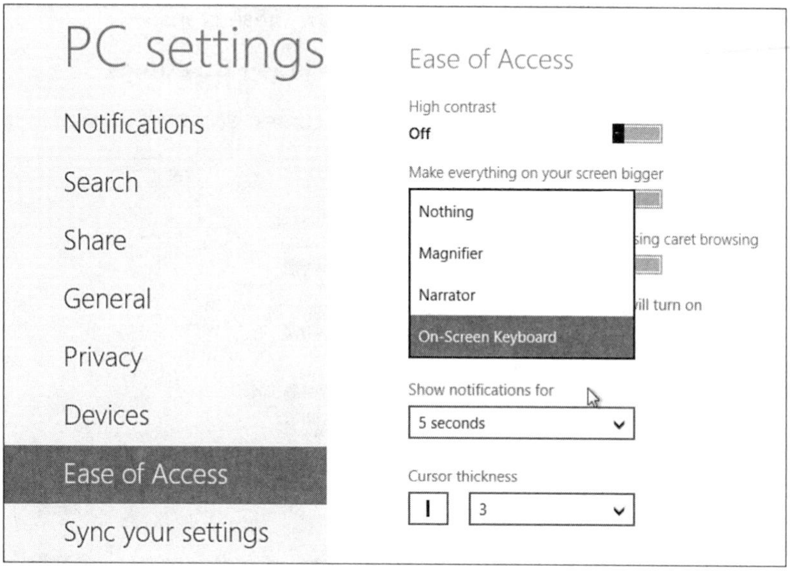

FIGURE 4.14

You can enhance certain aspects of Windows to make it easier to read and respond to prompts.

5. Select the notification durations from the **Show Notifications For** list. This option enables you to specify a longer period of time during which messages and notifications stay on the screen before they are closed. To do so, select the down arrow on the right side of the control; then select the duration you want.

6. Select the Cursor thickness from the list at the bottom of the screen. This option increases the thickness of the cursor, making it easier to see the location of the cursor between letters on the screen. To do so, select the down arrow on the right side of the control, and then select the thickness you want. You can see a sample of the cursor thickness you chose in the small square box adjacent to the **Cursor Thickness** list.

Personalizing How Notifications Work

You probably have noticed how some tiles on the Start screen are "live" in that they display information that changes periodically. For example, the Weather tile shows the local temperature. Certain apps even display status on the Lock screen. You can personalize whether apps display these notifications on the Start screen and on the Lock screen. You can also personalize which apps display notifications.

To personalize how notifications work, follow these steps:

1. Open the Settings charm and select **Change PC Settings**.

2. Select **Notifications**. The Notifications screen appears, as shown in Figure

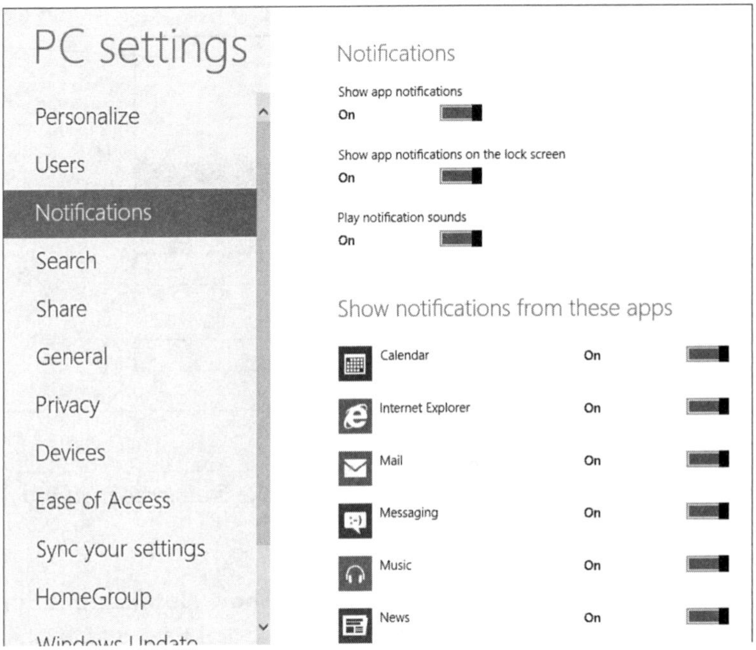

4.15.

FIGURE 4.15

You can control which apps display notifications.

3. To turn off all notifications, including on the Lock screen, move the **Show App Notifications** slider to the left for Off.

4. To turn off notifications on the Lock screen, move the **Show App Notifications on the Lock Screen** slider to the left for Off. The **Show App Notifications** slider must be in the On position, which is to the right.

5. You can set up your notifications to appear, but do so quietly so your co-workers or family do not become angry with you. To do so, be sure the **Show App Notifications** slider is in the On position, which is to the right, and the **Play Notification Sounds** slider must be in the Off position, which is to the left.

6. To turn notifications off from specific applications, move the slider for the particular app to the left, which is the Off position.

Personalizing How Your Windows 8 Settings Synchronize

As you learned in Chapter 1, "Starting and Stopping Windows 8," when you sign in to another computer with your Windows account, your personal settings, such as colors, pictures, apps, and more, are used on this other computer. What a relief not to spend time setting up this computer just to your liking.

Windows saves a number of categories of settings. The settings are stored on a server on the Internet. This server is checked for settings whenever you sign on to any Windows 8 computer. As such, Windows needs to keep that record of your settings on the server up to date with settings you change on a computer you sign in to. You can control which of these settings are synchronized with the server. Any settings you do not synchronize use the standard setting Windows would use when you first install it.

To specify which settings are synchronized, follow these steps:

1. Open the Settings charm and then select **Change PC Settings**.

2. Select **Sync Your Settings**.

3. To turn off all syncing, move the slider for **Sync Settings on This PC** to the left for Off.

4. Review the list of settings that can sync across computers you sign in to. There may be certain settings that you prefer not to sync. Move the slider to the left for Off for settings you do not want to sync. Be sure the slider is to the right in the On position for those you want to sync.

Personalizing the Desktop

One of the most enjoyable tasks in the computer world is to make Windows feel like home. This applies to the Desktop. You can tweak the color of everything from the window border to the text on the screen; use your favorite photo as a background on the Desktop; change the icon representing the Recycle Bin to one of 400+ icons provided in Windows; and change many other settings to make the Desktop reflect your mood and personality. In this section, you learn how to personalize the Desktop environment.

Changing the Desktop Background

The Desktop background is the best place where you can show your own personality and preferences in Windows. You can choose a stock image that comes with Windows, or you can choose a picture that you have imported from a camera or received in email. To change the Desktop background, follow these steps:

1. Right-click or tap-and-hold a clear spot on the Desktop; then click **Personalize**.

2. Select **Desktop Background** at the bottom of the window. The Desktop Background window appears, as shown in Figure 4.16.

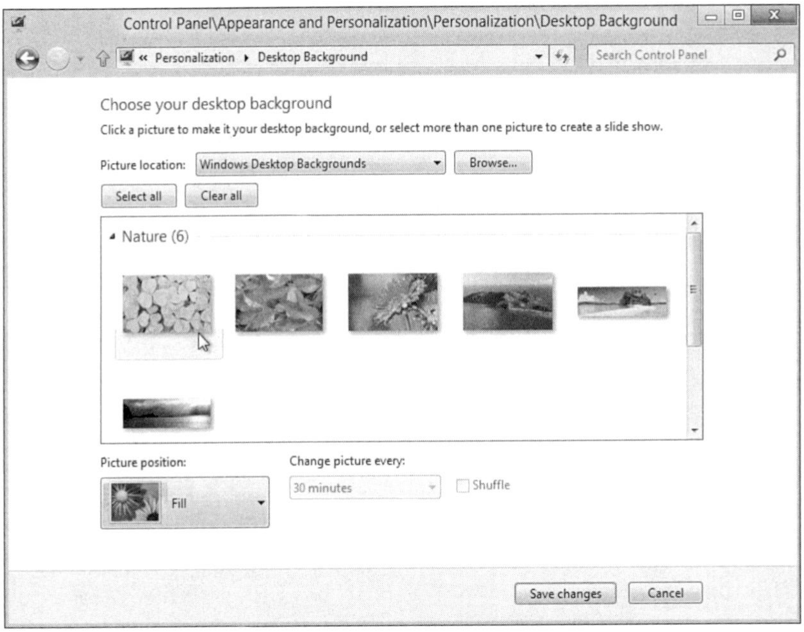

FIGURE 4.16

A number of options are available to format the Desktop background.

3. The **Picture Location** drop-down list includes four different locations on your computer where pictures to use as a desktop background are located. Select anywhere on the list to display the four locations. Then, select each item in the lists to see the pictures at each location. Of course, if you see a picture you like, there is no need to look further!

4. If you want to use just one picture or a color as your background, select the picture or color; then select **Save Changes**. At this point, you are done and can select the **X** on the top-right corner of the window to close it. If you want your background to rotate through a number of pictures, continue with the next step.

5. Select the check box in each picture you want to use.

6. At the bottom of the Desktop Background window (you should be there), select **Picture Position**, and then select how you want the pictures you chose in step 5 to appear.

7. Select the **Change Picture Every** drop-down list; then select the interval at which the picture should change, as shown in Figure 4.17.

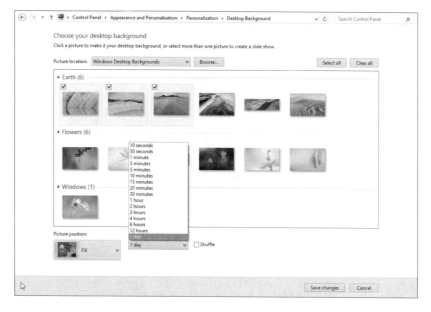

FIGURE 4.17

Select how often the Desktop background image will change.

8. Select **Shuffle** to randomly choose the order in which pictures appear.

9. Select **Save Changes**.

10. Select **Close** to close the Personalization window.

Changing the Mouse Pointers Used on the Desktop

You may want to customize the mouse pointers you use in Windows. You can adjust the pointers to reflect your personality and taste, or you might need to switch to pointers that are larger than normal to make it easier to see them. There are 10 different pointers you can customize, such as the selection pointer and the double-arrow head pointer. You can customize one or more of the pointers individually, or you can switch to a full set of 10 pointers.

To change the mouse pointers, follow these steps:

1. Right-click or press-and-hold a clear spot on the Desktop; then select **Personalize**.

2. Select **Change Mouse Pointers** near the top-left corner of the window. The Mouse Properties dialog box appears, as shown in Figure 4.18.

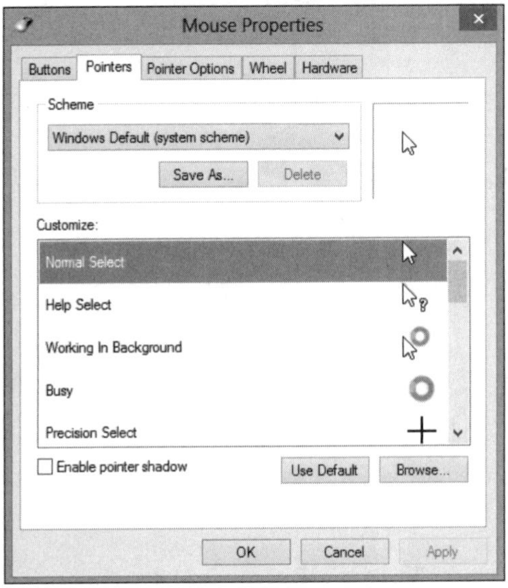

FIGURE 4.18

You can change many aspects of the mouse, including the pointer appearance, how fast the pointer moves across the screen as you move the mouse, and more.

3. To use a predefined set of pointers, scroll through the schemes at the top of the dialog box. Select a scheme to inspect the pointers. If you find a scheme you like, select **OK**. Select **OK** again to close the Personalization window.

4. To choose a specific mouse pointer without committing to a set, select the pointer in the large list.

5. Select **Browse**. A window appears displaying the mouse pointers available to you.

 NOTE You can change the way the selection of mouse pointers appear in the dialog box used to select a new pointer. Select the View Menu button from the toolbar, and then select the view you want. The Medium Icons view presents the most useful arrangement of icons.

6. Select the pointer you want to use from the list; then select **Open**. You should be at the Mouse Properties dialog box.

7. Select the next pointer you want to customize, and then repeat steps 5 and 6.

8. Select **OK** to close the Mouse Properties dialog box.

9. Select **Close** to close the Personalization window.

Change the Desktop's Color Scheme

You can change the color of the Taskbar and window borders. You can choose from a preset palette of colors. To change the Desktop color scheme, follow these steps:

1. Right-click or tap-and-hold a clear spot on the Desktop; then select **Personalize**.

2. Select the **Window Color** button at the bottom of the window. A window appears with a palette of color swatches.

3. Choose the color you like, and then select **Save Changes**.

4. Select **Close** to close the Personalization window.

Setting Up a Desktop Screen Saver

Screen saver programs became popular with the introduction of Windows as a means to prevent images from the new-at-the-time highly graphical software applications from creating a ghosted image on the display. This action came to be known as *burning in*. Display technology has advanced, and the risk of burning-in is negligible for modern displays, yet screen savers remain popular. If you want to use one, you can always find a screen saver that reflects your mood and personality. Follow these steps to configure a screen saver in Windows 8.

1. Right-select-and-hold an empty spot on the Desktop, and then click **Personalize**.

2. Select **Screen Saver** at the bottom of the window. The Screen Saver Settings dialog box appears, as shown in Figure 4.19.

3. Select the **Screen Saver** list to display the list of screen savers installed on your computer.

4. In the **Screen Saver** list, choose the screen saver you want to use. Notice that the monitor image at the top of the dialog box shows you a preview of the screen saver you selected.

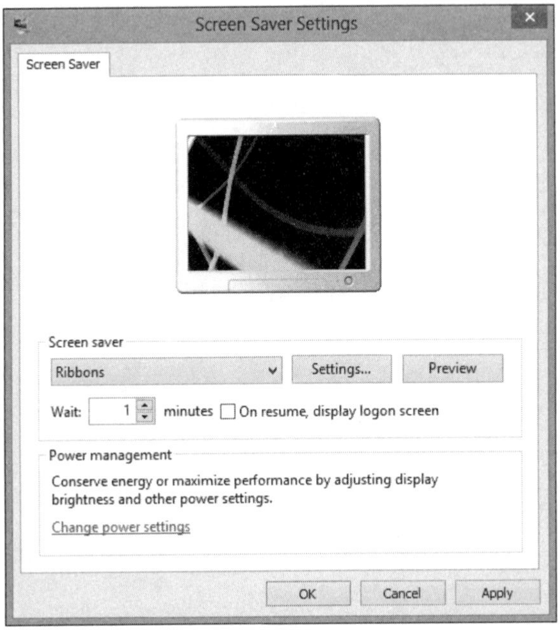

FIGURE 4.19

You can choose from the seven different screen savers that come with Windows.

5. Depending on the screen saver you selected, there may be options for you to set. For example, the 3D Text screen saver has a number of options. Select the **Settings** button to customize the screen saver. Click **OK** when complete.

6. Select **Preview** to review your screen saver as it will appear in use. Select anywhere on the screen to close the preview.

7. In the **Wait** box, enter the amount of time during which there is no activity on your computer before the screen saver starts.

8. If your computer is in a location where there are people that you would prefer not to potentially access your computer, enable the **On Resume, Display Logon Screen** check box. This requires a user to log on to clear the screen saver after it starts.

9. Select **OK**.

10. Select **Close** to close the Personalization window.

THE ABSOLUTE MINIMUM

Here are the key points to remember from this chapter:

- You can change a number of preferences and options in Windows 8 to suit your personality and mood. You can apply these preferences to any computer you sign in to with you Windows 8 password. You can determine which, if any, of these preferences are saved and then applied to other computers you use.

- Anyone can use the Ease of Access settings to enhance the readability and usability of Windows 8. A high-contrast color scheme can be used; everything on the screen can be made larger; a voice from Windows can read to you messages that appear as you work; and a magnifier can be configured to pop up as needed to read small text.

- Nothing says, "This computer is mine" more effectively than a custom color choice and personal photos used in various places. You can specify the color scheme to use throughout Windows 8, as well as the pictures that appear on the sign-in screen and the Lock screen. The pictures can be anonymous, such as a setting sun or another landscape or view. Or the pictures can be personal, showing you, family, friends, pets, or whatever.

- Many applications display information periodically without you having to open them. These messages, known as notifications, can be suppressed. For example, if you do not want to see the new email notification, preferring to check email status when you open the app, you can suppress this notification. You can suppress all notifications or individually choose which appear.

5

CONNECTING TO THE INTERNET

Although Windows 8 is jammed with cool and fun features, most of its power comes from its integration with the Internet. Your personal contacts are developed and maintained through social media, email, and messaging on the Internet. These contacts are the fuel that powers the sharing capabilities throughout Windows 8.

To help you connect wherever you are, this chapter provides several step-by-step lists of instructions. And to understand a bit of the fundamentals, there is a brief review of a number of key topics on Internet connections. You'll learn about connecting wirelessly, with a cable, via dial-up, and with a mobile broadband modem from your ISP.

Reviewing Important Internet Connection Basics

Connecting to the Internet from your desktop, laptop, or tablet usually runs smoothly after everything is set up properly. But there are lots of moving parts in the process, any of which can stop working or become dated as new capabilities are developed. One way to anticipate problems, as well as to be on the lookout for faster and better ways to connect, is to know the basics of connecting to the Internet. You won't necessarily become an Internet engineer after reading this section, but you can certainly gain a better understanding of what happens when you fire it up.

Learning About Internet Service Providers

The devices you use today to browse the web, send and receive email, play videos, and more cannot actually connect to the Internet on their own. Whether you are at home, in an office, on a plane, or in a coffee shop or another public place, you need a go-between to connect to the Internet. This go-between is known as an *Internet service provider*, or *ISP*. The ISP keeps a pipe open to the Internet. You pay your ISP to connect you to that pipe. Even large companies that provide their employees fast Internet access do so by working with an ISP. Figure 5.1 illustrates how your computer works with the ISP.

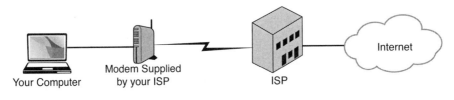

Your Computer   Modem Supplied   ISP   Internet
                        by your ISP

FIGURE 5.1

The ISP provides access to the Internet. Your connection does not run through your ISP's headquarters. The picture expresses your ISP managing your connection.

Checking the Hardware Required to Connect

Although Windows 8 is powerful, connecting to the Internet usually requires some hardware, all of it usually provided by the ISP, including the following:

- **Modem**—The modem is a device that bridges the Internet to your computer or home/office network. Each type of Internet connection—cable, DSL, and such—uses a different type of modem.

- **Ethernet cable**—Except for dial-up and mobile broadband connections, you need an Ethernet cable to connect your computer to the modem or to connect the modem to a router and your computer to the router. If an Ethernet cable was not provided by your ISP, you can purchase one at any store that sells electronics, especially computer equipment.

- **Wireless antennae**—If you want to connect wirelessly and your device does not have a wireless network adapter, you can purchase one and connect one easily. You can add a wireless network adapter usually just to a computer and not to a tablet device.

 NOTE Another common device you may have is called a *router*, which is discussed in the section, "Understanding Routers for Internet Connection Sharing." Routers are essential if you want to share your connection across multiple devices.

Learning the Internet Connection Services Typically Available

Each ISP uses a specific technology to connect your computer to the Internet. The combination of the technology the ISP provides plus the price the ISP charges, the availability of the service, how to use and configure the technology, and how convenient and reliable the technology is, all combine to define a service offered by the ISP. It may be that you have a number of different services available at your home. If that is the case, review each option carefully to make a decision. Price is important, but be sure to research the reliability of the service. Reliability is defined by how often the service is down, plus whether the connection is provided at the speed advertised and that you pay for. There may be just one ISP doing business in your neighborhood, and that ISP might provide just one service. In that case, your options are obviously limited.

Here's a list of the current services used to connect users, as well as a short explanation of how you connect to the service:

- **Cable**—Technology companies have learned to piggyback Internet traffic on the cable and hardware that provides cable TV service to their customers. Your ISP, which with this technology will be the company that provides your cable TV services, provides you a modem, which connects to one of the cable ports in your home using coaxial cable. If you would like the modem in a particular room in your home, you may need to have a new plug installed in that room.

You connect your computer to the modem with an Ethernet cable. You usually do not need a user id and password to access the Internet with a cable modem, but be sure to ask if one is needed when you have cable modem service installed.

 NOTE Many cable companies provide a choice for speeds of Internet service. Many services start at 3 Mbps, which stands for 3 megabits per second or *3 million bits per second*. At 3 Mbps, a song available for download on the Internet would take about 14 seconds (assumes song is 5 MB). Cable companies offer services (at a higher cost) up to 12 Mbps and faster.

- **DSL**—A popular broadband service is DSL, which, because it uses the same lines that support your regular telephone service (if you still have that), is provided exclusively by telephone companies. Telephone lines have the capacity to carry both the phone traffic and Internet traffic without one interfering with the other. The ISP provides a small device that splits the signal so that the phone signal goes to the telephone and the Internet signal goes to the modem. The modem is another piece of hardware provided by the ISP.

  You need access to a telephone port close to the location, ideally in the same room, where the model is installed. Like the cable modem, you connect your computer to the modem with an Ethernet cable. You usually do not need a user ID and password to access the Internet with a DSL modem, but be sure to ask if one is needed when you have the service installed.

- **Mobile broadband**—A relatively new option for connecting to the Internet brings the high-speed 3g and 4g cellular networks to laptops and tablets. Telecomm companies such as Verizon, AT&T, and others sell devices that connect to the provider's cellular network, sometimes by connecting the device to your computer's USB port and sometimes via Wi-Fi. It's a perfect option for connecting outside of the home or office. The device comes with software that you use to connect to the network whose service you chose.

- **Satellite**—DirecTV, the largest television and music satellite company, also provides Internet access through its satellite service. The signal is delivered to your home or home office from the satellite dish mounted on a building or based on the ground.

The signal is delivered into your office or home by a cable from the dish that connects to a modem, which is used to convert the signal for use with your computer, as shown in Figure 5.2. You connect your computer to the modem with an Ethernet cable. You usually do not need a user id and password to access the Internet with a cable modem, but be sure to ask if one is needed when you have cable modem service installed

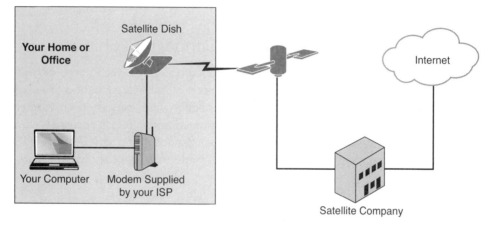

FIGURE 5.2

Satellite service is an option for locations that can't be served by cable or telephone companies.

The benefits of DirecTV Internet service is its availability where DSL and cable service is not available. You might also save money by bundling satellite entertainment service with Internet service. The disadvantage of satellite service for Internet is that under overcast skies the satellite signal is easy lost. The service is also approximately 75% slower than cable service. It's reasonable to say that satellite service should be used only when no other service is available.

• **Dial-up**—Dial-up Internet access is still in use where broadband access is not available. With this service, a modem is used to send and receive Internet traffic over telephone lines. Many computers have a built-in modem, but it's important to check if one is installed before you commit to using dial-up service. Dial-up service is slow, but using this technology may be your last resort when other services are unavailable. Your local telephone company may offer dial-up service. If you can get online, a popular and useful site that lists dial-up services is http://www.freedomlist.com.

- **Leased line**—The leased line service is used by companies needing the fastest connection to the Internet possible. This service gives customers constant access to a line attached directly to physical hardware on the Internet. This is an extremely expensive service. Unless you have a flourishing business at home or you have a demand for fast and reliable access (such as if you count on real-time access to financial markets), a leased line is probably overkill.

Understanding Routers for Internet Connection Sharing

To extend an Internet connection to several computers in your home or home office, you can use a router. A router is a piece of hardware (costing usually less than $75) that helps share the Internet connection with computers connected to the router. Routers today can provide both wired and wireless access. A router suitable for home or home office use can usually accommodate 5–10 wired devices. You connect your router to the Internet modem, as shown in Figure 5.3.

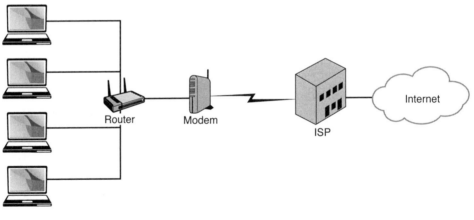

FIGURE 5.3

A router can be used to share a single Internet connection with several computers.

 TIP The modem provided by your ISP might also double as a router by providing support for sharing the connection with multiple computers, including permitting wireless access to the modem.

Understanding Network Adapters

The network adapter is the piece of hardware used to connect to a network. Often these adapters are internal, meaning you can't see them unless you open your computer (which is not recommended). A network adapter can be wireless or wired. You may be asked to disable or update a driver for one of these devices. Although troubleshooting isn't covered in this chapter, here's how to access the network adapter in Windows 8:

To view the network adapters set up in Windows, follow these steps:

1. From the Charms bar, select **Search**.

2. Select **Settings** and then enter **View Network Connections** in the search box.

3. Click **View Network Connections** in the results pane. The adapters configured on your computer appear on the screen.

Connecting to the Internet

Following are some of the most common Internet connection scenarios. You can follow the step-by-step procedures to connect to the Internet for each scenario in the following list:

- Connecting to a wireless network

- Connecting where free Wi-Fi is advertised

- Connecting where Wi-Fi access can be purchased

- Connecting to a wired network at work or home

- Connecting after you upgrade to Windows 8
- Connecting if you have been forced to restart

Connecting to a Wireless Network

To connect to the Internet through a wireless broadband network, follow these steps:

1. Open the Charms bar and select **Settings**.

2. Select **Network**. The pane showing network connections flies out, as shown in Figure 5.4.

FIGURE 5.4

You can review all the network connections in one place in Windows 8.

3. Select the network to which you want to connect. The pane opens to display connection statistics and the Connect button, as shown in Figure 5.5.

4. If want to connect to the network automatically the next time you sign in to Windows, select **Connect Automatically**.

5. Select **Connect**. You are prompted to enter the PIN of the router your wireless adapter connects to, as shown in Figure 5.6.

6. Enter the PIN and select **Next**. Skip to step 9.

   Alternatively, if you know the security key (passphrase) for the network, select **Connect Using a Security Key Instead**. The screen shown in Figure 5.7 appears.

FIGURE 5.5

You are able to review how much data has passed through your connection.

FIGURE 5.6

You can confirm you have access to the network by entering the PIN of the router.

FIGURE 5.7

You can confirm you have access to the network also by entering the security key set up on the router.

7. Enter the security key and select **Next**.

8. If you have not configured security on this network yet, you can specify whether sharing is allowed. You may answer Yes here and then control which items are shared, as well as with whom, with the homegroups feature in Windows 8.

9. Select **Close**.

Connecting Where Free Wi-Fi Is Advertised

There's little doubt that you have come across a store, a coffee shop, or another public location advertising Wi-Fi. If the place offers free Wi-Fi, follow the previous steps under "Connecting to a Wireless Network." At step 8, you need to provide the network passcode. A worker can provide you with this.

 NOTE Some sites do not require a passcode; although, they may require you to read an agreement or watch an advertisement to connect.

Connecting to Pay-as-You-Go Wi-Fi

Most airports and many small coffee and snack shops offer Wi-Fi today, which is almost always provided by a national service. You can usually tell which type of Wi-Fi is offered from advertisements or notices on the walls. Or you can ask someone. Most ISPs charge a fee based on the time you connect. If you connect from this location frequently, you may consider signing up for a plan that gives you access for a longer period at a reduced price.

If Wi-Fi is offered for a fee, you need to enter credit card information to pay for the access.

Follow these steps to connect to a Wi-Fi hotspot:

1. It might seem like a hassle or a waste of time, but if your device was powered on when you entered the store or shop that offers Wi-Fi, shut it down completely, and restart when you are at the location.

2. You need to first connect to the wireless service in place at your location. This does not provide you access to the Internet yet. You are simply joining the network at your location. Follow the instructions in the previous section, "Connecting to a Wireless Network." Someone working at or supporting your location can identify the network you should connect to; although, the name of the network (Paul's Bagel Shop Network) might make the selection obvious.

3. Open Internet Explorer. You should be brought to the sign-up page for the ISP in use at the location. Enter the information requested. You should connect shortly.

Connecting to a LAN/Wired Network

You might be at an office, a school, or a place of business, where Internet access, of course, is not advertised, but you have access to the local area network (LAN). Most corporate and school networks connect to the Internet over a LAN. This is no different than using a wired network connection in your home.

At an office or school, look for an unused Ethernet port. There is only one type of port that accommodates the Ethernet plug, so you should determine quickly if a port is available. At home, simply connect to one of the ports in your modem or router.

After you connect, wait a few seconds before you verify you are online. Start Internet Explorer to verify you are connected. If you are not connected to the LAN, it is a good idea to shut down your computer and restart. After you sign on again, open Internet Explorer to confirm you are connected to the Internet. If an error message appears, meet with a member of the information technology team or contact the support desk.

Connecting After Upgrading to Windows 8

If you upgraded your computer from Windows 7, and you could connect to the Internet before you upgraded, you should connect without issue in Windows 8. If you installed Windows 8 on a new drive or partition, you were probably prompted to connect to the Internet to complete the setup. You definitely need to connect to the Internet if you want to sign in with a Windows account.

Connecting After You Restart Your Device

Windows automatically reconnects to the wireless network you have been using. If you intentionally disconnected from a network, Windows 8 no longer automatically connects you to that network. Wi-Fi networks always have priority over mobile broadband networks.

Connecting in Other Scenarios

You can connect to a number of other Internet resources by walking through a few screens in Windows 8. Follow these steps to walk through the process to create a number of different Internet connections:

1. Open the Charms bar and then select **Search**.

2. Select **Settings** and then enter **network**.

3. Select the **View Network Status** app from the results pane. The Network and Sharing Center appears, as shown in Figure 5.8.

FIGURE 5.8

Select the Network and Sharing Center to create connections to other Internet resources.

4. Select **Set Up a New Connection or Network**. The Set Up a Connection or Network screen appears, as shown in Figure 5.9.

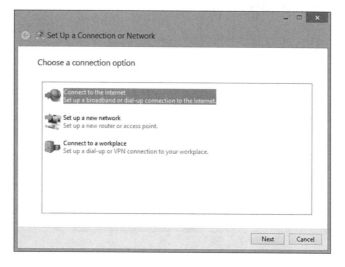

FIGURE 5.9

You have a choice of three different options with which to create a new connection to the Internet.

5. To use dial-up to get access to the Internet, select **Connect to the Internet** and follow the prompts on the screen.

6. To connect to a wireless network that doesn't appear automatically in the Network Connections pane, select **Manually Connect to a Wireless Network** and follow the prompts as they appear.

7. To connect to a virtual private network (VPN) based on instructions provided to you by your employer, select **Connect to a Workplace** and then follow the prompts as they appear on the screen.

THE ABSOLUTE MINIMUM

- There are a number of technologies in use today to connect people to the Internet. Because typically just one ISP serves a neighborhood, you might not have a choice of Internet connection technologies.

- The ISP is your most important partner in connecting to the Internet. The ISP provides the technology, connects you to the Internet pipe, and maintains service at an agreed-upon speed to its customers. Users can usually not overcome or work around problems at the ISP.

- Cable and DSL Internet connection technologies both ride their respective Internet signals piggyback on existing customer hardware. DSL providers use the same phone lines to carry the Internet service, whereas cable connection companies do the same on their cables infrastructure that provides you TV and movie service.

- Windows 8 permits you to use the PIN assigned permanently to your router to authorize you to use the Internet connection. This use of a PIN supplements the traditional use of a password or passphrase.

6

SURFING THE WEB IN WINDOWS 8

Surfing the web probably is the most popular activity in Windows, more so perhaps than checking email, and definitely more so than doing work! If you think the same way, you'll also agree how important it is to like your web surfing tool.

Microsoft thinks it's important, too, so important that Windows 8 comes with two versions of Internet Explorer. One version is new, reflecting the same look and feel as the rest of Windows 8. The other Internet Explorer is the Desktop version, which is much like the Internet Explorer you are accustomed to using in prior versions of Windows. You'll most likely use the new version of Internet Explorer more often than the legacy browser, especially because the new version is so readily accessible from the Start screen. This chapter helps you understand how to use the new Windows 8 browser, as well as when you may need to use the Desktop version.

As you learned in Chapter 3, "Learning Windows 8 Basics," Windows 8 reflects new principles, style, and rules about the screens appear and work. The Windows 8 browser leverages all the new controls and way-to-do-things presented in that chapter. To make the most of this chapter, review Chapter 3, paying particular attention to sections about charms.

Introducing Internet Explorer

Like the Start screen, the sign-in screen, the Mail, Contacts, and Calendar applications, and many other areas of Windows 8, Internet Explorer (IE) is new and different than previous version of Windows. The new version of IE is designed to run fast, provide a simplified experience, especially for those browsing from a touch device, and to maximize screen real estate.

The other version, referred to as the Desktop browser, is much like the previous versions of Internet Explorer. It provides more of the traditional browser features, such as playing movies from the Internet and working with custom toolbars, this at the expense of ease of use and speed.

You can use whatever version you prefer. The differences between the two probably won't lead to a permanent choice. You might switch between the two browsers based on the kind of browsing you want to do. Table 6.1 points out the major differences between the two browsers.

TABLE 6.1 Windows 8 Browser Versus Desktop Browser

Capability	Windows 8	Desktop
Perform downloads	✓	*✓
Run Flash content (Read the following Note.)	✓	✓
Maintain list of favorites		✓
Show most popular sites	✓	
Maintain list of sites you visit most frequently	✓	
Organize open websites in tabs	✓	✓
Pins sites to the Start screen	✓	
Uses toolbars		✓

NOTE The videos you play on YouTube, the exciting animation you see on the sites promoting new Hollywood movies, plus many online, animated games are built with technology known as Flash from a company called Adobe. Flash has come under criticism because it can use a significant amount of system resources, and sometimes errors in the content can cause a page to freeze. Microsoft has limited the sites it enables to play Flash content in the Windows 8 browser. You can see a message on the page with Flash content that has been disallowed by Microsoft. Most YouTube videos play in the Windows 8 browser. All Flash content is enables to run in the Desktop browser.

To start the Windows 8 browser, from the Start screen, select the Internet Explorer tile, as shown in Figure 6.1. Figure 6.2 shows the Windows 8 browser open to Microsoft's website.com. Notice that there are no on-screen controls—all you see is the website.

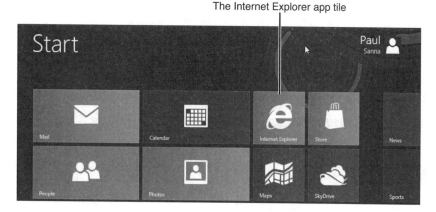

FIGURE 6.1

Start Internet Explorer from the tile on the Start screen.

Now that you know how to start the browser, it's time to dive into its features and capabilities. Let's start with some housekeeping:

As you can see in Figure 6.2, no buttons or other controls display in the Windows 8 browser. To display the buttons, tabs, and other widgets that you need to operate the browser, do one of the following based on the computer or device you use:

 Swipe up from the bottom of the screen.

Right-click anywhere on the page you are viewing. Avoid right-clicking any text, pictures, buttons, or links.

Press Windows+Z.

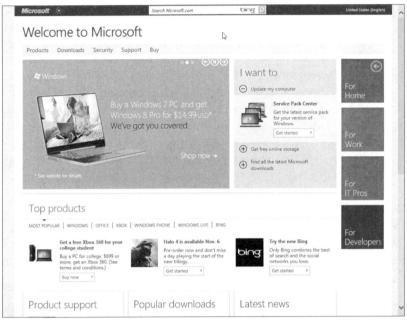

FIGURE 6.2

This screen shows Microsoft's home page in Internet Explorer.

Doing this displays the address bar and the tab switcher, as shown in Figure 6.3.

Tab Switcher

Address Bar

FIGURE 6.3

The address bar and the tab switcher appear when you need them to.

Navigating to Websites

The new versions of Internet Explorer in Windows 8 have lots of great features. But none of the new features that, for example, help you pin your favorites to the Start screen are worth anything if you can't perform a browser's core function— browse the web and stop at sites you're interested in. The following sections demonstrate a variety of ways you can get to your favorite websites or to websites you never knew existed.

Entering the URL of a Site You Want to Visit

Perhaps the most direct way to navigate to a site is to type the name of the site you want to go to. Don't worry, you don't have to memorize complicated website addresses. Many times just the main part of the address will do. For example, to visit Microsoft's website, you don't have to enter HTTP://WWW.MICROSOFT. COM, but just MICROSOFT will do.

As you visit more sites, the browser begins to recognize the site you want to visit after you enter just a few characters. As you enter characters into the address bar, the Windows 8 browser tries to match your input with sites on these lists, as shown in Figure 6.4:

- The sites you visit the most
- The sites you hit most recently
- The most popular sites

To enter the URL of the site to visit, display the address bar, click or tap anywhere in the address bar, and enter the name of the site you want to visit.

Searching the Web

Using Internet Explorer's search function can help you find both sites on the Internet you probably never knew existed and those you're specifically searching for. You can choose from a number of different search engines, such as Bing or Google. Depending on the topic you search for and the engine you want to use, you might see hundreds or even thousands of results returned.

To search the Web from the Windows 8 browser, follow these steps:

1. Open the Charms bar and select **Search**.

2. Type your search terms. Notice how the browser begins to retrieve results as you type, as shown in Figure 6.5.

FIGURE 6.4

Internet Explorer suggests sites as you enter characters into the address bar. In this example, the characters, l i v e are entered, and a number of matching tiles appear.

FIGURE 6.5

Internet Explorer begins searching as soon as you enter text into the search terms box.

3. If any of the search results are of interest to you, select it by either pressing the down arrow key to highlight the one you like and then press **Enter**; or simply click it with the mouse or tap it with your finger or stylus.

4. If the Windows 8 browser did not show any early results as you entered the search terms, just press **Enter** when you finish.

    After a moment, your search results appear on a web page (see Figure 6.6). Select any link of interest.

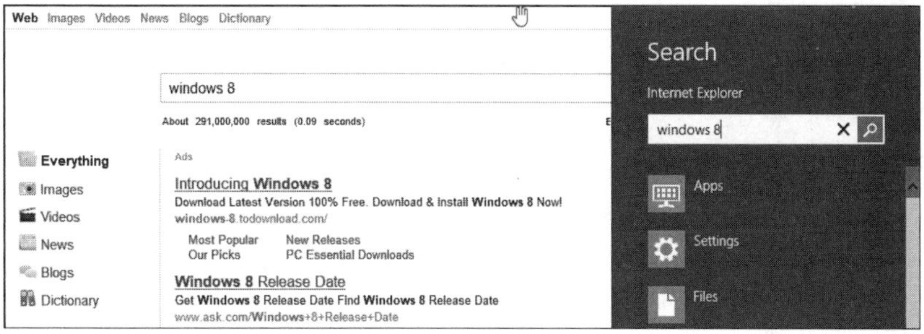

FIGURE 6.6

The Bing search engine returned approximately 290 million results on Windows 8.

Following a Hyperlink to Another Page

It's rare to come across a web page that does not have a link to another page. A link on a web page that brings you to another page is known as a *hyperlink*. A hyperlink normally has a color other than the rest of the text on the page, and often there is a line underneath the words of the hyperlink. A picture or even a word or headline large than the other text on the pages also can be a hyperlink. On many sites, almost every element on the page links to another page.

Follow these tips for working with hyperlinks:

-   Click or tap on a link to open the page targeted by the hyperlink.

-   Right-click or tap-and-hold on a link, which pops up a menu, as shown in Figure 6.7. From that menu, you can

    -   Copy the link so that you can use it somewhere else, like in an email or another web browser.

    -   Open a new tab containing the page the link points to.

    -   Open the page targeted by the hyperlink.

    -   Perform some action based on the type of link you selected, like saving a picture on the website to your computer.

FIGURE 6.7

The target pop-up shows you the web page that will appear when the link you point to is selected.

Revisiting a Site You Visit Often Plus Your Favorites

The Windows 8 browser keeps track of the sites you have visited recently and makes it easy for you to revisit any of those sites.

To see the list of sites you visit frequently, as well as see your list of favorites:

- Select the address bar. A row of tiles should appear above the address bar, as shown in Figure 6.8. Select a tile to visit the site it represents, or select the arrow buttons to scroll to tiles on the list but off the screen.

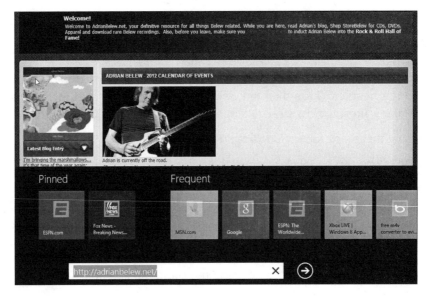

FIGURE 6.8

By just selecting the address bar, a row of your most frequently visited websites appears. Favorites are listed beyond Frequent sites.

Opening a Tabbed Site

A feature known as *tabbed browsing* enables you to have several websites open at one time. You can easily switch from one tab to another to see pages from as many sites as you like.

To access the sites you have open in tabs, follow these steps:

1. Open the tabs bar.

2. A pane with tabs appears at the top of the screen, as shown in Figure 6.9. Switch to the site you want to browse by selecting the tab that shows the site. To use your keyboard, press Ctrl+tab-number, where tab-number refers to the position of the tab you want to switch to in the collection of all tabs. For example, to navigate to the second tab, press Ctrl+2.

FIGURE 6.9

This figure shows the Windows 8 browser with a number of tabs open.

Using a Website's Jump List

A jump list is a terrific feature that was first introduced in Internet Explorer 8. In Windows 8, jump lists are a part of the Windows 8 browser. A *jump list* is a set of links specific to a particular application or site—developers decides what links to put on their jump list. A website might provide links to relevant pages on its site, whereas a music playing application might provide links to burn a music CD, import music from CDs, and more. The jump list appears only on sites pinned to the Start screen. Figure 6.10 shows how jump lists work.

Select commands from the Jump List

This button indicates a Jump List is available

FIGURE 6.10

Jump lists are another option for navigating to websites.

Navigating Back and Forth

You can easily go back to the last page you opened, and when there, you can move forward to the screen where you started. There is a forward and backward button on the page you are viewing, as shown in Figure 6.11. Point to the middle point on either the left or right border. Then click or tap to move forward or backward. To use your keyboard, press Alt+Right Arrow to go forward or Alt+Left Arrow to move back.

Although the Next Page button moves you to the page you left before visiting the page you're on, sometimes you need to move to the next page of the article you're reading. Many sites publish reports and articles that are organized across many pages. Although these sites usually provide a link to the next page in the story, it's not always convenient to access it. You can turn on a feature known as Flip Ahead that makes the Next Page button actually move you to the next page in the article you're reading.

To turn on the Flip Ahead feature, select the Settings charm, and then select **Internet Options**. Move the Flip Ahead browser to the On position.

Previous Page   Next Page

FIGURE 6.11

Move to the previous or next page by choosing one of the two buttons on the screen. You can also use your keyboard to switch pages.

Enhancing Your Browsing

A few features can make your browsing experience better. You can magnify the page you look at, which is known as *zooming in*. You can also *zoom out* to see a broader view of the page. You can also very easily open the site you're currently browsing in the Desktop browser, which gives you access to some features not available from the Windows 8 browser, like playing Flash movies or playing some games.

Zooming In and Out

Sometimes you come across websites in which the text and/or the graphics on the side have been formatted too small. Rather than abandon looking at the site, you can take advantage of a tool that enables you to enlarge or reduce the view used for the site.

To zoom in or zoom out of the Windows 8 browser, follow these steps:

1. Open the Windows 8 browser to the page you want to see.

2. Open the Settings charm. Select **Settings**.

3. Notice the Zoom slider bar about halfway down the Settings page. Tap or click on the slider to zoom in or out. Or drag the dark block on the slider until the browser, which you can see behind the Settings page, is at a resolution that enables you read the site clearly.

To zoom in or zoom out whenever you need to, you may also pinch with your fingers on the screen to zoom in or pull your fingers apart from the pinch gesture. With your mouse, you can turn the mouse wheel while holding the Ctrl key.

Viewing Web Pages in the Desktop Browser

You learned earlier in this chapter that there are actually two versions of Internet Explorer in Windows 8. One is the Windows 8 version that you have been reading about in the chapter, and the other is the Desktop version, which includes some capabilities not found in the Windows 8 version. If you go to a site with features that can be experienced only with the Desktop browser, you can view the site in the Desktop browser with just one click.

To open the page you are viewing in the Desktop browser, follow these steps:

1. Open the browser command bar. To do so, swipe up from the bottom of the screen, or right-click anywhere on the page.

2. Select the **Page Tools** button.

3. Select **View on the Desktop** from the menu that appears. The page you were viewing in the Windows 8 browser opens in the Desktop browser, as shown in Figure 6.12.

Pinning Websites to the Start Screen

Starting the Windows 8 browser in Windows 8 is a snap. After the browser is up-and-running, you are just a swipe or click or two away from seeing your favorite sites. As easy as it is to visit the sites you like in the Windows 8 browser, you can make it even more convenient by creating tiles on your Start screen for each of your favorite sites. This is known as *pinning*. Figure 6.13 shows an example of a Start screen with several websites pinned to Start.

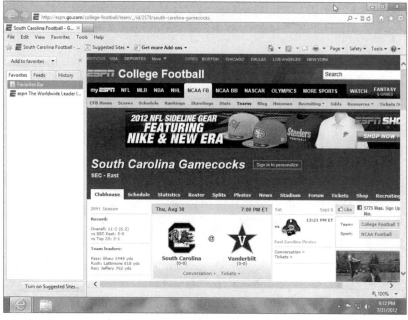

FIGURE 6.12

You probably notice less screen real estate available to pages in the Desktop browser.

FIGURE 6.13

Pinned sites are added to the right side of the screen, but they can be added to existing groups.

To pin a website to Start, follow these steps from the Windows 8 browser:

1. Display the address bar by right-clicking on a page or swiping up from the bottom of the screen.

2. Select the **Pin** button. Edit the label of tile and then select **Pin to Start** (see Figure 6.14).

FIGURE 6.14

You can see a preview of the tile to be used when a website is pinned to the Start screen, though the Internet Explorer logo may be used if a preview is not available. You can also supply your own label for the tile.

Sharing and Printing While You're Web Browsing

Most of the features discussed so far in this chapter have been related to browsing websites, especially seeing content as quickly as possible. It's also easy to accomplish the opposite, which is to share information from the websites you review with others.

Sharing Web Pages

Right after, "Wow," the first reaction most people have when they see something interesting on a website is to decide who to show it to. Well, Windows 8 can help with this reaction. The Share charm is tightly integrated with the Windows 8 browser, making it a snap to share content with other folks.

The Share charm actually connects the content you want to share with any app installed in your Windows 8 that is capable of sharing. When you open the Share charm from the Windows 8 browser, you immediately see a list of those apps (see Figure 6.15). Mail probably comes to mind as the application most useful for sharing, and because Mail comes with Windows 8, it happens to work well with the Windows 8 browser. You can read more about the Share and all charms in Chapter 3.

FIGURE 6.15

Any app is capable of sharing appears on the menu when you open the Shares charm. In this example, sharing from a website works with Mail and People.

The Mail app shares by sending a friend a link to the site you are looking at. Actually, the word link understates what is shared. Windows prepares a preview of the site including the image, colors, link, and a review of the site.

Printing Web Pages

You may want to print one or more pages from a website, perhaps to keep a paper copy of a receipt, a confirmation number, or perhaps just to retain interesting or valuable information. Unfortunately, the dimensions of a website don't always match those of a sheet of paper, so the print never looks as good as it does on the screen. But there are times when you are forced to print from a website regardless of how poor the formatting and print may turn out, such as of a boarding pass for a flight.

Windows 8 makes it easy to print from any page. The Charms bar, specifically the Devices charm you learned about in Chapter 3 is the tool you use for printing from websites. It provides access to all the hardware on your system, including printers, to all the Windows 8 applications.

To print from a website, follow these steps:

1. Open the Devices charm.

2. The Devices charm shows any devices that you could potentially use with the Windows 8 browser, such as the projector with which you can display your screen or a printer, which you can use to print open Web pages.

3. Select the printer. A sheet appears on the screen where you supply basic information about your print task, such as the number of copies, the orientation, and more. After you enter the information needed, select **Print**.

 TIP If you need to print one or more pages from a website but you do not have access to a printer while you have the site open, you can always print to a file. You can take the file with you on a portable drive or you can email the file to an account you can access on the web. When you print, be sure to select Microsoft XPS Document Writer from the Devices charm. A file will be created that you can print at a later time. Be sure to remember to either email the file or copy it from the machine before you depart!

THE ABSOLUTE MINIMUM

Keep these tips in mind as you work with the Windows 8 browser:

- There are two Internet browsers available in Windows 8. One of them is designed for a great user experience with a minimum number of buttons and other on-screen elements. The other supports all the traditional browse requirements, such as plug-ins, toolbars, and all Flash content. The first browser described is the Windows 8 browser. The second browser described is the Desktop browser.

- There are no visible controls in the Desktop browser. To show the controls necessary to enter the address of sites you want to visit, to pin sites to the Start screen, and much more, right-click, swipe in from the bottom, or press Windows +Z.

- To navigate to a site, simply start typing the name of the site into the address bar. The browser presents to you suggestions based on the sites you typically visit, today's most popular sites, and the sites you recently visited.

- To see the list of sites you typically visit, open the address bar again, and simply touch or click the long box where the address of the current site is shown.

- As you navigate to different sites, the sites are recorded in the tab switcher. This makes it easy to jump to any open site you like.

7

CONNECTING WITH THE PEOPLE APP

If you routinely visit four or five or more websites to see what your friends, family, and co-workers are up to, those days are over if you use the People app in Windows 8. The People app brings together all your contacts with all the ways they communicate on the web. This gives you an all-in-one socially aware record of your contacts infused with posts, status updates, and photos. This chapter helps you navigate through the different views of your contacts that the app provides you. You also learn how to link the app to the various social sites, saving you from entering your contacts by hand. Finally, you learn how to keep the app up to date at all times, ensuring you see the posts almost as soon as they are made.

The People app is a brand new piece of software that takes advantage of many of the new gadgets, widgets, and new ways to do things in Windows 8. To be sure you can easily follow the instructions in this chapter, consider reviewing some of the content in Chapter 2, "Interacting with Windows 8," and Chapter 3, "Learning Windows 8 Basics." In particular, review the section related to charms and the section describing use of the File Picker.

Introducing the People App

The People app is the hub for all your web contacts, both professional and personal. This hub has more than just people's names, email addresses, and phone numbers. With the People app, you can keep tabs on your contacts by viewing their status, news, views, and photos from many of the various social networking sites people use today. The People app is a component of the People, Messaging, Email, and Calendar bundle. These apps are provided free with Windows 8.

To start the People app, select it from the Start screen (Figure 7.1). The People app tile also has a live option, which replaces the standard People logo with a set of randomly chosen photos.

FIGURE 7.1

The Live version of the People tile shows randomly selected photos posted by you and your friends.

The main view in the People app gives you a consolidated view of all the persons in your personal and professional life, including their contact info, status, photos, profiles, and tweets.

You can also link to the various sections in the app:

- **What's New**—What's New is a scrolling view of events, activities, posts, and status updates, including photos and links, by all your people, as shown in Figure 7.2.

- **Me**—The Me page is all about you. It shows your updates, plus people's response to them, and all your photos, as shown in Figure 7.3.

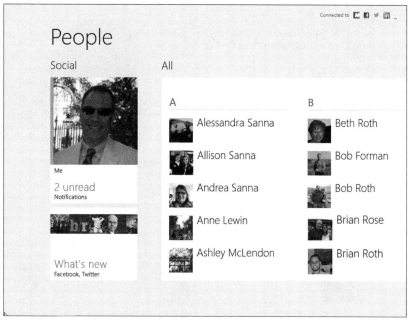

FIGURE 7.2

The home screen of the People app gives you a consolidated view of your personal and professional contacts.

FIGURE 7.3

What's new is a view of events, activities, and posts.

FIGURE 7.4

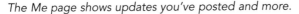

The Me page shows updates you've posted and more.

Depending on the number of contacts you have, the amount of information that can be shown in the People app can be significant. After you enter basic account information into Windows 8 for the various social media networks and email and contact accounts you use, Windows 8 connects with those networks and accounts and imports information into the People app. Here are the services used by the People app:

- **Facebook**—Facebook is the premier social media website, which enables people like you to share pictures, opinions, news, links, videos, and messages. The People app brings in your Facebook friends and both yours and their posts, photos, likes, and status.

- **Hotmail**—Hotmail is Microsoft's web-based email, contact, calendar, and task list service. The People app links to your Hotmail's list of contacts. Also, if your Hotmail contacts post their status through the Microsoft Windows Live service using the Share Something New feature, you can see those, too.

- **Google Mail Contacts**—Gmail is Google's email service. You can maintain an address book in Google to use with your Gmail service. The People app links to your contacts in Gmail. This enables you to connect with your Gmail contacts with People.

- **LinkedIn**—LinkedIn is a web-based contact and social media service for professionals that enables its users to exchange information about their professional expertise, employment, and views. It's fair to think of LinkedIn as the professional version of Facebook. The People app links connects to LinkedIn to import your list of professional relationships.

- **Microsoft Outlook/Exchange/Office 365**—Exchange is Microsoft's email, contacts, calendar, and to-do server product. Outlook is Microsoft's number one mail client, while Office 365 is a new solution for providing email, collaboration, and business tools over the Internet. The People app connects with each of these three solutions to bring your contacts list to Windows 8.

- **Twitter**—Twitter is the popular social networking application that enables you to post your views, news, photos, and comments in 140-character posts known as *tweets*. The People app links to persons you follow in Twitter, and it links to your tweets as updates, including photos.

Connecting with Your People

When you start the People app, you automatically see all the people with whom you have connections through email and social media sites. You also have quick access to the people you have deemed your favorites.

From this first view of the People app, referred to as the *People page*, you can review all your people. Using the skills you learned in Chapter 2, you can swipe left and right to see all your people, or you can use the scroll bars at the bottom of the screen.

There is a lot you can do in the People app besides simply scroll through your list of people. You can filter your list of contacts in certain ways, see information about one or more of your contacts, connect with any of them, or simply keep an eye on their social media activities. Try each of the tasks in this section to see how you can both review and contribute to the social chatter with your people:

- **Scroll through your people alphabetically**—If you have a large number of contacts loaded into People, it may be time-consuming to locate a particular person. To scroll immediately to contacts whose first name starts with a particular letter, select the **Alpha** button on the bottom-right corner of the screen (see Figure 7.5), and then select the appropriate letter, as shown in Figure 7.6.

Alpha Button

FIGURE 7.5

The Alpha button is located above right arrow button on the scroll bar.

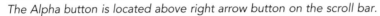

FIGURE 7.6

Select the letter to scroll to the contacts whose first name begins with the letter you chose.

- **Show online contacts only**— To hide contacts on the People tab that are not online, open the App bar and select **Online Only**. To see everyone, repeat these steps.

- **See a person's profile**—To see a contact's profile from the site(s) where your contact has an account, select the person you are interested in. Their portrait appears. Select **View Profile**, and then select the profile you want to see, as shown in Figure 7.7.

FIGURE 7.7

You can see details about any of your people. These are the details collected at the site or service where your contact is registered.

- **See a person's address and other info**—To see a person's address and other info, select the person you are interested. Select **View Profile** and then **More Details**.

- **See a person's recent status and posts**—To see a person's recent status and posts, select the person you are interested in. Scroll to the right to see **What's New**.

- **Look at a person's photos**—To look at someone's photos, select the person you are interested in. Scroll to the right beyond What's New to the Photos section. Select any album (the album cover is a photo) and then select it to review the photos in it. Use the scroll bar with your mouse or pan with your finger or stylus to scroll through the photos in the album. To enter a comment about a photo, type your comment into the box at the bottom of the screen, and then select **Comment**, as shown in Figure 7.8.

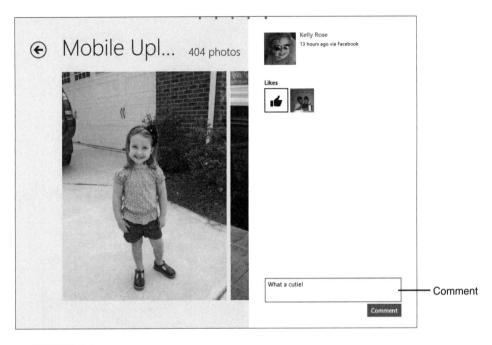

Kelly Rose
13 hours ago via Facebook

Likes

What a cutie! — Comment

FIGURE 7.8

You can scroll through a contact's photos in the People app, as well as enter a comment about a photo.

- **Send a message to someone**—To send a message to a contact, first select the person. Then, select **Send Message**. After doing so, the Messaging app appears where you write your message. If Select Message does not appear, your contact does not have an account with a service that provides messaging, such as Facebook. If you see a prompt to Twitter your contact, select it to open the Twitter page and tweet your contact.

- **Make a person a favorite**—Your favorite persons appear at the start of your person list, as shown in Figure 7.9. To make a person a favorite, select the person, open the App bar, and select **Favorite**. You can make as many contacts a favorite as you like. Be careful not to make so many contacts that you offend those that aren't!

- **Pin a person to the Start screen**—To create a tile for a person on the Start screen, select the person, and then open the App bar. Then select **Pin to Start**. Doing so creates a handy link to the person's details screen in the People app. If there are folks you email, message, or call frequently, selecting their tile created from the People app may be the quickest way to contact them.

FIGURE 7.9

Your favorite persons appear at the top of your Person list.

Checking What's New with Your People

The What's New page, which you access by selecting **What's New** on the People page, consolidates all the tweets and status updates from Hotmail, Facebook, and Twitter by all your people. Read through the following list to see how to review and contribute to the social conversations.

- **Seeing what's new for just one account**—You can select one of the networks or accounts you've linked to the People app as the sole source of What's New. To select one account, select **What's New**, show the App bar, and then select **Filter**. Select the account to filter on, as shown in Figure 7.10.

- **Make a post a favorite**—Your favorite updates appear at the start of the What's New page. To make a post a favorite, open **What's New**, scroll to the post, and then select it. A page appears on which the post is the only one displayed. Select **Favorite** on the right side of the page.

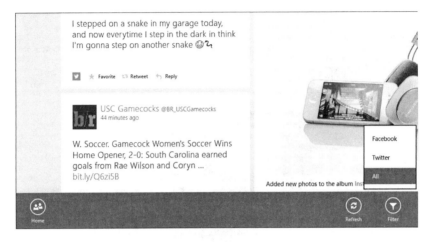

FIGURE 7.10

You can check what's new for just one account.

- **Retweet**—You can tell a Twitter post from the Twitter logo in the bottom-left corner of the post. If you see a tweet that you would like to share with the persons that follow you, you can repost that tweet, that is, *retweet* it. To retweet, select **Retweet** from the row of commands that appear below each post. A screen appears with the post and a list of people that have retweeted it (see Figure 7.11). Enter your comment in the box at the bottom of the screen, and select **Reply**.

FIGURE 7.11

You can retweet directly from the People app.

- **Reply to a tweet**—To reply to a tweet, select **Reply** from the row of commands that appear below each post. Enter your comment in the box at the bottom of the screen and select **Reply**. A reply to a tweet is different than a retweet. A retweet is a broadcast of an existing tweet to your followers. A reply to a tweet is simply a message sent to the author of a tweet.

- **Comment on a Facebook post**—Select **Comment** from the row of commands that appear below each post. In the screen that appears, enter your comment in the box at the bottom of the screen and then select **Comment**. You can also review the comments made by others. Like a reply to a tweet, a comment on a Facebook post is simply some message you leave about a post authored by someone else.

- **Read the post at the source**—You can read and respond to any post you see on What's New at the site/service that generated it. To open the website that generated the post, select the post, and then click the logo for the site.

- **Ensuring What's New is new**—When you open What's New, the People app automatically checks with the various sites and services you have connected to the People app to retrieve the latest posts, status, and so on. If you have had the What's New page open for a while and you want to update to retrieve the latest information open the App bar and select **Refresh.**

The Me Page

It's easy to see what your friends and professional contacts are up to by reviewing their activity on the main screen of the People app. The People app also gives you a view of your posts, people's comments about them, as well as of your photos. To access the Me page, which is about you, select your portrait on the People page. With your page open, read these items to get the most benefits from this section of the app:

- **Change Your Own Profile**—Open the Me page and then select **View Profile** under your portrait. Then select which profile to edit. You see one profile for each source—Facebook, Twitter, and so on—where you have an account. The web browser opens to show your profile for the site you chose.

- **See Older Posts**—This option is similar to the next one to see older notifications. A post is a comment made by you or one of your contacts, perhaps commenting on a photo or responding to a comment made by someone else.

  The Me page shows posts made on your Facebook wall, your status updates on Facebook, and your tweets, including those retweeted by others, over the last two days. To see all the updates, select **View All** next to What's New at the top of the screen.

- **See Older Notifications**—The Me page shows notifications sent to you on Facebook over the last two days. To see all the notifications, select View All beside Notification at the top of the screen.

Setting Up Your Contacts

One of the best features of the People app is how it brings together all the social media activity for all your contacts. To see all these posts, tweets, and photos, you have a little work to do to connect the People app to your social media networks/email accounts. Follow the instructions in the next six sections for whichever service you want to link to Windows 8.

Linking to Facebook

Follow these steps to link the People app to Facebook. You need the email address and password you use to sign in to Facebook:

1. Open the People app.

2. Open the **Charms** bar and select **Settings**. The Settings screen appears on the right, as shown in Figure 7.12.

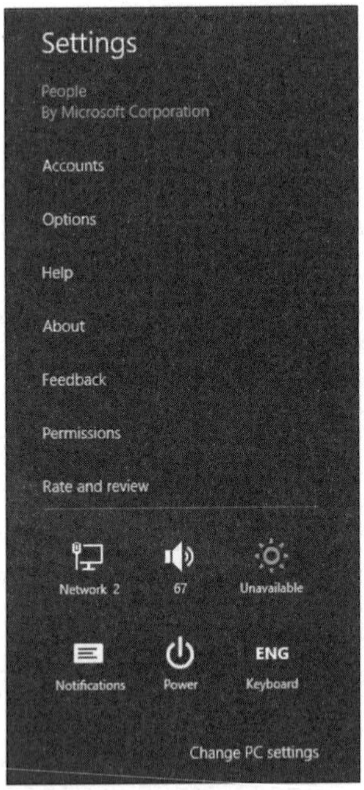

FIGURE 7.12

Open the Settings charm to link the People app to Facebook.

3. Select **Accounts**. The Accounts screen appears, which shows a list of the accounts that have been set up so far in the People app.

4. Select **Add an account**. The screen shown in Figure 7.13 appears, which presents the accounts you can link to in People.

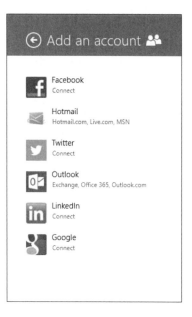

FIGURE 7.13

You can load information from six social media and email websites into People.

5. Select **Facebook**. The screen shown in Figure 7.14 appears.

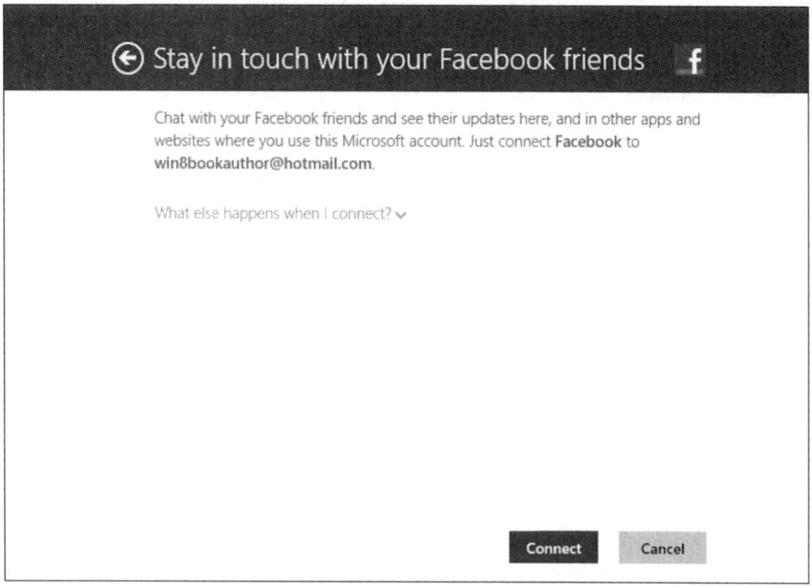

FIGURE 7.14

You may select Connect right away or read the info from Facebook by selecting the blue text.

6. Select **Connect**. After doing so, Windows connects with Facebook for you to sign in to Facebook.

7. Sign in to Facebook and select **Log In**. If you entered your username and password correctly, the screen shown in Figure 7.15 appears.

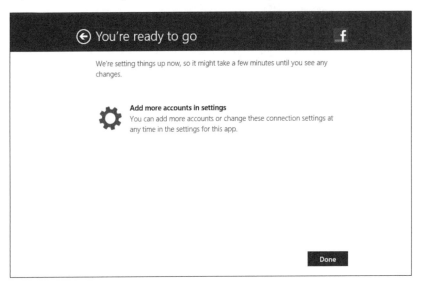

FIGURE 7.15

This screen indicates success in linking to your Facebook account.

8. Select **Done**.

Linking to Google, Hotmail, and Exchange/Outlook/Office 365

The steps for linking to Google, Hotmail, and Exchange/Outlook/Office are similar. Follow these steps, and pay particular attention to instructions specific to connecting to one of the networks:

1. Open the People app.

2. Open the **Settings** charm.

3. Select **Accounts**. The accounts screen appears, which shows a list of the accounts set up so far.

4. Select **Add an Account**. The screen shown in Figure 7.16 appears, which presents the networks and email providers you can link to in People.

FIGURE 7.16

You can load information from five social media and email websites into People.

5. Select **Google, Hotmail, or Outlook**. A screen that looks like the one shown in Figure 7.17 appears. The title and coloring on this screen can vary pending which kind of account you intend to add.

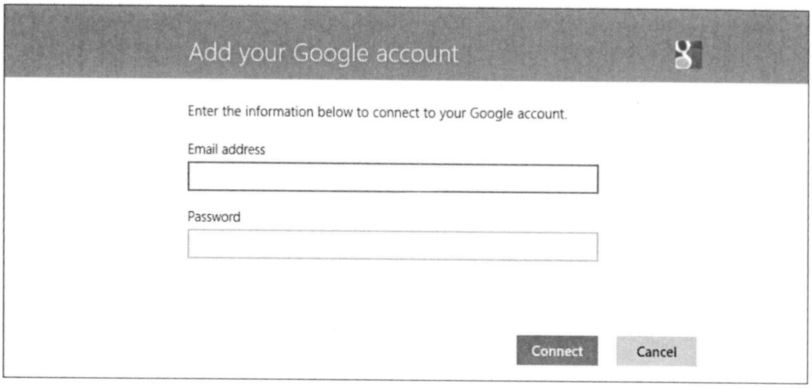

FIGURE 7.17

You need to enter your email and password to establish your connection to Google, Hotmail, or Exchange. This screen shows the connection to Google.

6. Enter your email address and your password in the fields provided.

7. If you want to link to Google or Hotmail, click **Connect**. If you have entered your email address and password correctly, the link is created, and posts from your Google and Hotmail contacts appear soon after.

   If you want to link to Exchange, Outlook, or Office 365, you have a little more work to do. Select **See more details** to see the screen where you enter more information about your Microsoft accounts (see Figure 7.18).

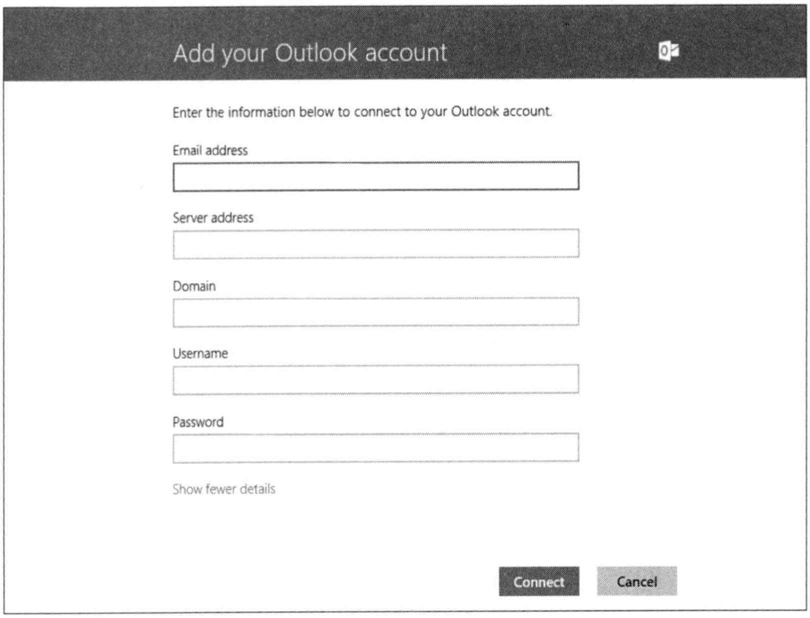

Add your Outlook account

Enter the information below to connect to your Outlook account.

Email address

Server address

Domain

Username

Password

Show fewer details

Connect   Cancel

FIGURE 7.18

Additional information may be required to link to Exchange, Outlook, or Office 365.

8. Enter the information required. The only field that might give you difficulty is Domain. If you are unsure of what to enter for Domain, check with a member of your technical team at your office. With each field filled in, select **Connect**.

   Windows 8 attempts to connect to Microsoft based on the server information you supplied. When it is successful, your Exchange/Outlook/Office 365 contacts begin to appear on the screen.

Linking to Twitter

Linking the People app to Twitter is a simple process, although explaining it will take more than 140 characters. Follow these six steps to see tweets from your Twitter friends in Windows 8:

1. From the People app, open the **Charms** bar and select **Settings**. The Settings screen appears on the right.

2. Select **Accounts**. A screen with a list of the accounts that have been set up so far appears (see Figure 7.19).

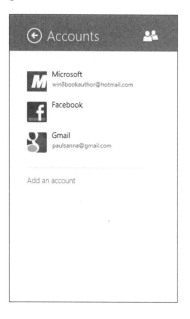

FIGURE 7.19

You can see which accounts you have linked to so far.

3. Select **Add an account**.

4. Select **Twitter**.

5. Click **Connect**. The screen shown in Figure 7.20 appears, in which you enter the username and password of your Twitter account.

6. Enter the username and password of your Twitter account. Do not enter the @ symbol at the beginning of your username. Select **Remember Me** so you don't have to enter your Twitter username and password again. Then, select **Authorize app**.

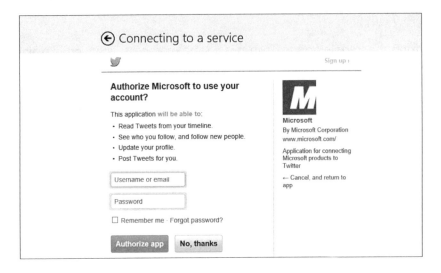

FIGURE 7.20

Enter your Twitter username and password.

7. The screen shown in Figure 7.21 appears. Click **Done**, which is the last step in linking to Twitter. In a short time, persons and organizations you follow in Twitter appear and their tweets appear in What's New.

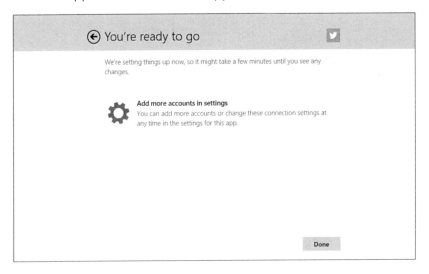

FIGURE 7.21

You can add a link to another Twitter account or finish.

Linking to LinkedIn

Follow these steps to link People to LinkedIn. You need the email address and password you use to sign in to LinkedIn. When connected, your professional contacts in LinkedIn appear.

1. Start the People app.

2. Open the **Charms** bar and then select **Settings**. You see the Settings screen fly out from the right.

3. Select **Accounts**. The Accounts screen appears, where you can see the list of the networks and/or email accounts that have been set up so far.

4. Select **Add an Account**. A screen appears, which presents the accounts and networks you can set up in People.

5. Select **LinkedIn**. The screen shown in Figure 7.22 appears.

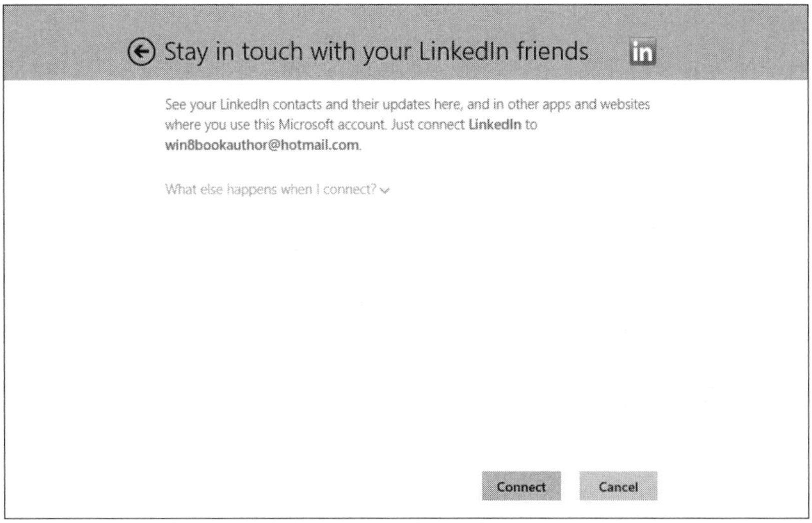

FIGURE 7.22

Windows show you a bit more information before you connect to LinkedIn.

6. Select **Connect**. After doing so, Windows connects with LinkedIn for you to sign in, as shown in Figure 7.23.

7. Enter the email address and password you use to sign in to LinkedIn. Leave Access Duration set to Until Revoked, which means your People account will remain linked to LinkedIn until you purposely disconnect the link.

Connecting to a service

Linked **in**.

Don't have an account? Join Now

Grant **Microsoft** access to your LinkedIn Account
Only allow access if you trust this application with your LinkedIn network information

Email:
Password: Forgot password?
Access Duration: **Until Revoked** change

Ok, I'll Allow It   Cancel

You can always revoke Microsoft's access through your settings page. By granting
access you agree to the LinkedIn User Agreement and Privacy Policy

FIGURE 7.23

Windows requires your LinkedIn username and password to create the link to the People app.

8. Select **OK, I'll Allow It**. Select **Done** from the next screen that appears, and in
a few minutes, your LinkedIn contacts begins to appear.

THE ABSOLUTE MINIMUM

The People app links to the social media networks plus your email accounts to
show you all your posts, notifications, photos, like, comments, plus those of your
friends and contacts, in one place.

The People app connects to Google, Exchange servers, Hotmail, Twitter,
LinkedIn, and Facebook.

You must supply the username and password you use to sign in to the networks
and accounts you want to see in People.

The People app is an address book that includes social media content. The What's
New page shows you just the latest content from the social media networks you
connect to. The Me page shows just content sent to you or from you.

8

USING THE MAIL APP AND MESSAGING TO STAY CONNECTED

This chapter introduces the new Mail application in Windows 8. Like the People, Calendar, Messaging, and many other apps, Mail is a new Windows 8 app that's launched directly from the Start screen.

There are certainly email apps, many of which run from the Desktop, available in the market with more features than those found in the Windows 8 Mail app. You might find a suitable replacement in the Windows 8 store, or you can use an email program you used previously with an older version of Windows. But this app is free, and it is extremely easy to use.

If your primary need is to exchange email with family and friends, including sending and receiving pictures and other attachments, this app should be perfect for you. It is integrated with all the important parts of Windows 8, such as displaying all your contacts when you address your message. This chapter leads you through the Mail app, explaining everything you need to know to use it and to set it up.

The chapter does include a brief summary of missing features you might find important, as well as alternatives to the Mail app. An alternative to sending text messages from your smartphone or the various messaging apps on social media site you visit is the Messaging app in Windows 8. The app is very easy to use. You can find some tips for using the Messaging at the end of this chapter.

Because Mail relies on many of the techniques covered in Chapter 3, "Learning Windows 8 Basics," you should refer to that chapter if you need help, or perhaps review the entire chapter if you need a refresher. Pay particular attention to these features, which play an important role in this chapter:

- Display the App bar, which reveals several formatting commands you can use to dress up your email.
- Open the Settings charm, where you specify the various email accounts you can consolidate in the Mail app.

Exploring the Mail App

To start the Mail app, select the Mail tile on the Start screen, as shown in Figure 8.1.

FIGURE 8.1

Select the Mail tile to launch the Mail app.

After starting the Mail app, you see a short bit of animation before the app starts. Depending on how many email accounts are set up in your Mail app, your screen will look more or less like the one shown in Figure 8.2. Your list of accounts and folders appears on the left in the Navigation pane. The middle pane shows the messages in the folder selected in the Navigation pane. The message selected appears in the pane on the right.

Navigation   Message Pane

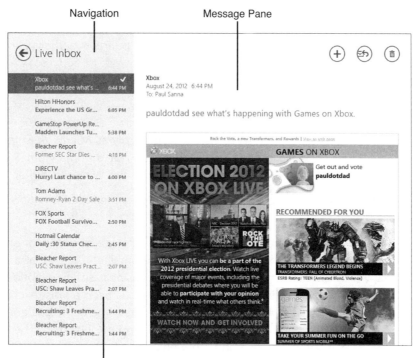

Message List

FIGURE 8.2

The initial view of email shows your accounts and folders, your inbox, and the selected message.

Setting Up Email

The Mail app requires little effort to set up. Unlike many email clients available in earlier versions of Windows, there are few opportunities to customize the screens, such as by showing just email that arrived in the last two days. So, you likely can set up Mail and take full advantage of all its features quickly.

NOTE   If the account you use to sign in to Windows 8 is a Microsoft account, an email account will be set up automatically for you using the same credentials you use to sign in.

Setting Up Your Email Accounts

One of the best features of the Mail app is how it brings together your email from all sources. To see all your email, you have a little work to do to set up the Mail app to retrieve and send mail from the different email services you use. The Mail app works with the following email providers:

- **Hotmail** —Microsoft's web email service is known as Hotmail; though you may at times see it referred to on the web simply as *Microsoft Email* or Live Mail. Regardless of the name, Hotmail is Microsoft's primary email service, and you can read and write Hotmail mail from the Windows 8 Mail app.

- **Gmail**—Gmail is Google's email service. You can learn information about Google email at www.google.com.

- **Outlook** —The Outlook option in the Email app is a catch-all for email accounts you have in Microsoft's new online email at Outlook.com, Office 365, which is Microsoft's collaboration and business solution cloud solution, and email accounts through Exchange, , which is used almost exclusively by corporate customers. Many users exchange their Microsoft Exchange email with Microsoft Outlook, which runs on the computer Desktop. The Windows 8 email app is one of the first apps that enable users to retrieve their Exchange email without Outlook.

You can create as many accounts in the Mail app as you need. If you use just one email service, and the service meets your needs, there is no reason to create more accounts. When you're ready to add an email account, follow these steps to set up any email account in the app:

1. Start the Mail app.

2. Open the **Settings** charm and select **Accounts**. A screen appears with a list of the mail accounts that have been set up so far.

3. Select **Add an Account**. A screen like the one shown in Figure 8.3 appears, which presents the email services you can set up.

From here, check out the following section that applies to the type of email account you want to set up.

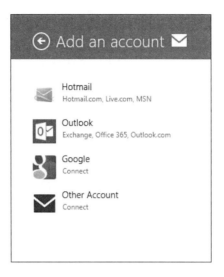

FIGURE 8.3

Select an email service.

Setting Up Your Hotmail Account

To set up your Hotmail account with the Mail app, start with the three steps at the end of the preceding "Setting Up Your Email Accounts" section and then continue with the followings steps:

1. Select **Hotmail**. A screen like the one shown in Figure 8.4 appears.

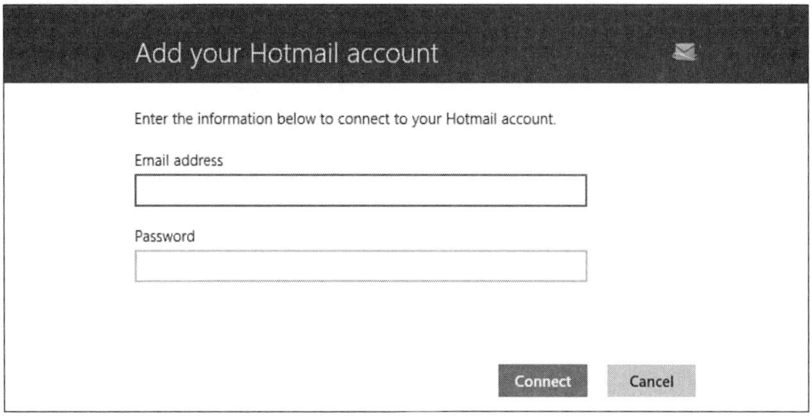

FIGURE 8.4

Hotmail requires just two pieces of information to connect to the server.

2. Enter the email address and password for your Hotmail or Live account.

    To verify you entered your password correctly, tap-and-hold or click-and-hold the password preview button at the end of the Password box.

3. Select **Connect**. The Mail app connects to Hotmail or Live.com to complete setting up your account. Your new account appears at the bottom of the list of accounts in the Navigation bar.

Setting Up Your Google Account

To set up your Google account with the Mail app, start with the three steps at the end of the previous "Setting Up Your Email Accounts" section and then continue with the followings steps:

1. Select **Google**. The screen shown in Figure 8.5 appears.

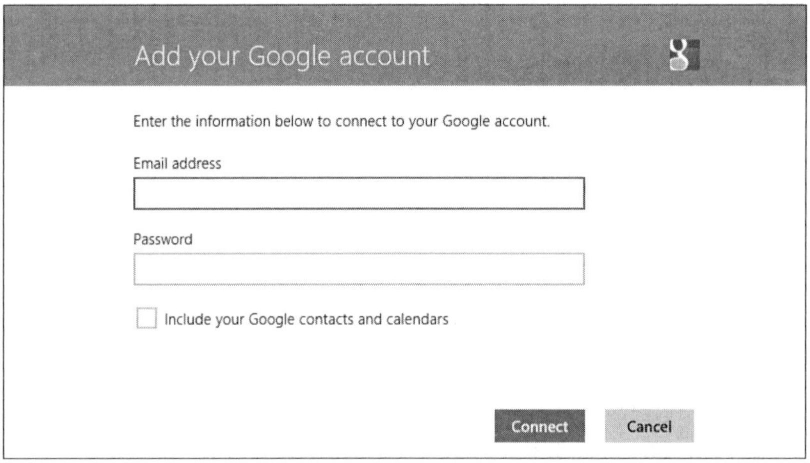

Add your Google account

Enter the information below to connect to your Google account.

Email address

Password

☐ Include your Google contacts and calendars

Connect   Cancel

FIGURE 8.5

Google requires just two pieces of information to connect to its email service.

2. Enter the email address and password for your Google account. If you would like the People app to be loaded with your Gmail contacts and the Calendar app to synchronize with your Google calendar, select the check box below the password field.

    To verify you entered your password correctly, tap-and-hold or click-and-hold the password preview button at the end of the Password box.

 TIP   Be sure you enter your full email address in the Email address field, including the "@gmail" portion.

3. Select **Connect**. The Mail app connects to Google to complete setting up your account. Your new account appears at the bottom of the list of accounts in the Navigation bar.

Setting Up Your Exchange/Outlook/Office 365 Account

To set up your Exchange/Outlook/Office 365 account with the Mail app, start with the three steps at the end of the previous "Setting Up Your Email Accounts" section and then continue with the followings steps:

1. Select **Outlook**.

2. Enter the email address and password for your account.

To verify you entered your password correctly, tap-and-hold or click-and-hold the password preview button at the end of the Password box.

3. If you are setting up an account to pull email from Exchange or Office 365, select **Show more details**. Fill in the domain and server fields as needed. You can learn the values for these fields from your administrator or from information on the service's site, if one is available.

4. Select **Connect**. The Mail app connects to the Exchange server to complete setting up your account. Your new account appears at the bottom of the list of accounts in the Navigation bar.

Reading Your Email

The Mail app retrieves email from your accounts every few minutes. To force the Mail app to retrieve mail right away, open the App bar and select **Sync**.

It's easy to read through email messages you receive. Return to the home screen by selecting the large back arrow button on the top left corner of each screen. The bottom of the list on the left side of the screen shows each of your accounts. When you select an account, the folders for that account appear (refer to Figure 8.6).

To read a message, just select the message from the list. The message you select appears in the Message pane on the right side of the screen. To see the messages in a different folder, select the folder from the list, and then select the message.

 NOTE Depending on the resolution of your screen, you might not see the Message pane, which is on the right side if the screen, If you resolution is too low, you might see just the Navigation pane and the message list.

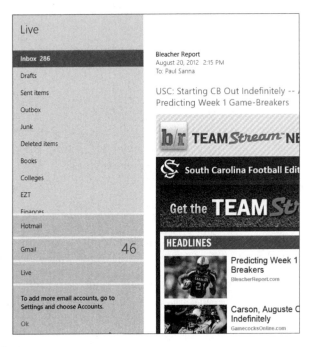

FIGURE 8.6

The home page in the Email app enables you to see email from each account you set up.

Replying to a Message

You can send a reply to a message you receive. You can send your reply message just to the author of the message you received, or send your message to everyone who received the original message. You can attach other documents or pictures to a reply, and you can format your reply however you like.

To reply to an email, follow these steps:

1. Select the message to which you want to reply.

2. On the top-right corner of the screen, select the **Respond** button. Then, select **Reply** or **Reply All** on the menu that appears, as shown in Figure 8.7

FIGURE 8.7

You can reply to only the sender, reply to everyone on the original email or forward the message to a new recipient using the Reply menu.

3. Write your reply message, as shown in Figure 8.8.

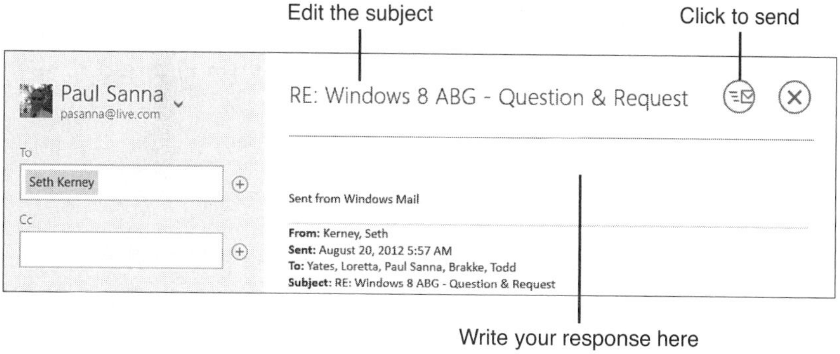

Edit the subject Click to send

Paul Sanna
pasanna@live.com

RE: Windows 8 ABG - Question & Request

To
Seth Kerney

Cc

Sent from Windows Mail

From: Kerney, Seth
Sent: August 20, 2012 5:57 AM
To: Yates, Loretta, Paul Sanna, Brakke, Todd
Subject: RE: Windows 8 ABG - Question & Request

Write your response here

FIGURE 8.8

Type your reply message.

4. Format the message based on the instruction in the "Formatting Your Email" section.

5. Address the reply message using the instructions in the "Addressing Your Message" section."

6. To send a file with your message, such as photo or a spreadsheet, follow the instructions in the next section, "Attaching a Photo or Another File to Your Message."

7. Select the **Send** button. Your message will be sent.

Filing a Message in a Folder

You can reduce the clutter in your inbox not only by deleting messages that have no value but also by filing messages that do. You can create folders in Hotmail, Google, Exchange, and many other email services to organize your email. You can usually file your messages into those folders on the email service websites, such as on Google's Gmail page, or with other email programs, such as Microsoft. These folders are visible in the Mail app. Here is how the folders work:

- When you create a folder in Hotmail, Outlook, you Live email account, or Google, the folder appears in the Mail app in that service's list of folders.

- When you file a message into a folder using Hotmail, Google, or Exchange, the message appears in the folder in the Mail app.

- When you file a message in a folder using the Mail app, the message is filed in the folder with the email service.

To file a message into a folder in the Mail app, do the following:

1. Select the message to file.

2. Display the App bar, and select **Move**, as shown in Figure 8.9.

FIGURE 8.9

You can file a message in any of the folders created with your email service.

3. Select the folder in which you want to store the message. The message will be moved to the folder you pick.

Deleting a Message

If you no longer need a message, you can delete it. The message disappears from your inbox.

To delete a message, select the message to delete. Then, select the **Delete** button on the top-right corner of the screen. The button is shaped like a trash can.

Forward a Message

When you forward a message, you send a message you received to someone else who did not receive it in the first place.

To forward a message, follow these steps:

1. Select the message to forward.

2. Select the **Respond** button; then select **Forward** the menu that appears (refer to Figure 8.6).

3. You can add your own text to the message you are forwarding. Your message appears above the forwarded message. To add your own message to the email you're forwarding, type it as shown in Figure 8.10. Format your message, if you choose, following the instructions in the "Formatting Your Message" section.

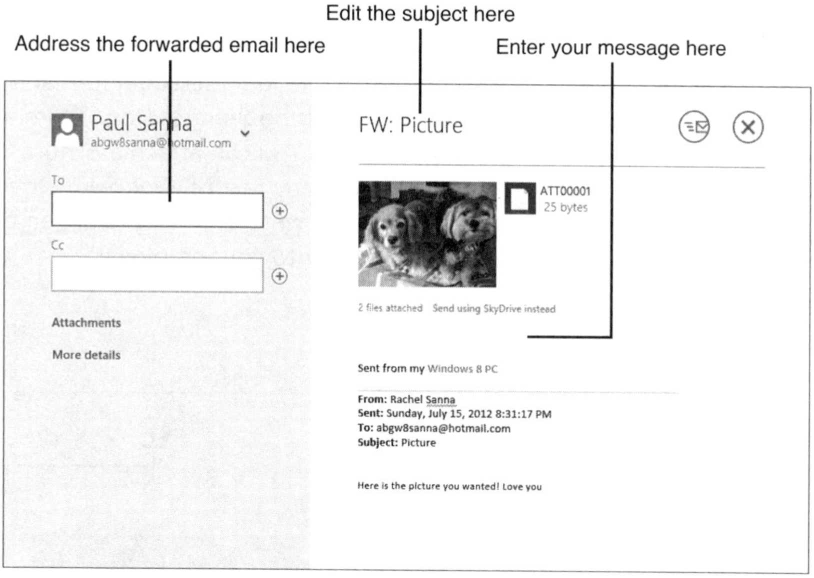

Edit the subject here

Address the forwarded email here

Enter your message here

FIGURE 8.10

You can type your own message to accompany the message you are forwarding.

4. Address the message to be forwarded using the instructions in the "Addressing Your Message" section.

5. Select the **Send** button.

Mark a Message as Unread

When you select a message by clicking it, tapping it, or moving the focus to the message using the arrow keys, the message appears in the Viewing pane. If you don't select another message or if you don't leave the Viewing pane in 5 seconds, your message will be marked as read. This means the message's bold formatting will be removed. This system of formatting messages differently for those you have read makes it easy to see quickly what messages are new and deserve your attention. Though some experts suggest that using the read/unread status is a poor method to manage your inbox, you can easily switch a message back to unread if you want to be sure you review the message again.

To mark a message as unread, select it, display the App bar, and select **Mark Unread**.

Writing an Email Message

Writing an email is a simple process. You write your message, format it as you like, address the message, and the select the **Send** button. There are no restrictions to the type of message you send. You can attach a picture or another document to a message and send it without any text of your own. Or you can write a 20-page letter if you choose. You can write a grocery list in an email message, or you can write a resignation letter to your employer.

To write a message, follow these steps:

1. Select the **New** button, as shown in Figure 8.11.

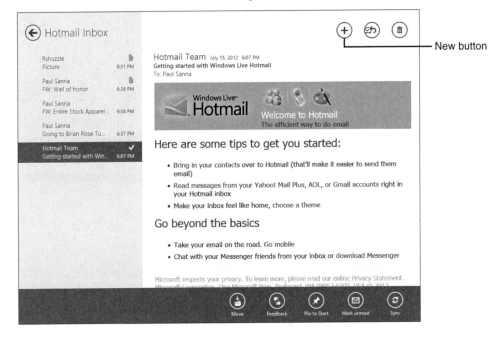

FIGURE 8.11

Select the New button to write a new email message.

2. If you have more than one account set up in the app, select the down arrow button next to your name. Select the account from which you want to send the email, as shown in Figure 8.12. If you have one account, move to step 3.

3. Type your message and subject, as shown in Figure 8.13.

4. Address your message using the instructions in the "Addressing Your Message" section.

5. Format your message using the instructions in the "Formatting Your Email" section.

FIGURE 8.12

Select the account from which the message will be sent.

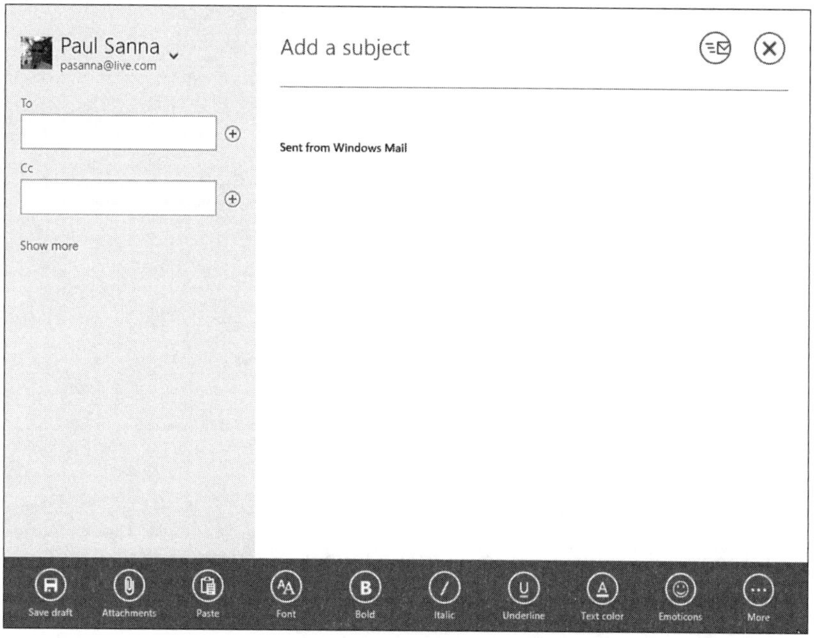

FIGURE 8.13

This screen shows where you type your email and its subject.

6. To send a file with your message, such as photo or a spreadsheet, follow the instructions in the "Attaching a Photo or Another File to Your Message" section.

7. If your message is ready to be sent, select **Send**.

Formatting Your Email Message

The Mail app has a number of options with which to format and personalize your email message. You can use colors, different fonts, and some text options, like bold, italics, and so on. You can also use emoticons to add personality to your message.

Using Text Formatting

To format the text in your message, select the text. To select text, click and drag with the mouse or press-and-drag with your finger over the characters to format. The App bar opens automatically when text is selected and display the formatting commands, as shown in Figure 8.14. Figure 8.15 shows examples of the formatting commands in use.

FIGURE 8.14

The App bar reveals several formatting options.

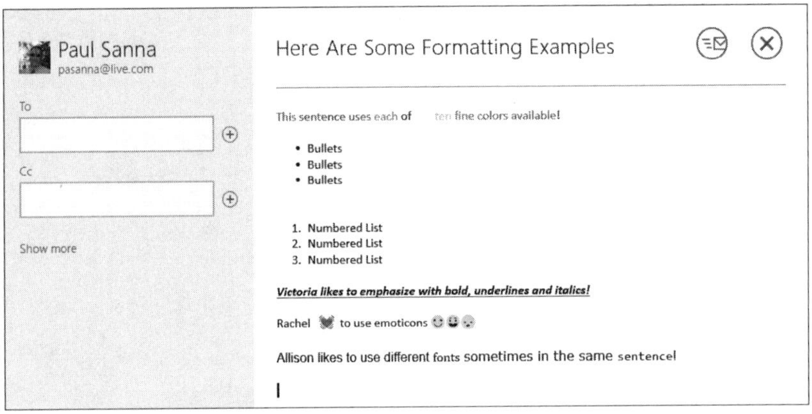

Paul Sanna
pasanna@live.com

To

Cc

Show more

Here Are Some Formatting Examples

This sentence uses each of   ten fine colors available!

• Bullets
• Bullets
• Bullets

1. Numbered List
2. Numbered List
3. Numbered List

Victoria likes to emphasize with bold, underlines and italics!

Rachel 🦇 to use emoticons 😊 😊 😊

Allison likes to use different fonts sometimes in the same sentence!

FIGURE 8.15

This screen shows examples of some of the formatting commands.

Using Emoticons

Who doesn't like a smiley face or a cheeseburger in messages they write? You can easily add emoticons to your messages. The Mail app has a surprising large library of emoticons to help you add character to your emails.

To add an emoticon to your message, do the following:

1. Click, tap, or use the arrow keys to move the cursor to the location in the message where you want the emoticon to appear.

2. Display the App bar and select the **Emoticons** button. The screen shown in Figure 8.16 appears.

FIGURE 8.16

Windows 8 has many emoticons you can use in your email.

3. Select the emoticons you like. You can add as many as you like while the emoticons flyout panel is on the screen. To select an emoticon, do one of the following:

    - Click it with your mouse.
    - Tap it with your finger or stylus.
    - Use the arrow keys to move the focus to the emoticon you want. Press the **spacebar** to select the emoticon.

4. Continue writing your email. The emoticons flyout screen closes.

Addressing Your Message

Follow these steps to address a message from the Mail app:

1. Click or tap the To button or the Cc button. The People selector screen appears. Although you can enter as many addresses as you like in the CC list, you must have at least one email address in the To field to send the message.

2. Select the portrait of the selected person. Select additional portraits until you have selected all recipients. Then select **Add**.

3. Repeat steps 1 and 2 to select recipients for the other list.

4. To secretly add recipients to the message, select **More Details**, which appears below the addresses of the receipts you selected in steps 1–2. When the Bcc field appears, choose the recipients you want to include. When your message is viewed by those recipients, they will not see any of the other addresses you might have included in this list nor will any other recipients see their address.

Attaching a Photo or Another File to Your Message

To send one or more files with your email, such as a photo, select **Attachments** under the two address fields. The File Picker window appears, as shown in Figure 8.17. The File Picker is a tool used throughout Windows 8 for navigating through the folders on your system and then choosing a file. You can read more about it in Chapter 3.

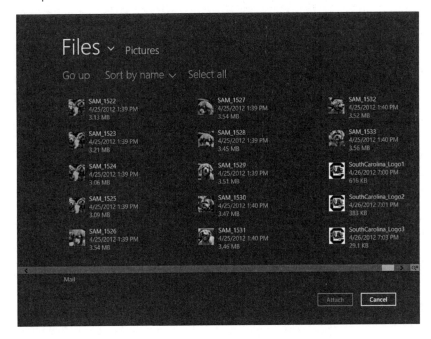

FIGURE 8.17

Select files using the File Picker tool.

Find the file you want to attach by moving through the folder and drives on your computer. Select the file by clicking or tapping it once. Then, select **Attach**. You can attach more than one file. Simply select additional files before you select **Attach**. You can click Attachments a second time to add more files to your email.

Checking Spelling in Your Message

If you are even mildly embarrassed to have an email you sent appear in your recipient's inbox with spelling errors or typing mistakes, it makes sense to take advantage of the built-in spelling checking in Windows 8. The spell checking features are universal in Windows 8, which means you don't need to turn spell checking on or off in each application you use.

There are two features available:

- **Highlight misspelled words as you type them**. This feature also enables you to correct the word or add the word as you spelled it to the dictionary. These two functions are carried out by right-clicking or tapping and holding on the highlighted word.

- **Autocorrect words as you type**. This feature simply fixes misspelled words as they are typed. You can try this on your own. Create a new email message and type, "mistpelled." With the autocorrect feature turned on, you should see the word you typed be corrected to, "misspelled."

To turn the spelling features on or off, follow these steps:

1. Select the **Settings** charm, and select **PC Settings**.

2. Select the **General** group of PC Settings.

3. Under Spelling, move the slider to the left for Off or the right for On for the Autocorrect Misspelled Words and for the Highlight Misspelled Words options.

Using the Messaging App

An alternative to email if a lack of formality is OK is the Messaging app. With the information you've set up in the People app, you can send and receive instant messages in Windows 8 from your regular circle of contacts. And the setup is almost non-existent. If you signed-in to Windows 8 with a Microsoft account, your Windows Live Messenger account is already set up. And if you are a Facebook user and you have added Facebook friends to the People app, Facebook messenger is ready to go.

To start the Messaging app, select the Messenger tile on the Start screen, as shown in Figure 8.18. With the app open, follow these tips to message like an expert. Also, refer to Figure 8.19 for assistance.

- The app uses the same service to send a message as required by the person you are sending to. When you choose a recipient, the Messaging app notes whether they are a Facebook or Messenger contact and sends your message using the appropriate service.

- You can only message with contacts who have accounts on the service as you. If you do not have a Facebook account, you will not be able to message persons on Facebook. The holds true for Windows Live Messenger, too.

- To turn off messaging temporarily, open the Charms bar and select **Settings**, select **Options**, and then drag the slider to the Off position (left).

- To set your status to Available or to make yourself Invisible, open the App bar, select Status, and then select the status you like.

- Open the App bar to also delete conversations and to invite someone to join messaging with you (as long as you have their email address).

FIGURE 8.18

Open the Messaging app from the Start screen.

FIGURE 8.19

The Messaging is perhaps the easiest app to use in Windows 8.

THE ABSOLUTE MINIMUM

- The Mail app is provided for free with Windows 8. You probably can find email programs with more functionality, but not likely so many additional toys and features as to justify paying for a program when the Mail app is free.

- You can bring together into the Windows 8 Mail app your email from many of your accounts and services, including Microsoft Exchange, Google, Hotmail, and more. This means you can read email from all accounts in one place but still author and send emails from any one account you choose.

- There are first-class formatting and email authoring capabilities in the Mail app, including colors, attachments, font choice and even emoticons.

- You set up email accounts from the system settings pane, which you reach by selecting Settings from the Charms bar. Settings for the message you are working on, such as formatting and folders, are reached from the App bar.

9

USING THE CALENDAR APP

Windows 8 provides an integrated Calendar app. The app is one of the new Windows 8-style apps, which means it matches the new apps built for mail, messaging, and contacts. Although the Calendar app is extremely easy to use, it has a few elements that deserve a bit more explanation. For example, you can synchronize your calendar with calendars you maintain online. You can create events and respond to invitations in the Calendar app, see those events appear in your online calendar, as well as invite your contacts listed in the People app. As a Windows 8 app, you can easily share your calendar with other parts of Windows, as well as take advantage of the centralized Windows 8 printing services.

Getting to Know the Calendar App

The Calendar app provides you a view of your calendar, as well as scheduling and event scheduling abilities. The Calendar is provided free in Windows 8. Here is a list of the things you can do with the Calendar app:

- Schedule one-time meetings and events.

- Schedule regular, recurring events.

- Set reminders so that you're notified before scheduled events.

- Review your calendar in a day view, a monthly view, or a weekly view.

- See events scheduled on Google, Hotmail, or Microsoft Exchange calendars that you have access to.

Starting the Calendar App

To start the Calendar app, select the Calendar tile on the Start screen, as shown in Figure 9.1. When the Calendar app opens, the view you last used—daily, weekly, monthly—appears automatically, as shown in Figure 9.2.

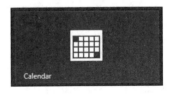

FIGURE 9.1

You start the Calendar app by selecting the Calendar tile on the Start screen.

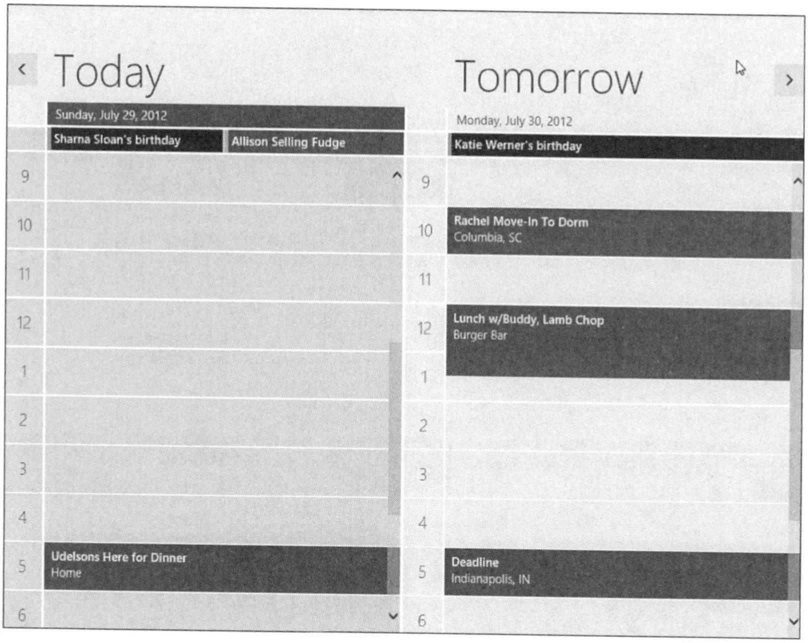

FIGURE 9.2

The 2-day daily view appears automatically appears because it was the view last used.

Controlling the Calendar View

You can review your calendar in three different views: Day, Week, and Month. You can easily change from one view to another. To do so, display the App bar, and then select the view you prefer, as shown in Figure 9.3.

The Week view shows up to 14 hours in a day and 7 days of the week. The default setting uses Sunday as the first day of the week. In the section "Customizing the Calendar View," you can read how to change the day the week starts on, as well as a number of other settings. The Week view is shown in Figure 9.4, whereas the Month view is shown in Figure 9.5.

App bar with Calendar options

FIGURE 9.3

You change views by making a choice from the App bar.

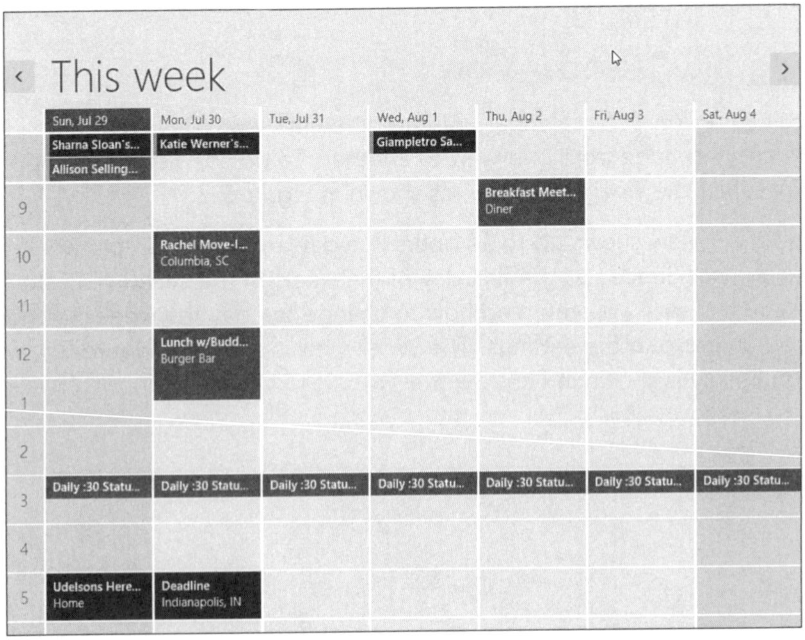

FIGURE 9.4

The Week view provides detail for each day of the week.

FIGURE 9.5

The Month view shows the current month, plus a number of days from the prior and next month.

You can switch to a different date using any of the three views. Each view includes arrow buttons you select to move to the next or previous date, as shown here. You can quickly switch to the present day by choosing the Today button from the App bar (refer to Figure 9.3).

Setting Calendar Colors

If you have set up just one account with the Calendar app, then all events will appear in the same color. A different color is used for events for each additional account you set up in the Calendar app. To set the colors used for each calendar, as well as to hide or show certain calendars, open the Charms bar and select **Settings**. Then, select **Options.** The screen shown in Figure 9.6 appears. Select the list under each calendar to select the color. You may have to scroll down to see other calendars. To hide a calendar, move the slider to the Hide position, which is left. You can also select whether birthdays, as well as holidays, appear from each calendar.

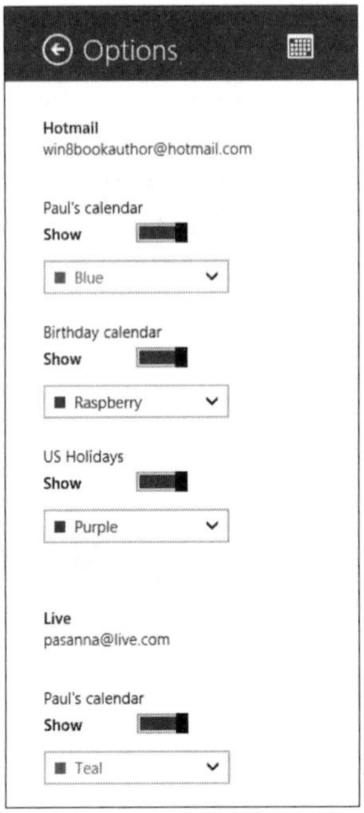

FIGURE 9.6

You can specify a diffent color for each calendar you've added to the app.

Synchronizing with Other Calendars

If you maintain a calendar online at Google or Outlook.com (which includes Microsoft Hotmail and Live), you can synchronize your those calendars in the Calendar app. You can also synchronize the Calendar app with Microsoft Exchange, which is useful if you use Microsoft Outlook to read and write email at work.

When you synchronize your calendar with Google, Exchange, or Hotmail, any events scheduled on the online Calendar appear on your Windows 8 calendar, merged with any appointments or events you entered here. You can synchronize your calendar with multiple accounts and with multiple services. You can see all your appointments booked on all your calendars in one place, including appointments on family members' calendars or work or corporate appointments.

Follow the steps in the next three sections to set up the Calendar app to work with these services.

Connecting to Your Hotmail Account

Hotmail is Microsoft's email, contacts, and calendar service, which is part of Microsoft's Live online platform. You can synchronize the Windows 8 People and Mail apps with Hotmail's email and contacts service, as well. You can use this option for Live accounts and new Outlook email accounts.

Follow these steps to connect your calendar to your Hotmail account.

1. Start the Calendar app.

2. Open the Charms bar, and then select the **Settings charm**.

3. Select **Accounts**. Another pane flies out; this one has a list of the calendars you have connected to, if any (see Figure 9.7). If you sign-in to Windows with a Microsoft account, the account you used to sign-in is already set up in the Calendar app.

FIGURE 9.7

The Accounts pane shows the calendars you have connected to.

4. Select **Add an account**. When you do so, a screen appears showing the online services you can connect to.

5. Select **Hotmail**. The Add Your Hotmail Account screen displays, as shown in Figure 9.8.

6. Enter your email address and password in the fields provided. To verify you entered your password correctly, tap-and-hold or click-and-hold the Password Preview button at the end of the Password box.

7. Select **Connect**. The Calendar app connects to Hotmail to complete setting up your account. Shortly, the Calendar app synchs to your Hotmail account, and you can see events and appointments on your Hotmail calendar appear in your calendar in Windows 8.

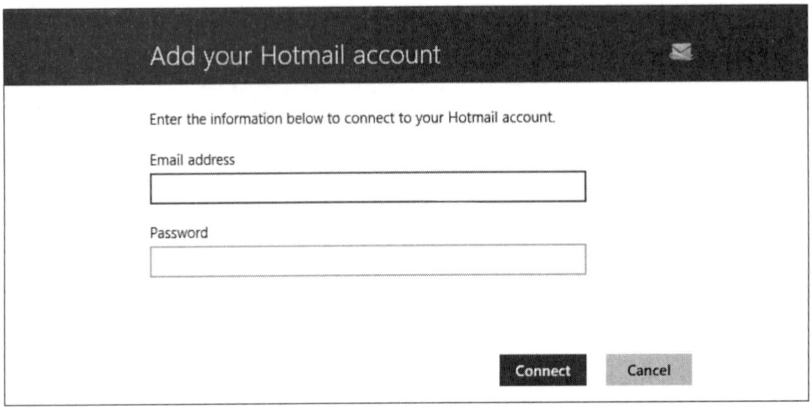

FIGURE 9.8

Hotmail requires just two pieces of information to connect to the server.

Connecting to Your Gmail Account

Gmail is Google's email and calendar service. You can find more information about Google calendar at www.google.com. Follow these steps to connect your calendar to your Gmail account:

1. Start the Calendar app.

2. Open the Charms bar, and then select the **Settings** charm. The Calendar pane flies out from the right.

3. Select **Accounts**. Another pane flies out; this one has a list of the calendars you have connected to.

4. Click the **Add an account** button. When you do so, a screen appears showing the online services you can connect to, as shown in Figure 9.9.

5. Select **Gmail**. The Add Your Google Account screen displays, as shown in Figure 9.10.

6. Enter your email address and password in the fields provided. To verify you entered your password correctly, tap-and-hold or click-and-hold the Password Preview button at the end of the Password box.

7. Select **Connect**. The Calendar app connects to Gmail to complete setting up your account. Shortly, the Calendar app synchs to your Gmail account, and you can see events and appointments on your Gmail calendar appear in your calendar in Windows 8.

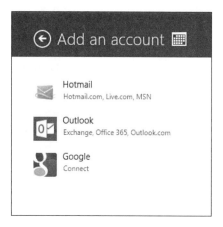

FIGURE 9.9

This screen shows the various calendar accounts you can display in the Calendar app.

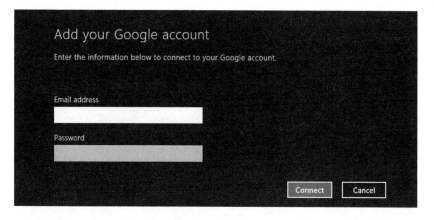

FIGURE 9.10

Gmail requires just two pieces of information to connect to the server.

Connecting to Your Exchange/Outlook/Office 365 Account

You can use the Outlook option to set up Exchange and Office 365, in addition to the new Outlook mail, which replaced Hotmail, to synchronize your calendar. Microsoft's server calendar, email, and contacts platform is Exchange, and Office 365 is a cloud-base office and collaboration platform. Almost all users integrate their Microsoft Exchange calendar with Microsoft Outlook, which runs on the computer desktop. The Windows 8 Calendar app is one of the first apps that enables users to retrieve their Exchange calendar without Outlook.

1. Start the Calendar app.

2. Open the Charms bar, and then select the Settings charm.

3. Select **Accounts**. A screen flies out from the right showing the list of the calendars you have connected to, if any (see Figure 9.11).

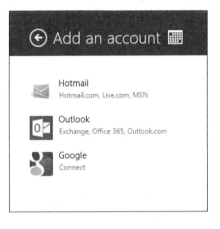

FIGURE 9.11

You choose the service where the calendar you want to link to is created.

4. Click the **Add an account** button. When you do so, a screen appears showing the online services you can connect to.

5. Select **Outlook**. The Add Your Outlook Account screen displays, as shown in Figure 9.12.

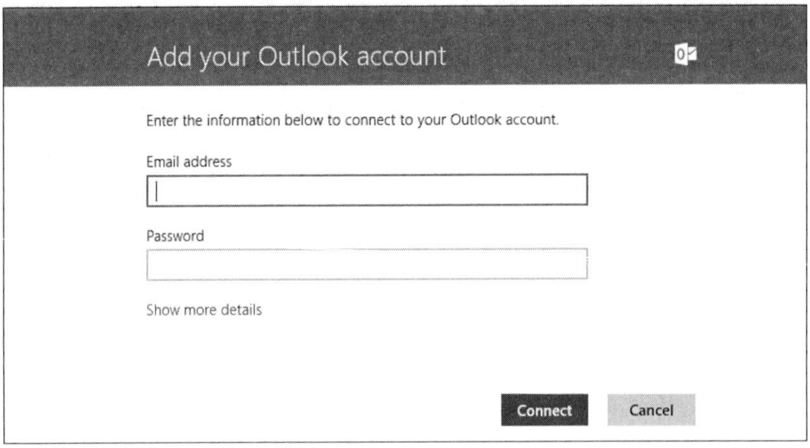

FIGURE 9.12

Exchange requires just two pieces of information to connect to the server.

6. Enter your email address and password in the fields provided. To verify you entered your password correctly, tap-and-hold or click-and-hold the Password Preview button at the end of the Password box.

   Select **Show more details** to enter the server name and domain name. This information can be provided by the help information available at the account you are synching with.

7. Select **Connect**. The Calendar app connects to Microsoft to complete setting up your account. Shortly, the Calendar app synchs to your account, and you can see events and appointments on your Outlook/Exchange/Office 365 calendar appear in your calendar in Windows 8.

Entering New Events into Your Calendar

You can easily enter a new event into your calendar, including inviting others to the event. You create your new event by selecting the date of your new event. Then you enter the details of your event. You can enter most of the details of your event by choosing from ready-made lists, such as the day, hour, frequency, duration of the event, and if the event recurs. This makes it easy to create your event.

To enter a new event into your calendar, follow these steps:

1. Open the Calendar app.

2. From any view, select the date of your event. If the event will be multiday or recurring, select the first date. If your view is daily or weekly, also select the time of your event. The Details pane opens for your new event, as shown in Figure 9.13.

    TIP You can select any date to start creating your new event. You need to switch the date of the event from the date you clicked or tapped to that of your event.

3. The first thing to do is select the calendar on which the event should appear. Select it from the Calendar list at the bottom of the Details pane. Don't forget this important point: the event you create will also appear in the calendar on the site of the service whose calendar you choose. So if you choose, for example, your Gmail account, the event will appear on Google.com.

4. Enter the details of your event in the fields provided. Although most of the information you enter is self-explanatory, there are a few items you should know about as you enter information about your event:

- Any field that has a down arrow includes a list of possible values for the field. Click or tap the arrow to see the items in the list, as shown in Figure 9.14.

Details

When

| August ⌄ | 20 Monday ⌄ | 2012 ⌄ |

Start

| 10 ⌄ | 00 ⌄ | AM ⌄ |

How long

| 1 hour ⌄ |

Where

| |

Calendar

| ☐ Paul's calendar—win8bookauthor@hotmail.com ⌄ |

Show more

Add a title Ⓗ ⓧ

Add a message

FIGURE 9.13

This screen shows the form in which you enter details of your calendar event.

FIGURE 9.14

Fields that include a down arrow contain a list of values from which you can select.

- Select the **Who** field to select persons to invite to your meeting. This calls the People Picker, which enables you to select from your contacts shown in the People app. To invite people who are not your contacts, enter their email address. For help with the People Picker, refer to Chapter 7, "Connecting with the People App."

5. Select **Add a Title** to enter a subject for the meeting. When you select the text, the words disappear giving you the opportunity to enter your own title.

6. Select **Add a Message** to enter a longer description for the meeting. You can enter any information you like for the meeting, including conference call information if this is a group meeting. When you select the text, the words disappear giving you the opportunity to enter your own title.

7. To save the event and, if others are invited, to send an invitation, select the **Save** button.

8. Review your calendar to be sure the event was created properly.

THE ABSOLUTE MINIMUM

Keep these points in mind after you finish reading this chapter:

- You can synchronize your Windows 8 calendar with your calendar on Google, Outlook, Live, or Hotmail, as well as with a Microsoft Exchange calendar. This gives you the ability to maintain your online calendars as you always do, but bring all your calendars together on one place in Windows 8.

- You select people to invite to events you schedule from the list of persons consolidated in your People app in Windows 8.

- You can schedule events in the Calendar app on the online calendars you synchronize with. This means the event appears on both the calendar in Windows 8, as well as on the online calendar.

SHARING YOUR WINDOWS 8 COMPUTER WITH OTHERS

The easiest way to share your Windows 8 computer or tablet with other users is to provide your username and password to whomever you want to share with! Well, you probably would prefer a more secure solution for giving others access to your Windows 8 computer—yet another reminder that the easiest way is seldom the best way. The best way to share your Windows 8 computer or tablet is to create a separate account for anyone to whom you want to provide access. As you read in this chapter, the process to create an account is easy, with just a few settings that require some thought. You learn how to handle these setting when you add a new user. You also read about the new password options in Windows 8, plus how to remove an account.

Windows 8 Users and Account Basics

You can give as many persons access to your Windows 8 computer as needed. As you give access, and you learn how to do so in this chapter, a new portrait appears on the Sign-in screen for each new user, as shown in Figure 10.1.

FIGURE 10.1

You may have a number of persons sharing your Windows 8 computer.

To give someone access, you create an account in Windows 8 for their own use. A new user in Windows 8 is automatically created as a *regular* user. A regular user contrasts with an *administrator* in that he doesn't have access to some of the more sensitive settings, including those related to security. This means only an administrator can add new users to Windows 8. So, to try out and then put to use the instructions and walkthroughs in this chapter, you must be an administrator-type user. If you are not sure if your account is an administrator-type, follow the steps in the section "Adding a New User with a Local account." If at step 3 of that section, you do not see the option to add a user, you are not an administrator. If you find your account is not an administrator type, try one of these fixes:

- If you were not the person to set up your computer, ask the person who did to change your account to an administrator-type. (You can't promote yourself to an administrator.)

- If you did set up Windows 8, the account you created when you installed Windows is an administrator-type. Sign in with that account.

Any person who wants to use Windows 8 must sign in with an email address and a password. The email address and password are associated with an account. The account may be one of two types. A Local account is used only with the computer where it was created. A Windows account is stored with Microsoft on its servers across the Internet. This means you can use a Windows account on any Windows 8 device anywhere, including servers, desktops, laptops, phones, and tablets.

You have a choice as to which type account to create and use. If you are the person who installs Windows, you can select which type of account to use to sign in to Windows 8 the first time. If someone creates an account for your use with Windows 8, be sure you understand which type of account is created for you. If you have a choice, it probably makes sense to use a Windows 8 account. Here's why:

- All of your Windows 8 preferences and settings, such as the color of the Start screen, a record of all the apps you downloaded, and approximately 10 more, are stored with your Windows 8 account. This means your preferences can be applied to any Windows 8 devices you sign in to. You don't need to spend time setting up any new computer you use. Refer to Chapter 4, "Personalizing Windows 8," to learn how to specify which settings and preferences are saved with your account.

- Signing in to Windows 8 with a Windows account automatically signs you in to any app that you downloaded from the Windows 8 store that requires you to sign in.

- Signing in to Windows 8 with a Windows account automatically signs you in to any website that requires a Microsoft account. If you start Internet Explorer and browse to a site such as www.outlook.com, you do not need to sign in to those sites.

 NOTE For the purposes of this discussion, a Windows 8 account and a Microsoft account are essentially the same thing. Your Windows 8 account connects directly to your Microsoft account.

- If you forget your Windows 8 account password, you can always reset it through Microsoft account services. If you forget the password to a local account, and you cannot recall it through one of the reminder features, you are probably out of luck and need to create a new Windows account.

You can create a Windows 8 account before you begin to install Windows 8. To do so, visit www.outlook.com or www.live.com (see Figure 10.2). If you already have a Hotmail, Live, or Outlook account, you are ready to sign in to Windows 8. Use the same credentials you use to sign in to those Microsoft online services to sign in to Windows 8. Your account must first be added to the Windows 8 device you intend to sign in to. This is covered next, in the "Adding a New User" section.

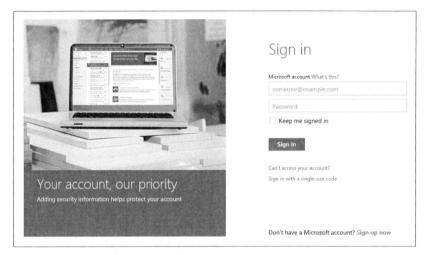

FIGURE 10.2

You can create a Windows 8 account before you add the account to your Windows 8 device.

 NOTE If you installed Windows 8, you are granted administrator rights, which mean that Windows 8 enables you to do anything with the software. Most relevant with administrator rights is you can add new accounts, hence giving other people access to Windows 8.

Adding a New User

There are a few things to keep in mind before you start the relatively easy process to add a new user to Windows 8:

- You must be signed in with an administrator-type account to add new users. For information about administrator-type accounts, see the "Changing a User's Type" section later in this chapter.

- You must select whether the new user has a Windows account or a Local account. You can find information about account types earlier in the "Learning About Account Types" section.

Because there are differences in the process to create a Local account versus a Windows 8 account, there are separate walk-throughs for each in the next two sections.

Adding a New User with a Local Account

To add a user account that will be recognized only on the device you work at, create a Local account by following these steps:

1. Open the **Settings** charm and select **Change PC settings** at the bottom of the screen.

2. Select **Users** from the list of settings on the left side of the screen.

3. Select **Add a User**, which appears at the bottom of the list of settings.

4. Select **Sign In Without a Microsoft Account**. You will be prompted one more time for the type of account you want to create, as shown in Figure 10.3. Select **Local Account**. The screen shown in Figure 10.4 appears.

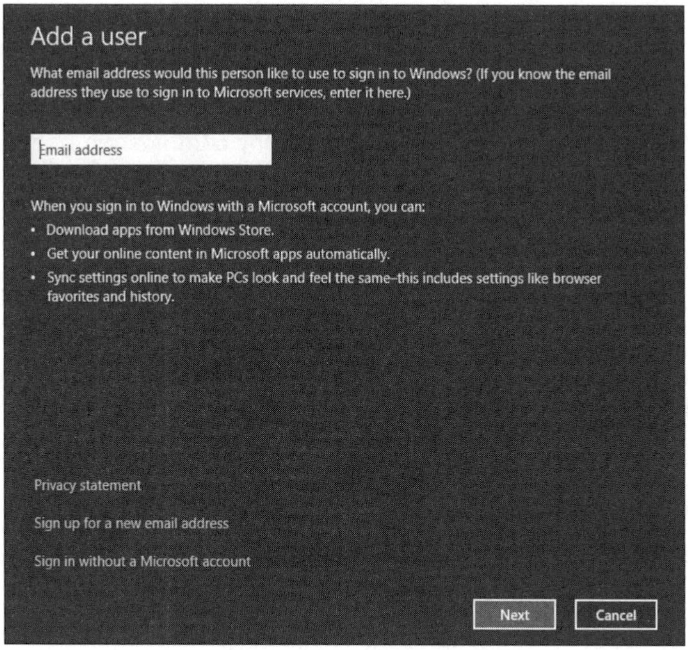

FIGURE 10.3

You get one more opportunity to select the type of account to create.

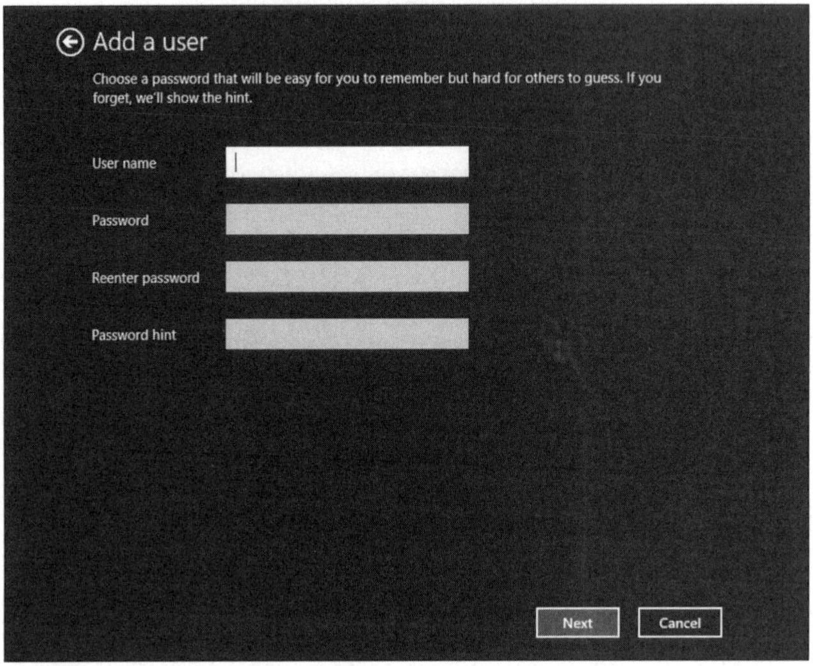

FIGURE 10.4

You need to supply just a username, password, and a password hint, to create a local account.

5. Enter a username (20-characters max; any combination of numbers and letters, including spaces; no ?|[]";|<>=+.?*%@), a password (any characters, including numbers, letters, spaces, and symbols), and a password hint into the fields provided. Select **Next**.

6. To track the user's online activity with Windows 8's Family Safety tools (Chapter 19, "Safe and Private Computing"), select the check box. Select **Finish**.

7. You return to the Sign-In options screen that appeared with step 2. Scroll to the bottom of the screen, and you should see your new user.

Adding a New User with a Windows Account

There are two scenarios in which you add a new user to your Windows 8 computer with a Windows account. You can add an account to your Windows 8 computer that already has been created, and you can add a user and create their Windows account at the same time. Both scenarios are covered in this walkthrough.

To add an account that can be used with any Windows 8 device, follow these steps to create a Windows account:

1. Open the **Settings** charm and select **Change PC Settings** at the bottom of the screen.

2. Select **Users** from the list of settings on the left side of the screen. Your screen should look like the one shown in Figure 10.5; though you may already have users added to your system while the screen has just one.

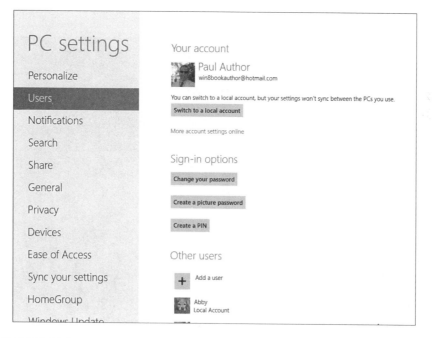

FIGURE 10.5

The Users screen enables you to manage most aspects of the accounts authorized to use your Windows 8 device.

3. Select **Add a User**. This option appears near the bottom of the screen.

4. If the user you want to add does not have a Windows account, and you would like to create one, select **Sign Up for a New Email Address**. Then, skip to step 6.

    If the user already has a Microsoft account, enter the email address associated with that account in the Email address box. Then, click **Next**. Windows attempts to verify the email address you entered.

5. If Windows does not recognize the email you entered, you will be prompted to sign up for a new email address, as shown in Figure 10.6. If you want to create an account with this email address, skip to step 6. If you want to change or correct the email address you entered, select **Cancel**. You will be returned to the screen described in step 3.

   If the email address is verified, the screen shown in Figure 10.7 appears. If the person using this account is a child and you plan to use the Windows Family Safety tools to manage her online use, select the child's account option. Select **Finish**. Skip to step 8.

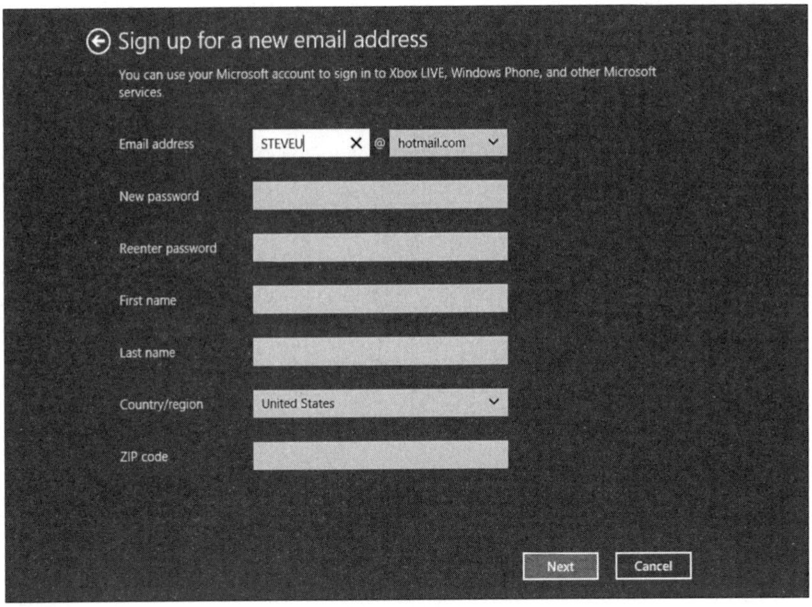

FIGURE 10.6

If you enter the email address for an account that does not exist, you are prompted to create an account with the address you entered.

6. The next three screens ask you to supply baseline contact information, such as your name and ZIP code, phone number, alternative email, and security question. Be sure to note the email address and password you entered by either writing it down or by storing the information in a password storage application. Read Chapter 19, for advice on storing passwords.

   When you've filled out all three pages of the form, select **Next** to continue.

FIGURE 10.7

Your work is done if you enter an email address associated with a working Windows account.

7. The last prompt from Windows checks if you want to monitor the new user's web activity with the Windows Family Safety tools. Select the option if you like, and select **Finish**.

8. You are returned to the screen where you started at step 2. You should see the new account you created in the Other users list at the bottom of the screen. At this point, you can modify the account, creating a PIN or Picture Password (as in the next section), or use it to log in to Windows 8.

Creating a PIN or Picture Password

When you create your new account in Windows 8, you need to supply a password, but you can use one of two new sign-in options, replacing the use of the password after you initially supply it. These two options are PIN and Picture Password. Besides saving you the repetitive stress of entering your password often, these two new options are impressive, and you'll want to use them to impress your friends!

Adding a PIN to Your Account

A PIN is a 4-digit number you use to identify yourself when you sign in to Windows. Any 4-digit combination of numerals is acceptable, including repeats such as 9999. A PIN is particularly useful to tablet users who normally don't have a physical keyboard. On a tablet, a virtual keyboard appears on the screen as you sign in to Windows, enabling you to enter just your PIN to access Windows.

To add a PIN to your account, follow these steps:

1. Open the **Settings** charm and select **Change PC Settings**, which appears on the bottom right of the screen.

2. From the menu of settings, select **Users**.

3. Select **Create a PIN**. The Create a PIN screen appears.

4. You first must verify your password. Enter your password and select **OK**. The screen in Figure 10.8 appears.

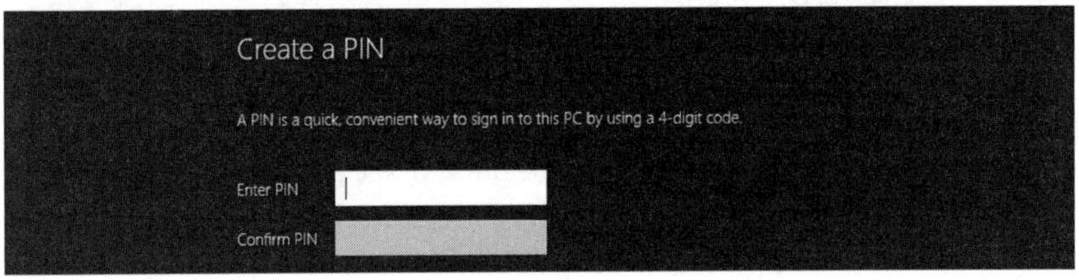

Create a PIN

A PIN is a quick, convenient way to sign in to this PC by using a 4-digit code.

Enter PIN

Confirm PIN

FIGURE 10.8

You can enter a PIN (and confirm it) to use as a substitute for your password.

5. Enter your PIN, and then enter it again in the **Confirm PIN** box.

6. Select **Finish**.

Adding a Picture Password to Your Account

If you are like the author and enjoy drawing mustaches and other funny shapes on pictures of your friends, family, and your editor, this is the password option for you. A picture password is a combination of a picture and touch gestures. To set up a picture password, you choose a picture from your Pictures folder and then make three gestures, which can be your choice of tapping or drawing a line or circle (see Figure 10.9). Windows records the position of the gestures, as well as the order in which you made them. This combination creates the picture password.

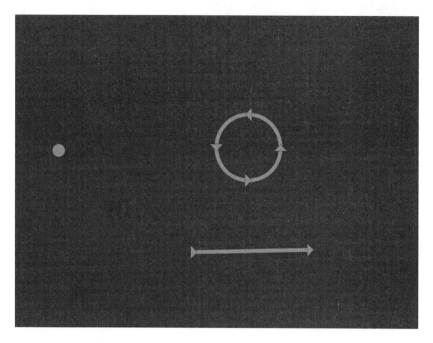

FIGURE 10.9

These are the three gestures you can use with your picture password.

 TIP It would be helpful if you had a picture in mind to use as your picture password. If you don't have a good candidate picture on your computer, you should locate or take a new photo and then load it onto your computer before you start this process. A good candidate photo has a number of recognizable items, as opposed to a broad, landscape photo. This way, it's easier to remember the objects on which you drew the required symbols.

To use a picture password with your Windows 8 account, follow these steps:

1. Open the **Settings** charm and select **Change PC Settings**, which appears on the bottom right of the screen.

2. Select **Users**.

3. Select **Create a Picture Password**.

4. You first must verify your password. Enter your password and select **OK**. If you entered your password correctly, the screen shown in Figure 10.10 appears.

FIGURE 10.10

The first step in creating a picture password is to choose a picture.

5. Select **Choose picture**.

6. Your screen displays the photos in your Picture folders. Look through the photos to find one to use as your picture password. Select the photo to use, and then select **Open**.

7. The picture you selected should be on the screen, as shown in Figure 10.11. The picture password screen uses only about three-quarters of the picture you chose. Click-and-drag or touch-and-drag the picture directly on the screen to a position you like. Tap or click **Use This Picture.**

8. The Set Up Your Gesture screen should be visible. This is the screen where you draw the three gestures. You'll be asked to draw them twice to be sure you can recall what they are and where they are drawn. Draw the three gestures. Figure 10.12 shows the example screen after one gesture has been drawn. The large number will be highlighted for each gesture drawn.

    Select **Start Over** if you want to redraw all the gestures. If you want to save creating a picture password for another time, select **Cancel**.

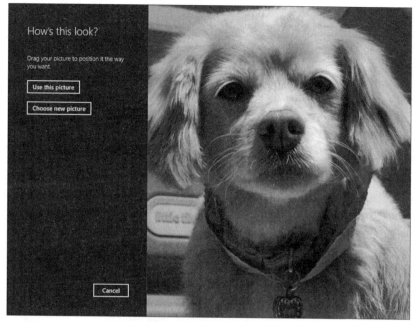

FIGURE 10.11

This is the picture you will use for your picture password.

FIGURE 10.12

Notice the numeral 2 is highlighted, indicating one gesture has been drawn. You can see the gestures on the screen when you redraw each as part of the verification step.

9. After you confirm the three gestures for the picture password, you are returned to your account setting screen. You can sign out to try out your new picture password. To return to the Start screen, from where you can sign out or start another activity, press the **Windows** key, or slowly move to the bottom-left corner with your finger or mouse to display the Start portrait. Select the portrait.

Making Changes to User Accounts

After an account has been created and a user has used the account to sign in to Windows 8, you can still make changes to it. You can change the account to an administrator from a regular type, or vice versa. You can also remove an account. While you add a new user account from a set of screens you access from the Windows 8 Start screen, any modifications are made from a set of Windows that you access through the Desktop app.

Changing a User's Type

You may want to give certain users more access in Windows 8, such as to add more users, install software, or change security settings. To do so, you need to change their account type to administrator. Closely related, you may want to remove an individual's administrator rights and instead give them regular user capabilities. Making either change is easy.

To change a user's type, follow these steps:

1. Open the **Search** charm. Enter **Change account type** and select **Settings**. Select the setting from the list of results. The Manage Account window should be on your screen.

2. Select the account to change, which opens another window with a menu of actions, as shown in Figure 10.13.

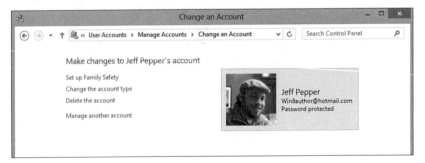

FIGURE 10.13

You can change several aspects of an account from the Change an Account screen.

3. Select **Change Account Type** from the menu, and then select **Standard** or **Administrator** as the account type to change to.

4. Select **Change Account Type**. You will be returned to the screen shown here.

Removing a User Account

You may need to remove an account from Windows 8. Perhaps the person who is associated with the account no longer should access to Windows 8, or perhaps the account was created in error. Regardless of the reason, it is easy to remove the account. You must be signed in with an administrator account to remove an account.

To remove a user account, follow these steps:

1. Open the **Search** charm. Enter **Remove user accounts** and select Settings. Select the setting from the list of results. The Manage Account window should be on your screen.

2. Select the account you want to delete. The Change an Account window appears.

3. Select **Delete the Account**.

4. You can delete the account but keep the files used by the account, such as music files, photos, files stored on the desktop, all files in the Documents folder, plus videos. To do so, select **Keep Files**. To delete the account and all the account files, select **Delete Files**.

 NOTE   If you deleted a user account but chose to keep the user's files, you can find the files in a folder in the Users folder.

5. You will be asked to confirm your choice. Select **Delete Account**. To keep the account, select **Cancel**.

6. You are returned to the Manage Accounts window. You can close the window if you choose, or you can return to the Start screen without closing it.

THE ABSOLUTE MINIMUM

Keep these points in mind as you wrap up this chapter:

- To give others access to your Windows 8 device, you need to add an account to Windows 8. This is also known as "adding a user" in Windows 8. Unless you are told otherwise, create a Windows account when prompted as you add the new account.

- A Windows 8 account includes information about your settings and preferences. If you sign-in to Windows 8 running on a computer other than your own, all your settings and preferences are applied to this new computer. This won't happen if you instead create a local account.

- A picture password replaces the standard password. To sign in with a picture password, swipe or tap three different times on a picture you choose. Windows checks your gestures against what it recorded when you created the picture password.

- You can also use a PIN to substitute for a password.

IN THIS CHAPTER

- Introductory Details About Home Networks
- How to Join, Leave, and Create a Homegroup
- How to Share with Other Homegroup Computers

11

SHARING FILES AND PRINTERS WITH HOMEGROUP

Say the word "network" to a novice Windows user and you're sure to notice a look of fear mixed with confusion. But for the person who simply wants to share a picture library or some music or perhaps all the family's important files among the computers in their home, there shouldn't be too much panic. Windows makes this panic-free sharing possible with a function called "homegroups." Homegroups provide exactly what you want from a small network to provide easy sharing without introducing any complexity. Much of the tough network concepts and procedures have been stripped away from the process to create a homegroup, and the focus has been made simply on sharing files, folders, printers, and other stuff. This chapter helps you understand just what you need to know about home networks and it walks you slowly but purposely through the easy process to set up sharing.

Setting up homegroup sharing is easy; although you need to leverage some information presented in other chapters. In particular, review the "Control Panel" section at the end of Chapter 3, "Learning Windows 8 Basics." Also, be sure to review the "Navigating Through Your File System" section in Chapter 15, "Organizing Files and Folders with Windows Explorer."

Networking with Homegroup

This section eases you into the idea to create a small network. Yes! You can boast to your pals that you know how to implement a computer network! Or you to be as modest as you like. The education begins with a brief review of the benefits of a small home network.

 NOTE   Homegroup is appropriate for smaller networks, but how small is small? There is no reason why 10 or more computers can't be set up in a homegroup, or even 20 or more. But most homes have between 5 and 10 networked devices to share (everything from PCs and tablets to DVRs and game consoles), and a small home office probably has a similar number of computers and devices.

If you have more than one computer in your home or home office, it probably makes sense to connect the computers into a small network. Although the advantages and conveniences might not make sense right now, the Microsoft and Windows 8 view of computing is growing wide and deep. Considering Windows Live, SkyDrive, and other Microsoft technologies that leverage the Cloud (that great mystical space in the Internet sky), it's clear that your computing world spans beyond the barriers of your own computer or tablet, even if the world spans just to the computer in the next room. Here are a few benefits to setting up a small sharing network at home:

- Consolidate all the files of a certain type, such as music or pictures, on one computer. This way, it's easy to find a particular song or photo if they are all stored in one place.

- Set up one computer as a kind of home media player, storing all your movies and music, and also having all your audio equipment attached to it.

- Buy just one printer with lots of bells and whistles, and then connect it to one of your homegroup computers. Then, share it with all computers in the homegroup rather than purchasing one printer for each computer.

There are usually a few settings to adjust plus possibly some hardware to acquire for a small group of computers to form a network. But the good news is that if all the computers that you would like to join to a network can connect to the Internet from home, you are likely ready to share. If each device uses the same device and service to connect to the Internet, such as your cable modem, DSL modem, or whatever, they are *already* joined to a network. It's as easy as that.

Using the Windows Homegroup

The Homegroup is an incredibly helpful feature in Windows 8 that enables you to share files with other computers that belong to the homegroup. As a member of a homegroup, you can see all the files that other members of the homegroup make available for sharing, and vice versa, as if the files were on your computer. You usually can open and edit the shared files, make copies of them, and delete them as if they were your own. Figure 11.1 shows Windows Explorer displaying some shared photos another homegroup computers.

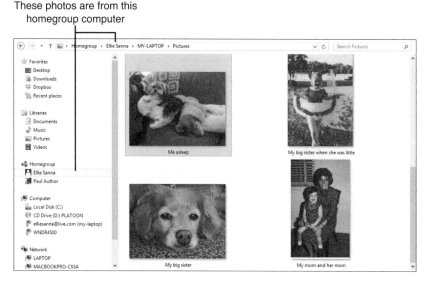

FIGURE 11.1

You can access shared files and folders as easily as files and folders on your computer's hard drive. In this picture, you can see pictures that Ellie has shared on her computer.

Here are a few things to know about homegroups and networks:

- Each computer whose files you want to share most join the homegroup; see the section, "Joining a Homegroup."

- There may be just one homegroup on your network.

- If one computer on the network has created a homegroup, then any computer on the network from which you want to share must join *that* homegroup.

- To create a new homegroup, all computers must leave the homegroup, including the computer that started it.

- One computer creates a homegroup, and all other computers then join it. This does not give ownership or responsibility for the homegroup to the computer that created it. All computers in a homegroup are on par with one another. None have any more responsibility or capabilities than any other.

- It might sound daunting to navigate through all your files and folders to find, discover, or identify what you might share. Windows 8 makes it easy to specify and organize the files you might share by leveraging the library. You specify which libraries to share with your homegroup.

 NOTE As a reminder, *libraries* are a convenient way to bring together all the files that share a particular use or function no matter where folders are located. A library is a special folder that "points" to several other folders. Whatever files and folders that reside in a folder specified by a library become members of that library. For a review of libraries, refer to Chapter 15.

Although libraries are set up for you, homegroups are not. You must create homegroup as the first step toward sharing on your home network.

There are three steps to set up a homegroup in Windows:

1. Create a homegroup.

2. Join a homegroup.

3. Set up homegroup sharing.

Each of these steps is covered in detail in the following sections.

Creating a Homegroup

Creating a homegroup is a simple matter of clicking a few buttons and then making a password. Before you can start, however, you need to get to the Homegroup screen. Here's how:

1. Open the Settings charm.

2. Select **Change PC Settings** at the bottom of the screen.

3. Select **HomeGroup** from the menu on the left side of the screen.

4. You should see a screen like the one in either Figure 11.2 or Figure 11.3 or Figure 11.4.

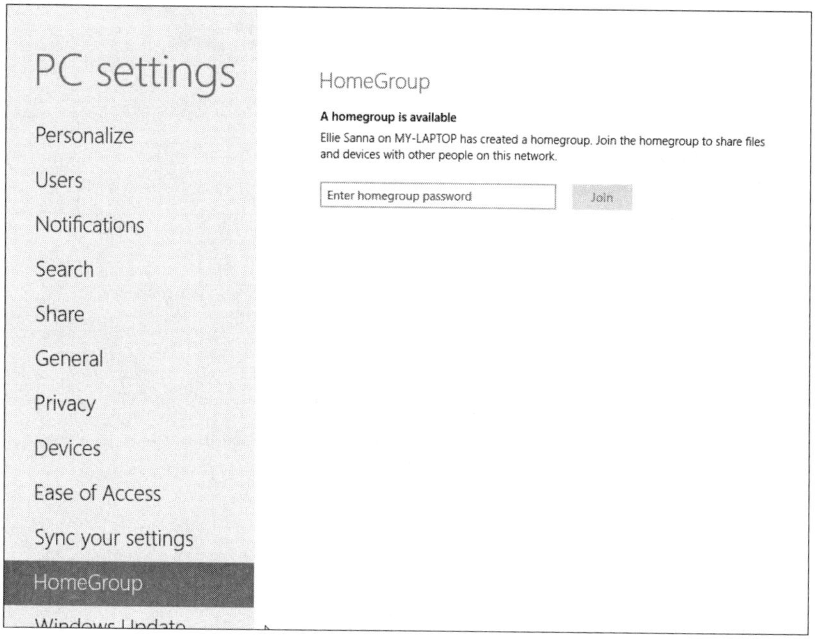

FIGURE 11.2

This screen indicates a homegroup already is set up on your network but you haven't joined it yet.

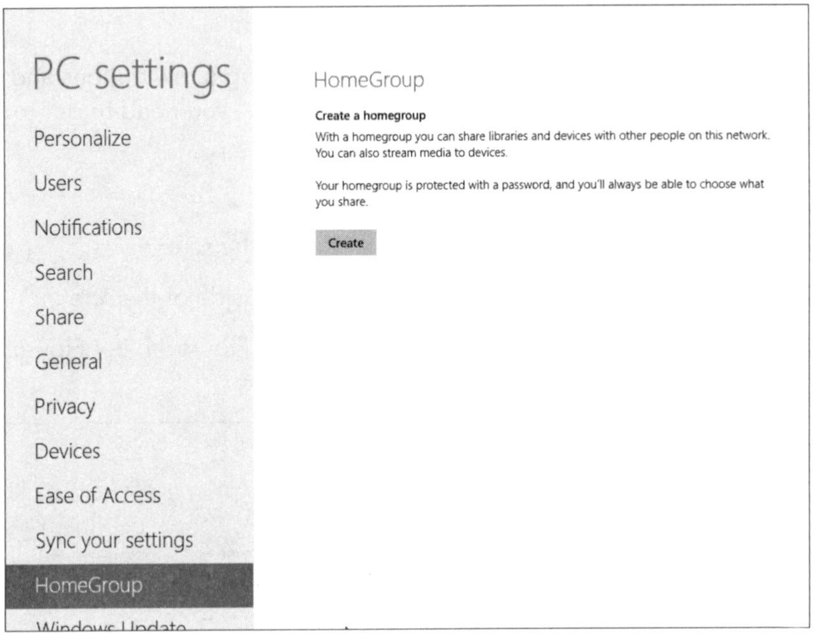

FIGURE 11.3

This screen indicates a homegroup has not been set up on your network.

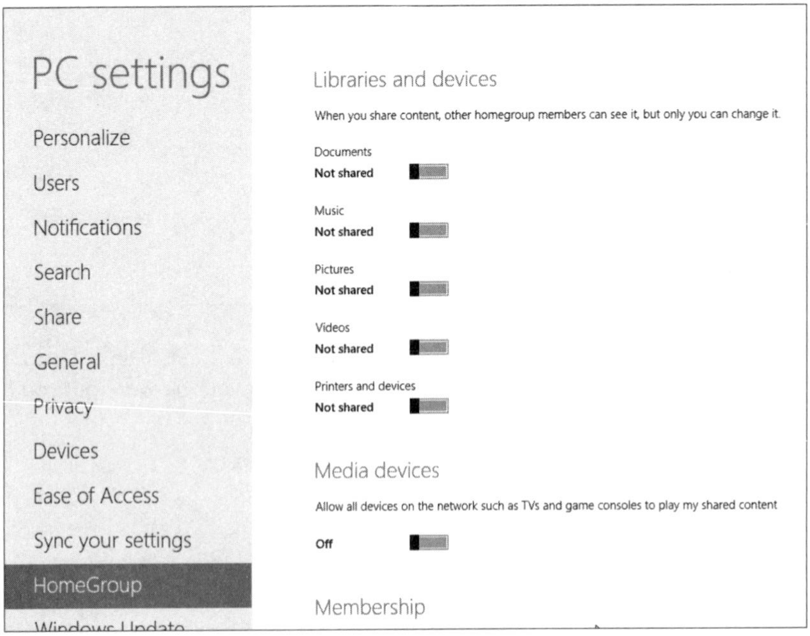

FIGURE 11.4

This screen indicates you belong to a homegroup but you have not shared anything yet.

NOTE If your device is already connected to an existing homegroup, but you want to create a new one anyway, skip to the section, "Leaving a Homegroup."

For now, we're only interested in Figure 11.3, which gives you the opportunity to create a homegroup. We'll get to the other two figures in a little bit. Follow these steps to create a homegroup:

If the option to create a homegroup is present you can do so by following these steps:

1. Select **Create**. After a moment, the screen shown in Figure 11.5 appears (scroll to the bottom).

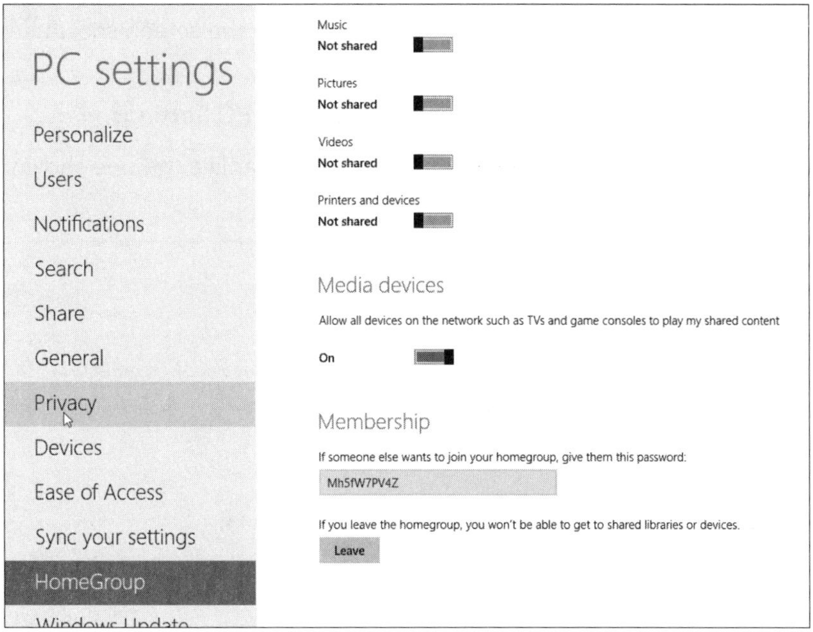

![PC settings screen]

PC settings

Personalize

Users

Notifications

Search

Share

General

Privacy

Devices

Ease of Access

Sync your settings

HomeGroup

Windows Update

Music
Not shared

Pictures
Not shared

Videos
Not shared

Printers and devices
Not shared

Media devices

Allow all devices on the network such as TVs and game consoles to play my shared content

On

Membership

If someone else wants to join your homegroup, give them this password:

Mh5fW7PV4Z

If you leave the homegroup, you won't be able to get to shared libraries or devices.

Leave

FIGURE 11.5

This screen indicates your computer belongs to a homegroup.

2. The box under Membership shows a string of 10 characters, indicating a homegroup has been created. The computer you've been using is a member of it.

3. Ignore the controls on this screen for now. Carefully write down the password shown in the box under Membership. Note the case used for letters (7abc8 is not the same as 7ABC8). You need this password so that other computers can join in the homegroup.

At this point, your computer has created and joined the homegroup. The homegroup, though, is a quiet one with just this computer as a member. In the next section, you learn how other computers in the network can join the homegroup.

Joining a Homegroup

You can join a homegroup as long as one computer that belongs to the homegroup signed on. Even if you know the computer that was used to create the homegroup, you do not need to wait for *that* computer to be signed in to join.

To join a homegroup, follow these steps:

1. Get the homegroup password. That password can be retrieved easily from another homegroup computer by bringing up the screen shown earlier (refer to Figure 11.5).

2. Open the **Settings** charm and select **Change PC Settings**.

3. Select **Homegroup**. Your screen should appear like the one shown in Figure 11.6.

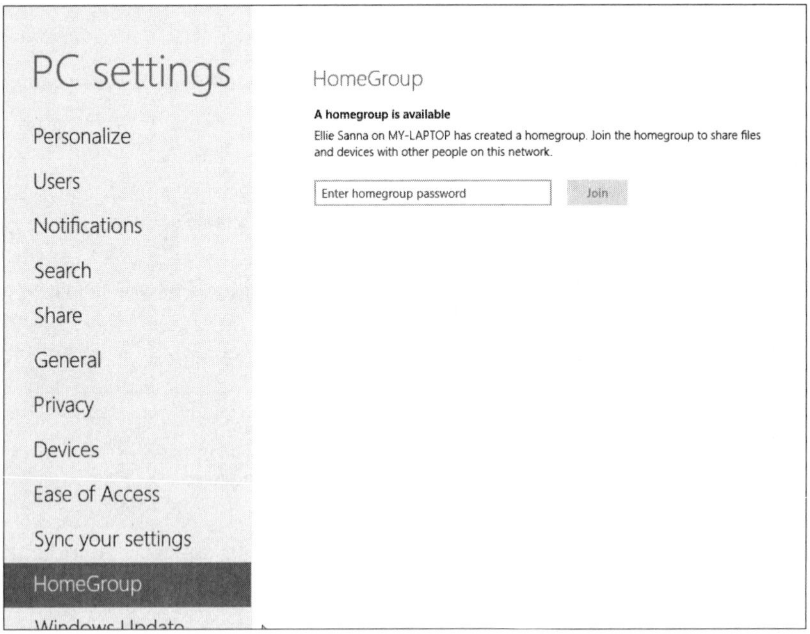

FIGURE 11.6

You are invited to join a homegroup when you visit the homegroup screen.

4. Enter the password into the box, and select **Join**.

5. If the password is accepted, the sharing options become available (refer to Figure 11.4). You can set the sharing options immediately. For guidance, however, read the section, "Setting Up Sharing."

Leaving a Homegroup

You read earlier that all computers must leave a homegroup before a new homegroup can be created. To leave a homegroup, follow these steps:

1. Open the **Settings** charm, and select **Change PC Settings**.

2. Select **Homegroup**, and then select **Leave**.

Troubleshooting Homegroup Connections

If you experience difficulty either joining a homegroup or leaving one, you can try one of these troubleshooting tips:

*   You may experience difficulties joining a homegroup if you use an antivirus program. If you don't mind disabling your antivirus program for a short time, you can attempt to join or leave the homegroup again after temporarily disabling the software.

*   You may experience difficulties joining a homegroup if you use an all-in-one Internet privacy or protection software suite. If so, disable the protection temporarily before trying to join the homegroup again. If you can connect, you may create an exception for Windows 8, enabling you to join a homegroup.

 CAUTION If you disable your antivirus or other Internet protection software, it's not a bad idea to disconnect from the Internet (but not your network) before you do.

*   Windows networks are of a specific type: home, office, or public. The type defines the level of security for each. For example, a home networks enables more computer-to-computer communication than a public network. A homegroup is allowed only on a home network.

*   **Warning: This fix is technical**. Get help restarting the Peer Networking Grouping and Homegroup Provider services. Another advice from geek-city is to be sure IPV6 is engaged. If this is Greek to you, you'll unfortunately need a bit more expert help than this book provides.

Setting Up Sharing

Windows 8 organizes everything you might share into five categories. With your computer joined to a homegroup, simply turn sharing On or Off for each of these item types:

- Documents

- Music

- Pictures

- Videos

- Printers and devices

You might recognize these options. They appear on the Homegroup settings screen, as shown in Figure 11.2. You might recognize the first four choices for another reason. They are each names of the default libraries in Windows 8. Libraries are a convenient way to bring together all the files that share a particular use or function no matter where folders are located (refer to Chapter 15). A library is a special folder that points to several other folders.

To share any of these items, you simply need to move the toggle switch associated with it (from left to right). Done.

Before you share everything your device has to share, however, here are some things you need to know about sharing:

- By default, every file in a library is shared with every computer in the homegroup (when you turn on sharing for that library, of course).

- You can prevent one or more libraries from being shared.

- You can prevent one or more files in a library from being shared even if the library is being shared.

- You can prevent one or more files in a library or one or more entire libraries from being shared with certain users in your homegroup.

The following sections show you how to deal with each of these cases.

Disabling Sharing for Specific Files or Folders

To prevent one or more files or folders in a library from being shared, follow these steps:

1. Start Windows Explorer.

2. Navigate to the folder where the file or folder you want to restrict from sharing is located. You can find assistance with navigating in Chapter 15.

3. Select the files or folders. You can use the multiselect approach (also described in Chapter 15) to restrict all the files or folders at once, or you can do them in small batches, or you can set sharing for each file or folder one at a time.

4. Under the Share tab in the **Share With** group, select **Stop Sharing**.

5. You may have to repeat these steps a few times.

Sharing Files and Folders Only with Specific Users

To share certain files or folders only with specific persons:

1. Start Windows Explorer.

2. Navigate to the folder where the file or folder you want to share with only certain people is located.

3. Select the files or folders. You can use the multiselect approach (refer to Chapter 15) to restrict all the files or folders at once, or you can do them in small batches, or you can set each file or folder one at a time.

4. Under the Share tab in the Share With group, select the down arrow button on the right side of the box, as shown in the top picture in Figure 11.7. A list of the persons you can share appears, as shown in the bottom picture in Figure 11.7

5. Select **Specific People**. The dialog box shown in Figure 11.8 appears.

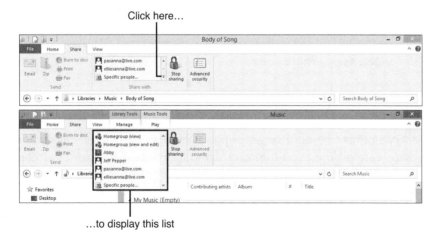

Click here...

...to display this list

FIGURE 11.7

Select the small down arrow to display the list.

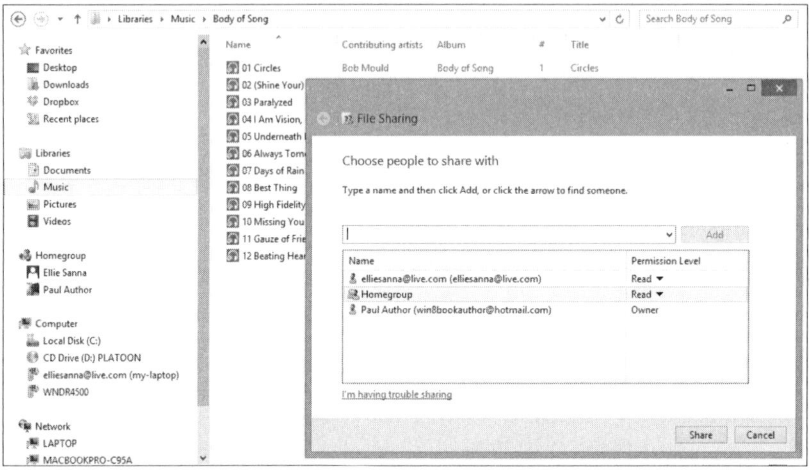

FIGURE 11.8

Select persons to filter sharing.

6. Enter the email address or the name of the person, and then select **Add**.

7. Repeat the last step if needed to select more persons with whom to share the files you selected.

8. To allow all the users you selected to edit the files and folders you share, select **Share**. You're done.

   To allow some or all the users you selected to *read* only the file you're sharing and *not change anything*, select **Read** from the Permission Level column for any user you won't allow to change the files you're sharing. Otherwise, leave the setting in the Permission Level column as Read/Write. To save your changes, select **Share**.

Sharing Your Printer

Sharing a printer in your homegroup is as easy as sharing files and folders, perhaps easier. When you turn on sharing for Printers and devices (refer to Figure 11.2), each of your printers, scanners, and other devices become available to all computers in the homegroup. Here is how to share specific printers:

1. Open Control Panel, and then open Hardware and Sound. Finally, open Devices and Printers.

2. Locate the printer you want to share. Right-click or tap-and-hold the printer, and from the menu that appears, select **Printer Properties**.

3. Select the **Sharing** tab.

4. Select **Share This Printer**. You'll notice a name for your printer is automatically filled in for you. This is the name everyone will see on the network. You can change it if you like.

 TIP A person looking to use a shared printer can see what computer shares the printer. There is no reason to add this type of information ("Abby's printer") to the printer name.

5. Select **OK**.

6. Close the Devices and Printers window by selecting the **Close** button in the top-right corner of the window.

Seeing Stuff Shared By Others

While its good share, it's also really good to receive. Whatever your homegroup partners decide to share, you can access very easily. You'll do using the capabilities of the Desktop app, which is reviewed in detail in Chapter 13. Follow these steps to review the content being shared by others.

From the Start screen, start the Desktop App.

1. Open Windows Explorer. If you are unclear how to open Windows Explorer, refer to Chapter 15.

2. Be sure the Navigation pane is displayed. To do so, from the File tab on the Ribbon, select **Navigation pane**. From the menu that appears, select **Navigation Pane** (yes, again) if there is no check besides the command. If the Navigation pane command is checked, then the pane is in view.

3. In the Navigation Pane, scroll down to about the third major group. It should show "Homegroup" at the top entry in the tree. Click the small arrow beside the word Homegroup to display homegroup computers, as shown in Figure 11.9.

4. Select the computer whose shared files you want to see. Then, navigate through the folders in the Content pane as you would if browsing through file on your own computer, as shown in Figure 11.10.

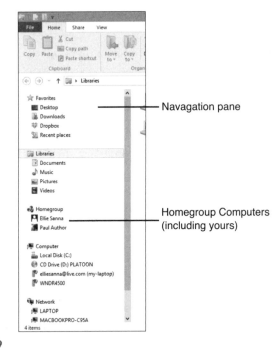

Navagation pane

Homegroup Computers
(including yours)

FIGURE 11.9

Computers in the homegroup that share content appear in the Navigation pane.

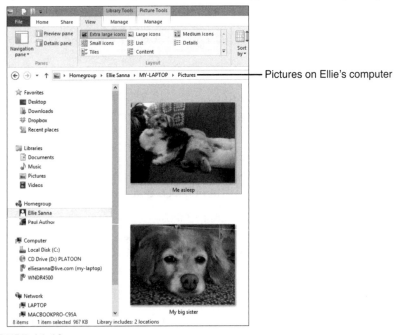

Pictures on Ellie's computer

FIGURE 11.10

Browse through the folders shared on a homegroup computer as if the folders are on your own computer.

THE ABSOLUTE MINIMUM

- Homegroups is a feature in Windows 8 that makes it extremely easy to share files, such as pictures, music, and other files, with other nearby computers. Homegroups also enable you to share printers.

- Computers and tablets that connect to the Internet at your home or home office are already part of a network for which you can create a homegroup.

- There can be just one homegroup in a network.

- Use libraries to determine what files get shared. When you turn on sharing, all the files in that library are shared. You must use the settings available through Windows Explorer to restrict sharing.

- The printers connected to your computer are automatically shared with all other computers in the homegroup as soon as you turn on sharing for printers and other devices on the Homegroup screen.

IN THIS CHAPTER

- Learn Windows 8 Apps' Basic Information
- Change a Windows 8 App's Settings
- Manage Windows 8 Apps
- Shop at the Windows Store

MASTERING WINDOWS 8 APPS

You have probably noticed that Windows 8 is different than previous versions of Windows. Much of the new look, colors, appearance, layout, and even placement of buttons and lists in the new Windows comes from a set of design principles know as *Windows 8 style*, developed by Microsoft. All the programs and tools that Microsoft and other companies build for Windows 8 also follow the Windows 8 style. Given that, it's not surprising that the new Windows 8 programs are as different from Windows 7 programs as Windows 8 is from Windows 7. The goal of this chapter is to bring you up to speed as quickly and clearly as possible on these new software programs, covering everything from starting up an app to using two apps together on the screen.

This chapter introduces you to a number of new concepts and techniques, all intended to help you manage Windows 8 apps. Many of these techniques are dependent on some of the skills presented earlier in the book. Be sure to review Chapter 2, "Interacting with Windows 8," and Chapter 4, "Personalizing Windows 8," if you are confused while reading the step-by-step procedures. In particular, review the sections related to the Start screen and the Charms bar in Chapter 3, "Learning Windows 8 Basics."

Learning Basic Windows 8 Apps Info

Windows 8 apps are software programs developed by Microsoft and other software companies specifically for use in Windows 8. The term Windows 8 apps is a shortened version of Windows 8 style apps for Windows 8.

Windows 8 refers to the set of design principles and philosophies about building software for users that was used to build Windows 8. Although a majority of the software used in previous versions of Windows, especially Windows 7, can run in Windows 8, the opposite does not hold true—Windows 8 apps cannot run in older versions of Windows. Here is more basic information you need to know about Windows 8 apps:

- Windows 8 apps run full screen, and only in certain conditions can two apps be viewed on the screen at the same time.

- Windows 8 apps are sold in the Windows Store, which is built into Windows 8. The Windows Store is covered at the end of this chapter.

- The Windows Store also handles the installation of Windows 8 Apps, saving you the confusion of installing new software into a new operating system.

- Windows 8 apps leverage the Charms bar consistently for printing, setup, and search. The Charms bar is described in Chapter 3. This requires a bit of a change in thinking on your part, because you traditionally look *inside* of your app for important tools, such as for printing. Now, you should check the Charms bar first for everyday tools and functions.

Unfortunately, much of what you know about Windows programs from your experience with older versions of Windows doesn't mean anything with Windows 8 Apps. Programs that were built for the prior version of Windows can still run in the Desktop app, but if you look for some of the standard Desktop features you're used to when running Windows 8 apps, you're not going to find them. Some of these include

- Resizing windows
- Arranging multiple windows on the screen
- Minimizing windows
- Using standard menus, such as File New, File Open, File Print

In the rest of this chapter, you can find enough hands-on instruction to make you a near-expert with Windows 8 apps before you charge off on your own working with them. Here's what's covered:

- Starting and stopping Windows 8 apps
- Managing Windows 8 apps
- Arranging multiple Windows 8 apps on the screen
- Shopping for Windows 8 apps

Running Windows 8 Apps

Starting an app probably seems like a basic topic, perhaps one that doesn't merit its own section in a book. But innocent situations, such as if another app is running when you start a new app, deserve some explanation. So, this section explains what happens when a Windows 8 app starts up, what happens when a Windows 8 app is running when you start a new one, as well as how to close a running app.

Starting a Windows 8 App

To start a Windows 8 app, select the tile from the Start screen that represents the app you want to start. Figure 12.1 shows a representative set of Windows 8 app tiles. Immediately after you tap/press/click the tile, you see a bit of fancy animation that quickly transitions to the open app, which fills the screen.

FIGURE 12.1

Windows 8 apps are started by selecting a tile from the Start screen, and the tiles can be formatted with colors and graphics.

You'll notice Windows 8 apps appear flat, borderless, and broad. There are no buttons, sliders, or other controls that appear to be raised off the screen, as shown in Figure 12.2, which presents the Internet Explorer browser built for Windows 8. Most controls are hidden until you follow the app's instructions to reveal any controls the app requires. An app's settings likely can be revealed by opening the App bar, which is covered later in this chapter. A Windows 8 app typically does not have borders because the app fills the entire area of the screen.

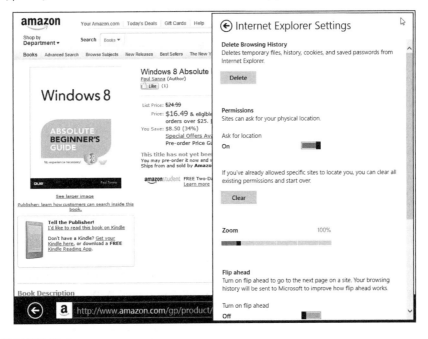

FIGURE 12.2

Notice how Windows 8 apps fill the entire screen and how controls appear flat against the screen.

Starting Additional Windows 8 Apps

If you are already using an app and would like to use another, just return to the Start screen, and start the additional app. You don't need to close the app you are working with before starting another app. When you start a Window 8 app, it opens full screen, replacing whatever was on the screen previously. The app you previously had open doesn't actually close. It's just hidden, so you can always switch back to it or to any other app that you started. You'll learn more about that in the section, "Managing Windows 8 Apps."

Stopping a Windows 8 App (If You Must)

You generally do not need to close or exit an app when you are done with it. Windows handles the housekeeping with apps it believes you no longer are using. But if you are instructed to close an app, perhaps for troubleshooting purposes, or you simply want to impress your friends, here are a few ways to close an app:

 Be sure you are in the app you want to close. Slowly drag your finger on the screen down from the top of the screen. By the time you reach the bottom of the screen, the app should disappear from view. When you start this gesture, be sure your finger or stylus is close to the edge of the screen that borders the rest of your device.

Press Alt+F4.

If there is another app open (or a few apps open) in addition to the one you are stopping, point at the top-left corner of the screen. A portrait of the most recent app you started appears. If that is the app you want to close, right-click and then select **Close**. Otherwise, move your mouse down from the top-left corner until the app you want to stop appears. Right-click it, and then select **Close**.

Point to the top-middle border of the app. Adjust the position of the mouse pointer until it changes to the shape of a hand. When it changes shape, click-and-drag down as if you were dragging the border of the app. The app reduces to a size not much larger than that of a large tile on the Start screen. The app follows your mouse cursor as you drag down. When you reach a point about two-thirds down the screen, the app closes down and disappear.

Using the App Bar to Change a Windows 8 App's Settings

Almost all Windows 8 applications have at least one setting that you can adjust. For example, the Photo app enables you to use one of your photos as the apps' tile on the Start screen, as shown in Figure 12.3.

You summon the settings for all apps in the same way. App settings appear on the App bar (see Figure 12.3). Although the App bar appears at the bottom of the App in the figure, the App bar also can appear above the app. The developer of the app determines whether the App bar settings appear above or below the app.

App bar

FIGURE 12.3

The links on the bottom left of the Photo app enables you to set the picture as the app tile or background image or use it on your lock screen.

To open the App bar, do one of the following based on the device you use:

- Swipe in from the bottom of the screen.
- Press Windows+Z.
- Right-click any empty area of the Start screen.

Managing Windows 8 Apps

With the new design of Windows 8, applications also have been redesigned to be more engaging and efficient. One way to do this is to keep the screen organized and clutter-free. Restricting the number of apps that can appear at once on the screen is a helpful step toward that goal. But there are always exceptions. In this section, you learn how to switch between open apps, how to actually organize two apps on the screen at once, and how to use the app switcher to quickly get to the app you want.

Using the App Switcher

One of the important tools you use to navigate between open apps is the app switcher. The *app switcher* displays a list of open apps and apps you opened recently. You simply select an app from the app switcher, and Windows brings that app to the freground.

To use the app switcher, as shown in Figure 12.4, do the following:

Swipe in from the left in the middle of the screen. When the portrait for the last-used app appears, swipe back to the left. The app switcher appears. Tap the app you want to use.

Press Windows+Tab. The app switcher appears immediately. Keeping the Windows key depressed, tap the Tab key until the app you're interested in is selected. Release the keys and your app opens.

Point to the top-left corner of the screen. When the portrait for the most recent app appears, move your mouse pointer down slowly and deliberately. The app switcher appears. Click the app.

List of open apps

FIGURE 12.4

The app switcher enables you to quickly switch to any app.

Switching to the Previous App

You might be involved in a task that requires you to work with two applications, switching back and forth between them. Windows makes this kind of task easy with a gesture that switches you to the previous app with which you were working:

To switch to the previous app, do one of the following based on the device you use:

 Swipe in from the left.

Press Windows+Tab.

Point to the top-left corner of the screen. A portrait of the previous app appears, as shown in Figure 12.5. Click the portrait.

FIGURE 12.5

The most recent app you used appears in the top-left corner of the screen when you point or tap there.

Showing Two Windows 8 Apps on the Screen

As you use Windows 8, you'll encounter all sorts of instances in which it's useful to have two apps visible on the screen at once. For example, say you are creating a presentation or perhaps designing a birthday card with one of those snappy greeting card programs and you'd find it helpful to also have Internet Explorer open to search for graphics to use. As another example, many people like to have the People app open so they can monitor the social chatter while they do their work in a different app. You can probably think of many other reasons to have two apps visible at one time.

Windows 8 enables you to use two apps on the screen at once. It does so by enabling you to dock one app on the left side of the screen and another app on the right side of the screen. When two apps are docked on the screen, the apps do not share the screen space evenly. One app always uses approximately two-thirds of the screen, and the other app gets the remaining one-third, as shown in Figure 12.6. You choose which app—the one on the left or the one on the right—gets the larger slice of the screen and which gets the smaller slice. You can easily switch an app from the larger slice to the smaller slice or vice versa.

allrecipes app   Mail app

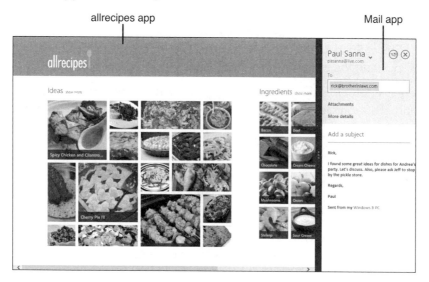

FIGURE 12.6

You can view two apps at once on the screen.

You can use your touch, keyboard, or mouse interface to manage the two apps on the screen at once. If you use your mouse or finger/stylus to place and maneuver apps on screen, which you'll learn shortly, you can see that the apps seem to jump into the slices of the screen closest to them. This is known as *snapping*. For example, you can snap your app into place on the left side of the screen.

Unlike prior versions of Windows, you can't see *more* than two apps on the screen at once.

The screen resolution must be at least 1366x768 to show two apps on the screen. Refer to Chapter 17, "Setting Up Hardware the Easy Way," for help in setting screen resolution.

Setting Up Two Apps on the Screen at Once

Follow these steps to arrange two Windows 8 apps on your screen:

1. Start the two apps to be shown together on the screen. The order you open them doesn't matter.

2. Switch to the app that will occupy most of the screen. That app should occupy your screen. Switching to an app is discussed earlier.

3. Open the app switcher as discussed in the section, "Using the App Switcher."

4. Right-click or tap-and-hold the app with which you want to share the screen. Select **Snap Left** or **Snap Right** depending on what side you would like to position the second app.

Here is another option for setting up two apps on the screen at once. This approach requires use of a mouse or hand/stylus via the touch interface:

1. Start the two apps to be shown together on the screen. The order you open them doesn't matter.

2. Point to the top border of the app in the middle of the screen. Move the mouse pointer carefully up and down near the border until the mouse pointer changes shape to a hand.

3. Click-and-drag down, which has the effect of dragging the app on the screen down with your mouse pointer (see Figure 12.7).

4. At approximately the halfway point down the screen, stop dragging the app down. Instead, change directions and now drag the app horizontally to the side of the screen that you would like it docked.

5. Drag across the screen until a black vertical bar appears. Drag the app beyond the bar close to the border of the screen and release. The app should fill the smaller slice of the screen.

6. Next, open the other app you want to view on the screen. It should snap into the larger slice of the screen.

FIGURE 12.7

The mouse pointer changes to the shape of a hand as you drag the app downward.

Snapping an App to the Other Side of the Screen

You can easily move an app docked on one side of the screen to the other. This won't affect the app occupying the larger slice of the screen. It changes the arrangement of your screen, moving the two slices of the screen to the opposite sides, with each slice still occupied by the same app.

To do so, repeat the previous second set of steps in the "Setting Up Two Apps on the Screen at Once" section (the section that leverages the mouse or touch). The only changes follows:

- Ignore the first step. Both apps should be on your screen already.
- At step 2, rather than pointing at the middle of the screen, point at the border above the app to be moved.

Swapping Slices on the Screen

You can easily switch an app from the larger slice to the smaller slice when you have two apps visible at once. Of course, this has the effect of moving the other app to the now open slice. To do so, simply drag the vertical border separating the two apps across the larger slice of the screen, as shown in Figure 12.8.

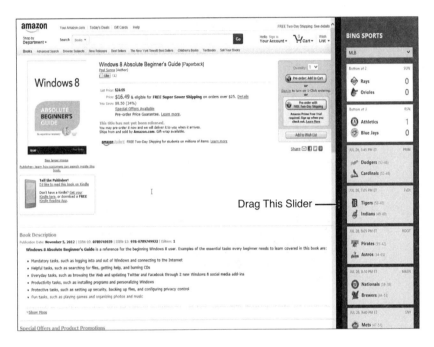

FIGURE 12.8

Drag the vertical slider across Internet Explorer to move the sports scores to the larger slice of the screen.

Shopping at the Windows Store

The Windows Store is an online marketplace integrated into Windows 8 that sells Windows 8 apps developed by Microsoft and other companies. You buy the apps at the store, and then Windows installs the apps into your copy of Windows 8, usually without a single additional step on your part required.

The Windows Store organizes and provides updates to the apps you acquire from the store. This means when Windows 8 software companies release an update to an app you own you can install the updates directly from the store or let Windows install the updates automatically.

The Windows Store is a Windows 8 app, so you should be as comfortable shopping in the store as you are writing and reading email in the Mail app or creating a slide show in the Photo app. You open the store by selecting the store's tile on the Start screen, as shown in Figure 12.9.

The Windows Store app tile

FIGURE 12.9

Enter the store by selecting its tile on the Start screen.

With the store open, you can scroll through the store to look at all the apps available. The store is organized by departments or categories, so it should be easy to find some apps that might meet your needs. You can read overviews and details of the apps to help you determine if you want the app. A minimum age for use rating is provided, too. Finally, you can check the ratings assigned to the app by others that have acquired it, as well as written reviews, as shown in Figure 12.10.

Purchasing an App

Purchasing an app should take no more than two clicks, provided you have set up your account information (see "Managing Your Account" next). To purchase an app, select its portrait in the store, and then select **Install**. You see two confirmations that your purchase was successful and the product installed properly. The first message appears in the top-right corner of the screen, and the second appears in the middle of your screen, as shown in Figure 12.11.

FIGURE 12.10

You can read what other shoppers think of the app by their reviews and ratings assigned.

FIGURE 12.11

After you select an app to purchase, you recieve one notification that the purchase was successful and another that the install was successful.

Managing Your Account

Although some apps in the Window Store are free, most aren't. You must enter payment information into the store to purchase software. You can enter credit card information or a PayPal account number. In addition to setting up your payment option, you can also specify whether a password should be entered each time you purchase an app.

To manage your account in the Windows Store, follow these steps:

1. Select the **Settings charm**. The Settings options for the Windows Store appear on the right, as shown in Figure 12.12.

FIGURE 12.12

You manage account information, app updates, and other preferences for the Windows Store in Settings.

2. Select **Your Account**. The Windows Store Your Account screen appears, as shown in Figure 12.13.

3. To specify that your password is entered each time you buy an app, move the Always Ask for Your Password When Buying an App Slider to **Yes**.

4. To enter payment information, select **Add Payment Method**. The Payment and billing screen appears, as shown in Figure 12.14.

5. Enter the required information, and then choose Next. Your information is saved. You can continue shopping at this point or leave the store.

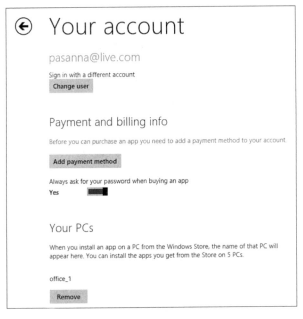

FIGURE 12.13

This screen presents options for managing your account.

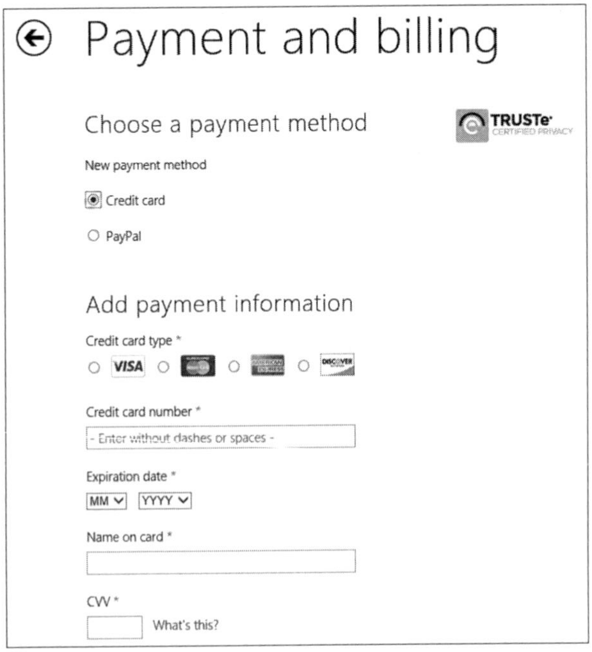

FIGURE 12.14

You enter payment instructions for all purchases in the Windows Store.

THE ABSOLUTE MINIMUM

- Windows 8 apps are software programs developed by Microsoft and other software developers that are designed to run exclusively in Windows 8. This is different than older Windows applications that ran in Windows 7 and earlier. These programs run in the Desktop environment.

- The App bar gives you convenient access to the most important options and settings available to the app you are using.

- Usually just one application may be seen at one time in Windows 8. The exception is when you choose to dock a Windows 8 app onto the screen in one of two reserved positions, allowing a second app to occupy the rest of the screen.

- With two apps on the screen at one time, any new app you open always takes over the larger of the two screen slices occupied by the two apps already on the screen.

- A number of touch gestures, plus keyboard and mouse support, make it easy to snap apps in, out, and around the screen.

- If you do not want to view two apps at once and you want to work with an app other than is on the screen, simply switch to the other app. The app you were working with disappears from view.

- Windows 8 apps are available for purchase from the Windows Store. Sometimes, apps are made available at no charge. You enter payment methods, such as a credit card and PayPal information, to pay for apps purchases in the Windows store.

13

WORKING WITH THE DESKTOP APP

If you have any experience with previous versions of Windows, such if Windows 8 has been upgraded over your old version of Windows, you probably had a typical reaction after signing in for the first time: "Where is my stuff? Where is that program I used for this or that?" If you are missing something that you *just know* should be part of Windows, it's probably hiding on the Desktop. The Desktop is the kind-of secret place where Windows 8 keeps many of the tools and programs that were an important part of previous versions of Windows. This chapter helps you understand when to access the Desktop, as well as how to do so; and you'll learn how to set up the Desktop so it's easy to use.

Introducing the Desktop App

One of the goals Microsoft pursued in designing Windows 8 was to rebuild the user experience to support the use of touch-screen devices, such as tablets, slates, and touch-screen monitors. Microsoft had other goals, of course, but this redesign for mobile devices was at the top of the list. This new design of Windows is known as the Windows 8 style.

Changing the user experience that had been a part of Windows since 1995 certainly presented a challenge to Microsoft. Keep in mind, thousands of programs have been built over the years that depended on Windows looking and behaving consistently. So how does Microsoft build and rollout a brand new way to interact with Windows without breaking everything that has been built to run in Windows for decades? The core of the answer is the Desktop!

The Desktop, the home for all those great Windows programs, has been dropped in the middle of Windows 8. Programs that have not been converted to the new Windows 8 app style run on the Desktop in a way that's cosmetically identical to past Windows versions. In addition, some of the more complicated Windows tools and features still run on the Desktop. This effectively gives Windows 8 two appearances: one as the Windows 8 style and another that's almost exactly like Windows 7. Figure 13.1 shows the Windows 8 Desktop, which perhaps is familiar to you if you have used previous versions of Windows. Either way, you're certain to find it different than the Windows 8 user interface (UI), as shown in Figure 13.2.

Finally, keep in mind that the Desktop is essentially an app. You'll start the Desktop app, which opens an environment known as, you guess it, the Desktop. So at times we'll refer to the Desktop app, and other times we'll refer to this Windows 7 friendly work area also as the Desktop. We'll try to be careful not to confuse you!

Now that you have a basic understanding of these two environments, let's dive into the Desktop mode, learn how to get work done, and have some fun along the way.

Starting the Desktop

There are three methods to start the Desktop app, both methods originating from the Start screen:

- Select the **Desktop** tile (refer to Figure 13.2).

- Change a Windows 8 settings whose window or dialog box for doing so runs on the Desktop, such as hardware and sound, appearance and personalization, clock, language, region, system and security, and more. You can enter these terms in the Search charm for settings to access the Desktop.

FIGURE 13.1

The Windows 8 Desktop is similar to the Desktop of previous versions of Windows.

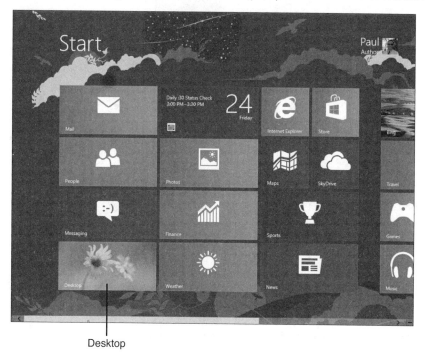

Desktop

FIGURE 13.2

The Windows 8 user experience is different from that of previous versions of Windows.

- Start a program that runs on the Desktop. When you start one of these programs, the Desktop app also starts. Examples of Windows programs that you might use today that run on the Desktop are Microsoft Office (Word, Excel, PowerPoint, and so on), Skype, Adobe Reader, and more.

Considering that the Desktop is basically a streamlined version of Windows; there is lots more you can do there besides run a game or save your to-do list. First take a look at some of the tools that appear on the Desktop, as shown in Figure 13.3.

Desktop icons   Desktop

Programs pinned to taskbar   Taskbar   Notification area

FIGURE 13.3

The Desktop app is an environment almost identical to Windows 7.

Returning to the Start Screen

While you are working on the Desktop, you may need to return to the Start screen to start another application. You are not forced to exit the program you are working with or to close files you have open before switching back to the Start screen. The Desktop remains unchanged until you return to it.

To return to the Start screen from the Desktop, do one of the following:

⊕ With your hand or stylus, swipe in from the right, and tap the Start charm.

⌨ Press the Windows key.

⊛ Select Start from the Charms bar.

Keeping the Desktop Organized

You can use the area of the Desktop above the Taskbar much as you use your desktop in your office or at home. You can keep the files associated with a project you are working on anywhere on the Desktop. You can organize the files into folders, and the folders can also be kept on the Desktop. Back at home or in the office, when you acquire new files or folders or other items, you might drop them onto your desk to file away or store later. In Windows, when you download content from the Internet or when you create a new document, you can just as easily drop the content onto the Desktop. With all the files potentially moving on and off of the Desktop, even organized users might find their Desktop in a state of disorder and mess, as shown in Figure 13.4.

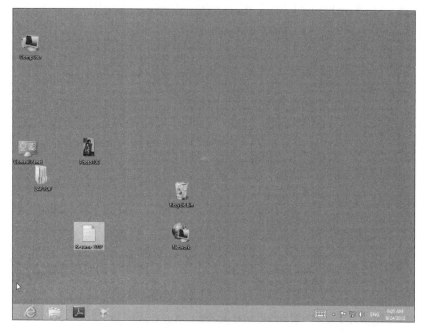

FIGURE 13.4

It's not hard to discover your Desktop has changed into a cluttered mess.

Fortunately, it's not hard to keep the Desktop clutter under control.

Automatically Line Up Icons on the Desktop

The Desktop has an invisible grid that keeps every item positioned in uniform columns and rows. When you save, move, download, or copy a file to the Desktop, or if a program you use saves a file to the Desktop, Windows immediately snaps the file into an empty cell in the grid. Windows normally fills the grid from left to right and top down, but you can turn this option off. Turning this option off allows you to place an item anywhere on the Desktop, though still lined up in one of the invisible rows and columns.

To configure Windows to automatically line up icons on the Desktop, follow these steps:

1. Right-click or tap-and-hold an unused spot on the Desktop and point to **View**.

2. If **Align Icons to Grid** is checked, then the invisible grid is in use. If **Align Icons to Grid** is not checked, select it to turn the grid on.

3. Right-click or tap-and-hold an unused spot on the Desktop, and point to **View** again.

4. To snap icons to the first empty cell in the grid, select **Auto Arrange Icons**. To keep icons anywhere you like on the Desktop (but still lined up), select **Auto Arrange Icons** to clear the check mark. Figure 13.5 shows the Desktop from Figure 13.4 with all its icons aligned.

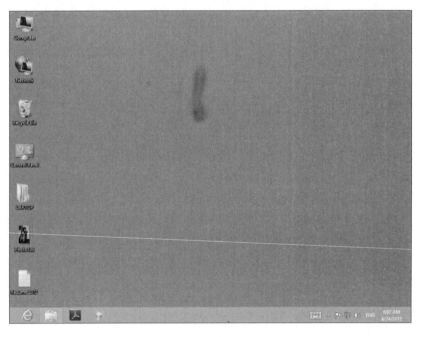

FIGURE 13.5

Notice how with the Align Icons and Auto Arrange Icons to Grid settings turned ON the icons are arranged more evenly.

Arrange the Desktop by Icon Type

If the Auto Arrange icon option is turned on (see the previous section), you can also keep the icons sorted (by rows). Windows can order the icons in the invisible grid according to each icon's name, type, size, or the date the icon was last changed.

To sort the Desktop icons by type, right-click or tap-and-hold an unused spot on the Desktop, and point to **Sort By**. Select **Name**, **Size**, **Item Type**, or **Date Modified**.

Change the Size of Desktop Icons

You can change the size of the icons that appear on the Desktop. Your choices are Large, Medium, and Small. The default icon size is medium. Note that the size of some special objects that appear on the Desktop, such as gadgets, are not affected by this setting. Figure 13.6 shows the Desktop with this option set at Large.

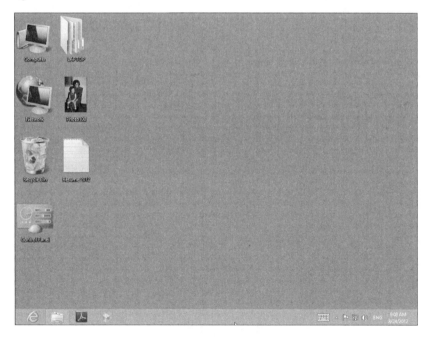

FIGURE 13.6

You can configure the Desktop to show icons in different sizes. Large is the setting used here.

To change the size of the Desktop icons right-click or tap-and-hold an unused spot on the Desktop and point to **Sort By**; then select **Large Icons**, **Small Icons, or Medium Icons**.

Hide All Desktop Icons

If you want a clean Desktop environment, you can hide all Desktop icons. Right-click or tap-and-hold an unused spot on the Desktop, and point to **View**. Select **Show Desktop Icons** to clear the check mark. To make the Desktop icons appear again, repeat these steps.

Working with the Taskbar

An important element of the Desktop is the Taskbar. Although the Taskbar takes up little space, it performs a number of important tasks. Here is the full list of the Taskbar's capabilities:

- Lists the programs running on the Desktop, even if a program is obscured from view

- Enables you to switch to a running program by just selecting the program's portrait on the Taskbar

- Shows you the status and messages from the many small programs that run silently, performing a service or waiting for you to do something

- Displays the current time and date

- Displays a toolbar that enables you to quickly open any file on the Desktop

- Displays a toolbar that enables you to quickly access a website from your Favorites list

- Enables you to quickly jump to a website or any folder by displaying an address bar where you enter the URL or folder name

- Enables you to set up a list of the last 10 documents or sites visited

- Enables you to arrange the open windows on the Desktop

Receiving Alerts and Notifications

The Notifications section of the taskbar organizes the small icons that keep you informed about important events and the status of some important Windows tasks and systems. When one of these notification icons has something it wants you to know, it pops up a small window with information about it. Although programs you install can be added to the icons listed in this area, Windows sets up some notification of its own, such as the status of your network connection (see Figure 13.7).

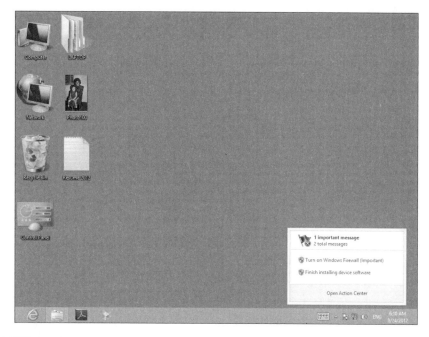

FIGURE 13.7

Windows alerts you if the built-in firewall is not engaged.

The event reported on depends on the software doing the reporting. For example, as shown here, the Action Center icon notifies you if a problem develops with the security software guarding your system, or if Microsoft has released an update to Windows. To look at a notification, just click or touch the icon showing the notification.

You don't need to live with a cramped notification area. You can control which notification icons are always visible and which ones appear only when they have something to report. You can also set a notification icon to be hidden all the time.

To customize how the notification items work, follow these steps:

1. In the Notifications Area, select the **Show Hidden Icons** button. Then, from the pop-up window that appears, select **Customize**.

2. In the Notification Area Icons window that appears, click either **Show Icon and Notifications**, **Hide Icon and Notifications**, or **Only Show Notifications** from the drop-down list for each icon, as shown in Figure 13.8.

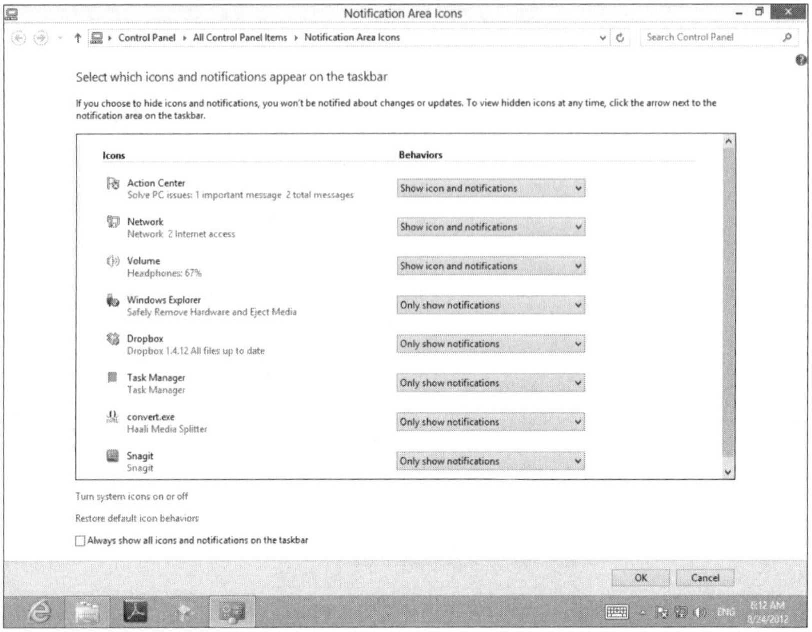

FIGURE 13.8

You can customize the behavior of each potential notification alert.

3. Select **OK**.

4. Select **Close** to close the Personalization window.

Adding Toolbars to the Taskbar

In Windows, toolbars are usually a set of like functions assigned to clickable icons arranged together on a bar on the screen. They're mostly common to various Desktop applications, but you can also enable a set of toolbars on the taskbar. In this case, however, the toolbar label for this feature is curious. Referring to any of these five components as *toolbars* is a stretch. These features are certainly useful, though, as described here. Five toolbars are available to show on the taskbar.

To show a toolbar, right-click or tap-and-hold on the taskbar, and point to **Toolbars**. Then, select the toolbar you want to display.

Here is a short description of each toolbar:

- **Address**—This toolbar is actually a box into which you can enter any address, including a website name or a folder name. After entering the address and pressing **Enter**, a window opens set to the address you entered.

- **Links**—This toolbar is a list of links to favorite websites or folders on your computer. This list mirrors the Favorites List you keep in Internet Explorer.

- **Desktop**—This toolbar is a list of the files that appear on your desktop. This list is composed of files you have placed on the Desktop and files that were placed there by Windows, such as shortcuts.

- **Touch Keyboard**—Launching this toolbar places a small keyboard icon in the Notifications area. When you need a keyboard, such as when you use the Desktop on a tablet device, touch the Keyboard icon to display the virtual keyboard.

- **New Toolbar**—Windows enables you to create your own toolbars to use alongside the toolbars Windows provides you. The toolbars you create are like the Desktop toolbars. You choose a folder to associate with a toolbar so that when you select the toolbar, it displays the contents of the folder.

Displaying Special Icons on the Desktop

You have read in this chapter how the Desktop can be leveraged to keep files and folders you're working with in a convenient, handy location. The Desktop also can keep a few important icons readily available that give you access to some key tools and features. Although the PC Settings screen on the Start screen gives you access to a large number of settings, the Desktop, through the icons, also gives you access to a number of settings. These icons can be hidden or displayed:

- **Computer**—This icon opens the File Explorer window that displays the big, important, expensive parts of your system, including hard drives, network connections, and more. Figure 13.9 shows the computer view opened in File Explorer.

- **Network**—This icon enables you to see all the interesting resources on the network, such as other computers, printers, and more. It's convenient to have this icon available on the Desktop. You can quickly locate a resource you need, like a family member's computer, and connect to it. If you do not use your computer on a network and you don't have any devices connected wirelessly, then you can hide this icon. Refer to Chapter 11, "Sharing Files and Printers with Homegroup," to learn more about navigating through your network at home.

- **Recycle Bin**—The Recycle Bin stores all deleted files, folders, and icons. These items stay in the Recycle Bin, a wonderful fact for many Windows users, until the Recycle Bin is emptied. Having the Recycle Bin on the Desktop is a convenience. The Recycle Bin operates the same way whether it is displayed. You can learn everything the Recycle Bin, including how to recover files you mistakenly deleted, later in the "Using the Recycle Bin" section.

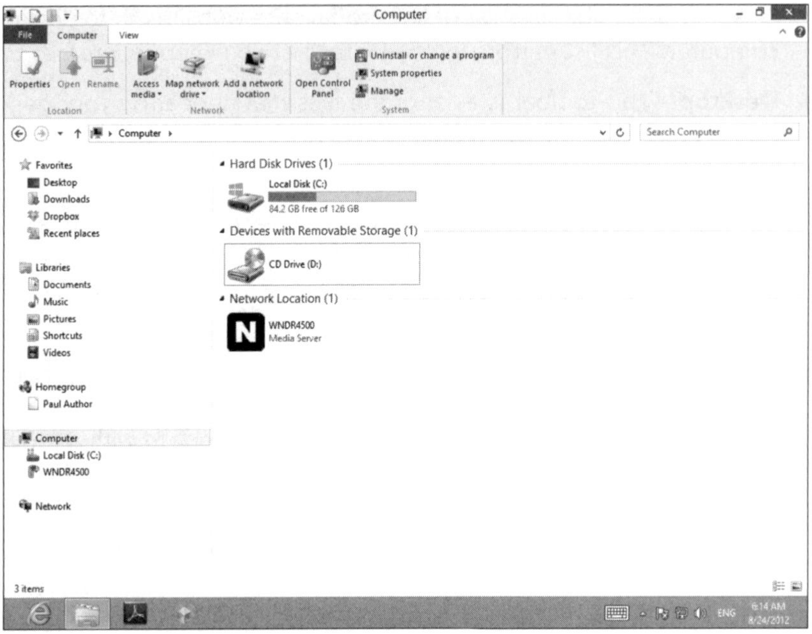

FIGURE 13.9

You can see all the elements of your computer in one window.

- **User's Files**—The User's Files icon, which appears actually as a folder with your name below it, gives you access to the set of files and folders that Windows reserves for your personal use. Selecting this item starts File Explorer open to the main folder that contains all your personal files and folders. You can find a chapter's worth of information about files and folders, including the user files, in Chapter 12, "Mastering Windows 8 Apps."

- **Control Panel**—There is a set of small programs that each help you set up some part of Windows. This collection of programs is called Control Panel. The Control Panel icon brings you to the front page of Control Panel, where you can select the tool you need, as shown in Figure 13.10.

To display (or hide) Desktop program icons, follow these steps:

1. Right-click or tap-and-hold an empty spot on the Desktop, and then click **Personalize**.

2. Select **Change Desktop Items** at the top-left corner of the Personalization window. The Desktop Icon Settings dialog box appears, as shown in Figure 13.10.

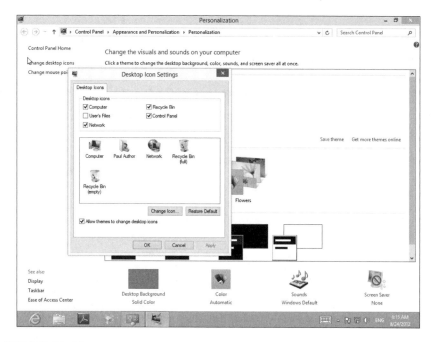

FIGURE 13.10

Display or hide icons for some important Desktop tools.

3. Under Desktop icons, select the check box for each item you want to appear on the Desktop. Remove the check mark for any item you do not want to appear on the Desktop.

4. Select **OK**.

5. Select **Close** to close the Personalization window.

THE ABSOLUTE MINIMUM

Keep the following points in mind as you work on the Desktop:

- The Desktop is a special application you can use to run programs that were built for previous versions of Windows.

- Some of the important tools and components of Windows 8 are run from the Desktop. If you are missing a program that you believe is important to Windows, check the Desktop.

- You can customize the Desktop to keep files organized on the desktop, show and hide icons, and pin programs to the taskbar.

- The notifications area of the Desktop shows important information, so you should check the Desktop regularly for these updates.

- You can start the Desktop app by selecting its tile from the Start screen or by starting a program or opening a setting that runs on the Desktop.

14

USING WINDOWS DESKTOP PROGRAMS

Chapter 13, "Working with the Desktop App," covers the Desktop from a broad perspective, not focusing on one specific task and instead helping you find your way around, this chapter has a more specific viewpoint. You see how to start and then manage programs that run on the Windows desktop. You see how to organize program windows as well as to install them and remove them. If you are comfortable working with programs in Windows 7 or earlier, you might have less to learn in this chapter than others; though it pays to review the troubleshooting section at the end of the chapter.

Introducing Windows Desktop Programs

You may have read elsewhere in this book about how you work with the programs developed for previous versions of Windows. The new software applications that have been built specifically for Windows 8 are known as Windows 8 apps. The programs that have not been updated for Windows 8 are known as Windows Desktop Programs. The programs are run in the Desktop app. Think of the Desktop app as windows-in-windows. The Desktop app is a streamlined version of Windows 7 running within Windows 8. The Desktop app serves as a comfortable, reliable environment for all those great Windows programs.

To start a Desktop program, select the tile representing the program on the Desktop. Figure 14.1 shows Microsoft Excel open on the Windows 8 Desktop. Notice that an icon for the program, known as a *portrait*, appears on the taskbar.

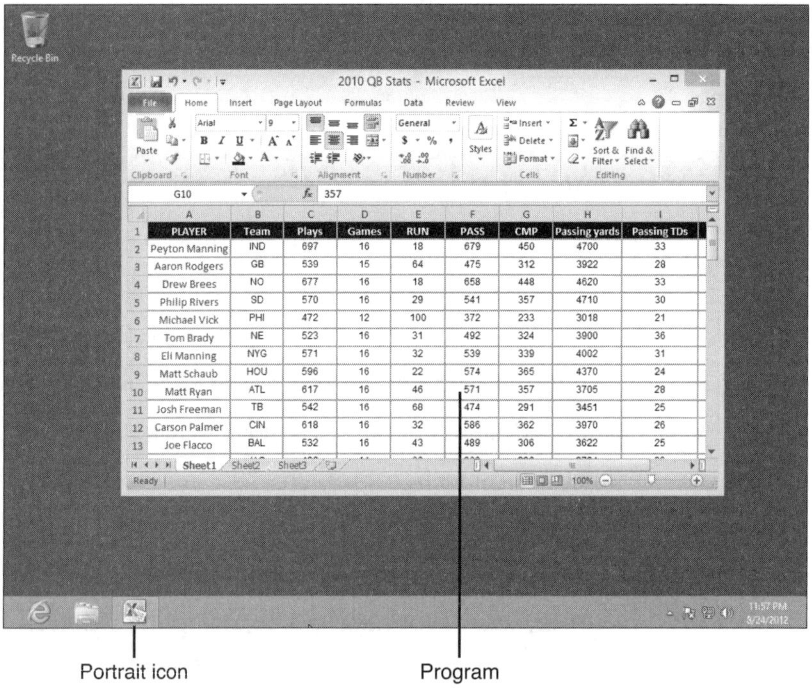

Portrait icon   Program

FIGURE 14.1

Microsoft Excel running on the Desktop.

Running Programs on the Desktop

This section helps you understand how programs operate in the Windows 8 Desktop environment. You learn how to manage a single program, as well as how to organize the Desktop with multiple program windows open.

Running Multiple Windows Desktop Programs

As you become more proficient and comfortable with Windows, it is likely you will run multiple programs on the Desktop at the same time. For example, you might need to read instructions in the Adobe Acrobat Reader for a software program you are also using on the Desktop. You must be at the Start screen to launch a program, so you must first return to the Start screen to start the next program. When the program starts, it appears on the Desktop in a window on top of the other programs that are running, as shown in Figure 14.2.

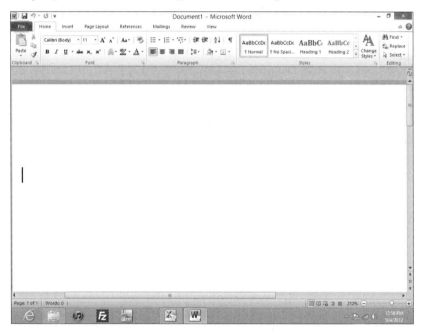

FIGURE 14.2

Notice how Microsoft Word opened on the Desktop, obscuring Microsoft Excel that was running there already.

In addition, a portrait representing the program appears on the Taskbar. After starting a number of programs, the Taskbar starts to fill up with an array of colorful portraits, as shown in Figure 14.2.

To switch from one program to another, select the program's portrait on the Taskbar. When you do so, the program you selected appears on top of any other windows on the Desktop.

NOTE A quick way to switch to a program or document without moving the cursor is to use a keyboard shortcut. Press and hold the Alt key and then press the Tab key. A screen appears showing portraits of each program or app window open in Windows 8. While holding the Alt key, tap the Tab key repeatedly to move the highlight to the next window on the screen. Release both keys when you have selected the window you want to switch to.

Certain applications enable you to work on more than one file or workspace or project at one time. In Microsoft Word, you can have your resume open in one window, a cover letter you are writing to accompany your resume in another open window, and a table in a document in a third window detailing your work experience. You can usually identify a program that enables you to multitask this way by the existence of a Window menu. In Windows-speak, regardless of the type of program being referred to, these files you create are known as *documents*.

When you have more than one document open in a program, the Taskbar behaves a bit differently than when you have just one document open. When you move the mouse pointer over the program portrait, another row of portraits, one for each document, appear above the main portrait.

To switch to a different document, select the program portrait to display the document portraits. Tap or click the document portrait to switch to that document. The Taskbar with document portraits appears, as shown in Figure 14.3.

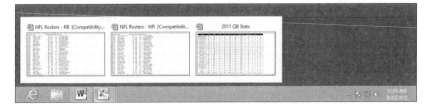

FIGURE 14.3

The Taskbar displays a portrait for each of the documents you have open in a program.

Making It Easy to Start Your Favorite Desktop Programs

You can save trips to the Start screen to start your favorite or most used Desktop programs by pinning a portrait of each of your favorite programs on the taskbar.

To pin a portrait of a program to the Desktop, follow these steps:

1. Return to the Start screen.

2. Right-click or tap-and-hold on the tile representing the program you want to pin to the Taskbar.

3. Select **Pin to Taskbar** on the apps bar.

To start one of your pinned programs, select its portrait on the taskbar.

 TIP You can pin as many programs to the Taskbar as you like. If there are a number of programs you use frequently on the Desktop, follow the numbered steps in this section for each program.

Saving Files to the Desktop

Windows reserves a private set of folders where each user can save their own files, such as documents, music, pictures, and more. One of the private folders a person can use is Desktop. Each user has a Desktop folder, and the contents of the folder are always displayed on the Desktop, as shown in Figure 14.4.

Saving to the Desktop is convenient, especially when you work on a project, and you need quick access to some of the files related to the project. You can start working on the file by double-tapping/clicking the file on the Desktop.

To save a file to the Desktop, choose Desktop from the list of folders presented in the program where you created the file, as shown in Figure 14.5.

FIGURE 14.4

Items that appear on the Desktop are stored in a special Desktop folder that you can also see in Windows Explorer.

FIGURE 14.5

The Desktop is presented as a choice where you can save a file.

Exiting Desktop Programs

Windows does not require you to shut down a program when you finish working with it. But there are a few reasons why you should consider routinely closing Desktop programs when you finish. If you have a number of programs running concurrently, your computer's speed may be negatively impacted. If your computer seems to be running more slowly than normal, consider shutting down some programs.

TIP You may have read that Windows 8 has a new system to manage the memory consumed by applications running but not being used. This is true, but unfortunately, this innovation does not apply to programs running on the Desktop. Although Windows may reduce the memory used by the Desktop as it idles, it can't do this at the detriment of programs running in the Desktop app.

To close a program running on the Desktop, follow these steps:

1. On the taskbar locate the portrait for the program you want to close.

2. Right-click or press-and-tap the portrait.

3. From the menu that appears, select **Close** (or **Close All Windows** if you have multiple windows open). The program disappears from the Desktop, and the program's portrait disappears from the Taskbar. Note that a program that you have pinned to the Taskbar remains pinned even after you have closed all its document windows.

Working with Windows

You don't necessarily need to be a Windows expert to work with multiple programs at once with several windows open on the Desktop. You may be working in an Office program, such as Microsoft Word or Excel; you might have Internet Explorer open to check in at some of your favorite social media sites; and you might have a Windows explorer window open to organize a folder. So innocently, you might have three windows fighting for screen real estate. It's easy, though, to arrange, move, and resize windows to leverage all of the room on the Desktop. Figure 14.6 shows the controls at the top of a typical window with the important parts pointed out for you.

FIGURE 14.6

These controls are common to virtually all Desktop app windows.

The following list summarizes the various methods available to manage windows on the Desktop:

- You can easily **resize** and reshape a window. You can't change the window's shape from rectangular to circular, but you can make the window short and wide, narrow and tall, perfectly square, or anything in between. To resize a window using a mouse, point to any border of the window you want to resize. If you use touch, tap-and-press on any border of the window you want to resize. When the pointer becomes a double-arrow head, drag the pointer to move the border.

- You can enlarge a window so it fills up your entire screen space (known as maximize), obscuring every other window you have open. Select the **Maximize** button or double-click/tap on the window's title bar.

- You can also remove a window from view without closing the program. Select the **Minimize** button to hide the window.

- You can minimize all open windows simultaneously, exposing the Desktop. To do so, click or tap on the Taskbar between the time and date and the edge of the screen.

- To return a window to its most previous state, select the **Restore** button. You can also restore the window by choosing **Restore** from the Control menu on the top-left corner of the window. The Restore command works only when the window is in a maximized state.

- You can **move** a window around your Desktop. You move a window by dragging the window by its title bar.

- When you start multiple programs on the Desktop or if you open several documents, it can become difficult to arrange and size the windows so that you can work efficiently. You can move and resize the windows manually, but Windows provides a few quick commands to arrange the windows on the Desktop. These commands are found on the Taskbar. Right-click/press-and-tap on the taskbar to find these choices:

  - Cascade Windows

  - Show Windows Stacked

  - Show Windows Side by Side

Figures 14.7, 14.8, and 14.9 show you each of these arrangements.

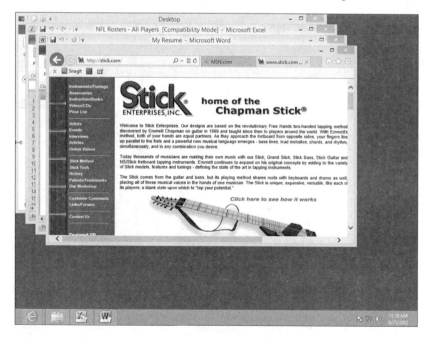

FIGURE 14.7

This Desktop has been arranged using Cascade Windows.

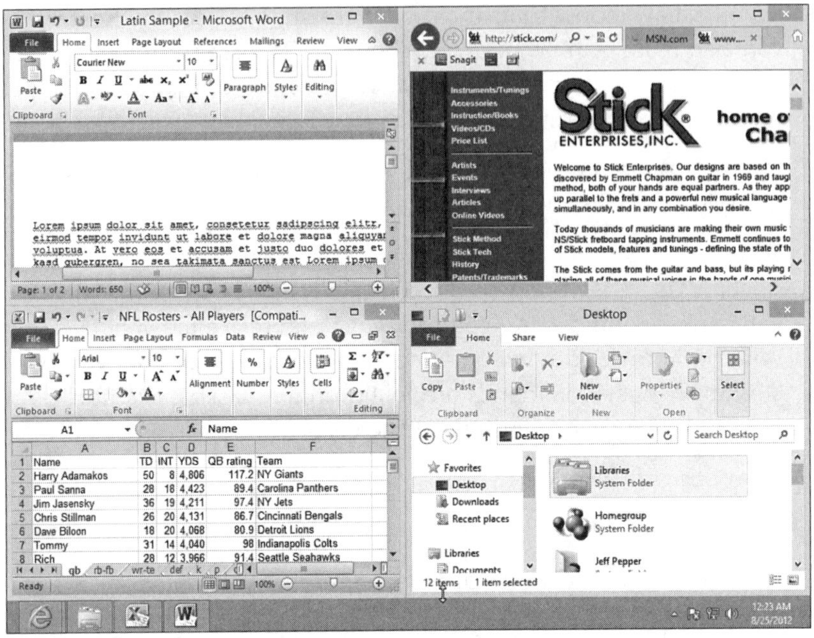

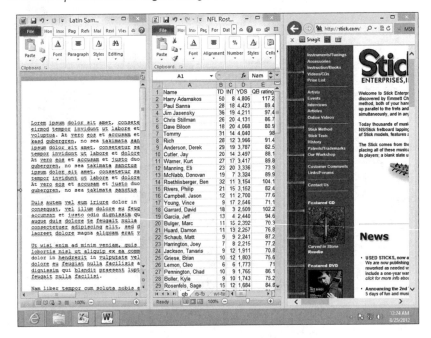

FIGURE 14.8

This Desktop has been arranged using Show Windows Stacked.

FIGURE 14.9

This Desktop has been arranged using Show Windows Side by Side.

Installing and Removing Programs

Windows Desktop programs do not get installed from the Windows Store, like Windows 8-style apps. Rather, each program you install comes with its own installation tools. Programs are removed the same way; though you kick off the uninstall process from a central location in Windows. You can learn about the Windows Store in Chapter 3, "Learning Windows 8 Basics."

Installing Program

The installation process for new programs into the Windows 8 Desktop has lots of variations. Keep in mind, the setup process is designed by the company that developed the software you are installing, meaning anything can happen:

- For software installed from a CD or DVD, the installation program usually starts as soon as the disc is inserted into the drive. If a program does not start, you should navigate to the disc using Windows explorer (see Chapter 15, "Organizing Files and Folders with Windows Explorer.") Look for a program named install.exe, autoplay.exe or setup.exe. Double-click the file to start the installation program.

- Setup programs are not perfect. You may need to uninstall a program if the setup stops unexpectedly to run the setup program again.

- Setup programs sometimes require that the person installing the software have administrator rights. To run the setup program as an administrator, locate the setup program (possible names are setup.exe and install.exe), right-click the program and select **Run as Administrator**. You likely will need an administrator password to do this.

Removing Windows Programs

You may need to remove an installed program for a number of reasons, including

- You are running out of free disk space.

- There seems to be a problem with the software, and you need to reinstall it.

- You no longer will use the software.

- You plan to install new software that is incompatible with an installed program.

There is no harm in leaving a program installed if you have enough free disk space and if the program does not interfere with another program. If you need to remove a program, follow these steps:

1. Save any unsaved work.

2. Open the Add or Remove Programs dialog box. To do so, select the **Search charm**. Select **Settings** and enter **Add Remove Programs** in the Search box.

3. From the results on the left, select **Add or Remove Programs**. The dialog box shown in Figure 14.10. appears.

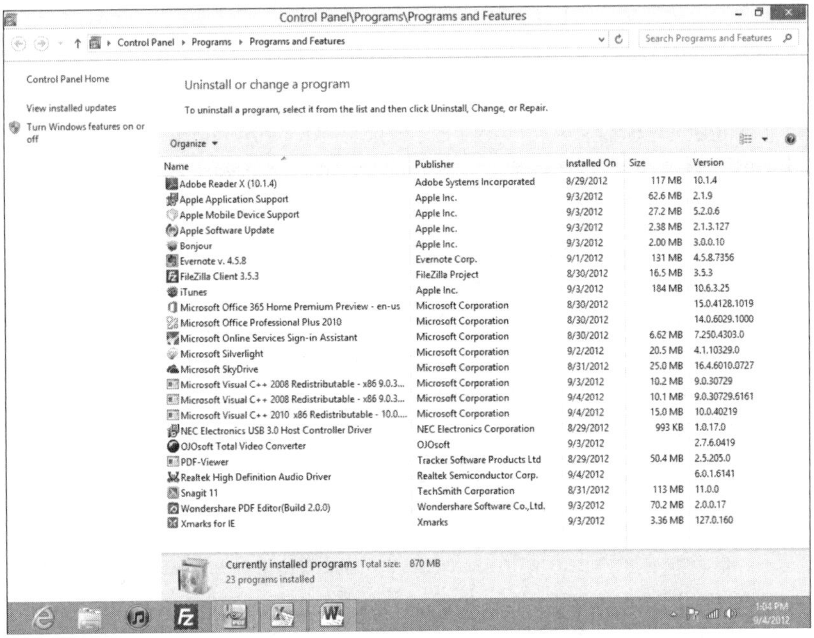

FIGURE 14.10

Programs are uninstalled from the Add or Remove Programs dialog box.

4. Select the program and then select **Uninstall**. The program's own uninstall process starts. Follow the instructions and answer any prompts that appear.

You may be prompted to restart Windows to complete the uninstall process.

THE ABSOLUTE MINIMUM

Keep these points in mind after you've completed reading this chapter:

- Programs that were used in Windows 7 and earlier can run in Windows 8 in an environment provided by the Desktop app. The Desktop app is a windows-in-windows environment, appearing and operating almost identically to Windows 7.

- You can run multiple Desktop programs at one time, as you could with Windows 7. Start subsequent programs on the Start screen.

- To switch to a different program, click the portrait representing the program on the Taskbar. Alternatively, press and hold the **Alt** key and then press the **Tab** key. A screen appears showing portraits of each program or app window open in Windows 8. While holding the **Alt** key, tap the **Tab** key repeatedly to move the highlight to the next window on the screen. Release both keys when you have selected the window you want to switch to.

- To arrange the open windows on the Desktop, right-click/tap-and-hold on the taskbar to reveal a menu. Select **Cascade windows** or one of the three Show windows commands to arrange the open windows.

- Windows 8 Desktop programs are installed and removed in the Desktop app.

15

ORGANIZING FILES AND FOLDERS WITH WINDOWS EXPLORER

The exciting new Windows 8 environment, with its simple active tiles, gives the perception that everything you do in Windows can be accomplished through the immersive, colorful screens you see on your computer, as well as on the web in advertisements, videos, and reviews. The reality is that you'll certainly work with the native Windows 8 apps and features often, but you'll also spend a lot of time just managing your files and folders, something you'll do from the Desktop, using the Windows Explorer tool. This chapter helps you understand the basics about files and folders and how to keep them all under control. You read how to handle common but important tasks, such as copying and moving files. You also learn skills that you can use in lots of area of Windows, such as selecting files.

Files and Folder Basics

Before diving into the methods and how-to's of managing your files and folders, it's a good idea to have a firm grasp of the basics. The following sections offer an overview of both, as well as a look at how you can use libraries to manage them all.

Understanding Files

At their absolute simplest, files store data. Different types of files serve many different purposes. But for this discussion, its best to categorize all files two ways:

- System files
- User files

System files are the parts of the Windows 8 engine. Windows 8 uses these files to do its job, from connecting to the Internet to recognizing a mouse-click from a hand-tap on the screen to figuring how much time you have before your battery runs out. There are 16,000 system files in Windows 8, so clearly there are thousands of jobs and services accomplished by these files, and it's usually a number of files working together to perform a job as opposed to just one.

These system files are important, and not only does Windows 8 expect that that they remain located on your computer, but also that they are in a specific location. You generally do not need to worry about accidentally erasing a system file and causing Windows to stop working. System files are stored in *System Folders,* and these folders are in a location generally difficult to access unless you are an administrator. Even so, it's best to avoid these folders and all their subfolders:

> \Windows
>
> \Program Files
>
> \Program Files (x86)

Many programs enable you to select the folders into which the system files for the program are installed. Unless you know better, it's best to use the default folder option they offer.

These system files contrast with *user files.* User files are the files you use and create every day, such as your work files, music, photos, and many more. These user files and the folders that contain them are the main subject of this chapter. Software programs define the format of the user files that work with their program. You usually cannot use a user file created in one program in another, although there are exceptions.

User files are normally stored in a person's own folders. As you read next, all users in Windows 8 have their own set of folders that other users usually cannot access.

Understanding Folders

Whereas files store data, folders store files (and sometimes more folders). A folder can contain other folders, and those folders can contain other folders, and so on. A folder in Windows 8 is represented by, no surprise here, the Folder icon, as shown in Figure 15.1.

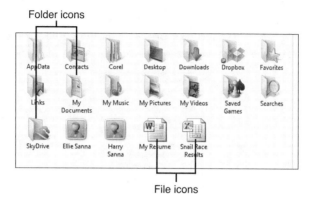

FIGURE 15.1

You can easily tell which of the items in Windows are files or folders.

When new users are added to Windows 8 by creating an account for them, a set of unique user folders are created. These folders are created in a parent folder. The folder is named after the user's first name if the account is a Windows 8 type account. If the account is a local account, the folder name is the same as the username you provided when you created the account. (Refer to Chapter 20, "Performing Routine Maintenance.") This folder is known as the user's *home folder*. This set of folders is shown in Figure 15.2.

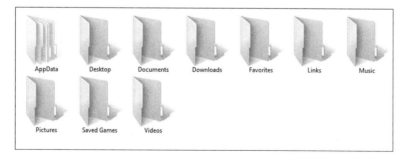

FIGURE 15.2

A set of folders is created for each Windows 8 user.

You can store files anywhere you like in your own home folder and subfolders. You can create as many folders and subfolders as you like in your home folder. It makes sense to store certain special files, such as music files, in the folders specially designed for them. You cannot save or create files in any other folder in Windows, including the home folders of other users, unless you are an administrator of the system.

With some planning, you can create a hierarchy of folders to help organize all the files related to a task, subject, project, hobby, and so on. Figure 15.3 shows an example of a folder tree used to store recipes. As you'll soon see, you do not need to be a Windows 8 expert to create this organization of folders.

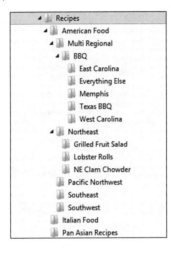

FIGURE 15.3

You can design a folder system for specific needs.

CAUTION Software programs you purchase also leverage folders to organize their file. When you install programs, they often create their own folders. You should never move or delete program folders even if you know you will never use the program again. Sometimes these folders contain files that are used by other programs. When you delete a folder that contains files, all the files are deleted along with the containing folder.

Exploring Your Files and Folders with Windows Explorer

The tool used to manage your files and folders is Windows Explorer. Windows Explorer has been around for many years, and the version that comes with Windows 8 probably is the easiest to use. At the same time, this version has more capabilities and features packed under the hood than ever before.

You can start Windows Explorer from within the Desktop app. If you need to use Windows Explorer a lot (and you probably will), it makes sense to add a tile to the Start screen for it. To do so, use the Search charm to locate an app named "explorer." When Windows Explorer appears in the list of results, right-click the icon and select **Pin to Start** (see Figure 15.4).

After selecting the Windows Explorer tile, Windows Explorer opens, as shown in Figure 15.5. The image in Figure 15.5 points out all the important parts of Windows Explorer.

FIGURE 15.4

Search for "Explorer" to locate the Windows Explorer tile.

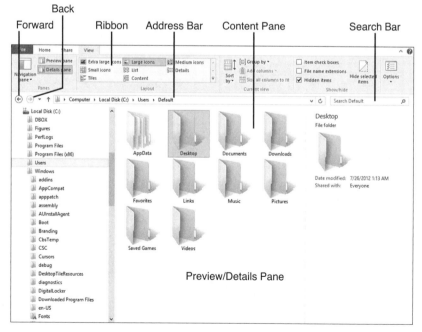

FIGURE 15.5

Windows Explorer includes a number of controls to enable you to navigate through your file system.

The Navigation pane, as shown in Figure 15.5, drives almost all the activity in Windows Explorer. Whatever you select in the Navigation pane determines what appears in the Content pane.

Working with Libraries

The library is a useful tool to organize your files. Referring to a library as a tool may not be 100% appropriate because libraries, which are a standard part of Windows 8, are deployed all over the place. A library is actually just a label that points to one or more folders that you can access from Windows Explorer. When you select a library, all the files in all the folders designated by the library appear as if they were in the same folder. A library does not actually store a file the way a folder does. Windows 8, by default, creates a number of libraries, including one for pictures, one for documents, and another for music files. You might create a library to organize all the files related to your career, or you might consolidate all the receipts for products you purchased online.

To see the folders specified in a particular library, select the library in Windows Explorer. Then, under Library Tools, on the ribbon's Manage tab, select **Manage Library**. Figure 15.6 shows the window that appears if you select to **Manage the Pictures library**.

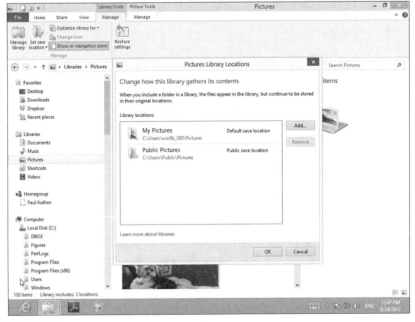

FIGURE 15.6

Edit a library's settings to add additional folders to include in the library.

- To add a folder to a library, select **Add**. A small Windows Explorer type window appears. Navigate to the folder to include and then select **Include Folder**. You can read how to navigate in Windows Explorer later in this chapter.

- To remove a folder from the library, select the folder and then select **Remove**.

- To define where files are stored when you save to a library, close the dialog box. With the library still selected in the Navigation pane, under Library Tools, on the Manage tab, select **Set Save Location**. Then, select the library folder to which files are to be saved.

- To create a new library, right-click/press-and-hold on Libraries in the Navigation pane and select **New Library**. An empty library appears in the list of libraries. Enter a name for the new library and press **Enter**. Next, add folders to the library.

Navigating the Folder Tree

The center of attention of the Navigation pane is the folder tree. The folder tree shows all your computer's drives and folders, plus some other stuff, such as libraries and your drives, in a format that makes it easy to see how everything is related. Think of your computer as the main trunk of the tree, and think of those leftmost positioned items as the primary branches growing from the trunk. In many cases, those branches have other branches growing from it, such as Libraries with branches for Pictures, Music, and Documents, but in other cases, those main branches have just leaves growing, such as Favorites.

Each of the five primary branches in the Navigation pane folder tree contains related kinds of items.

- **Favorites**—Just as you can specify websites as Favorites, making it easy to reach these sites by choosing from the Favorites menu, you can do the same with folders. Folders that have been made Favorites appear off the Favorites branch.

- **Libraries**—As you read earlier in this chapter, a library organizes related folders, making it easy for you to see and work with all the related files and folder. The Libraries branch contains all your libraries. The branch below the library name shows all a library's folders.

- **Homegroup**—This node shows all the content shared with the workgroup that your Windows 8 belongs to. The tree is organized by the user that joined the computer to the workgroup. Under each user are the computers the user has access to.

- **Computer**—The Computer branch contains all the computer's physical objects, such as hard drives, folders, removable drives, network drives, and so on. This branch excludes the virtual items, such as libraries and Favorites.

- **Network**—The Network branch shows all the computers on the network that the computer connects to.

You can tell a branch that has other branches growing from it by the appearance of the small triangle symbol besides its name. That triangle icon is black or white, as shown in Figure 15.7. If it is black, the branches growing from it are hidden. When the triangle is white, the branch's subbranches are visible.

To display more branches in the tree, click or tap the black, triangle-shaped icon. To hide the branches growing from a main branch, click or tap the white, triangle-shaped icon.

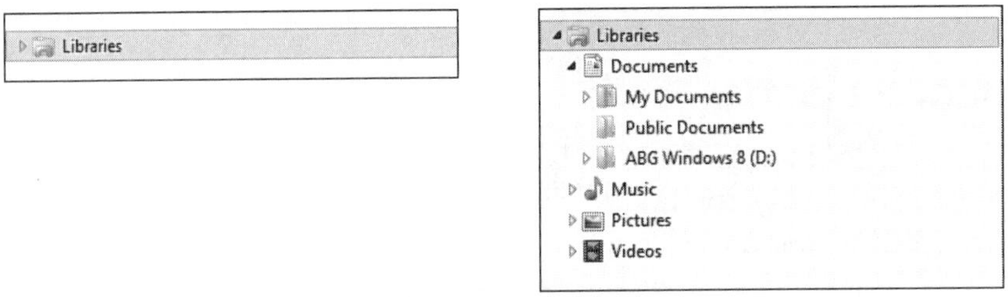

FIGURE 15.7

Show and hide branches in the folder tree by clicking the triangle-shaped icon.

Here are a few options to help you organize the Navigation pane. Each of the following, with the exception of the Navigation pane width, can be set by accessing the Navigation pane options menu. On the **View** tab in the ribbon's **Panes** group, select the **Navigation** pane down-arrow (refer to Figure 15.5).

- **Show/hide the Navigation pane**—After you navigate to the folder you want to work with, you can close the Navigation pane to maximize your screen real estate.

  To show or hide the Navigation pane, on the **View** tab in the **Panes** group, select the **Navigation** pane down arrow. Then, select the **Navigation** pane to toggle the appearance of the pane on and off.

- **Change the width of the Navigation pane**—If your folder names are particularly long or if you have several levels of folders in your file system, you can increase the width the Navigation pane. You can also decrease the width of Navigation pane to see more of the Explorer pane.

To change the width of the Navigation pane, point to or tap-and-hold on the right edge of the slider bar that separates the Navigation pane from the Content pane. When the pointer becomes a double-headed arrow, drag the bar to change the width of the Navigation pane.

- **Showing/hiding Favorites**—If there are folders you tend to work with more than others, even temporarily as you work on a project, you can add a folder to the list of Favorites. Keeping a folder on the Favorites List makes it easier to access the folder than having to navigate through your file system each time you want to work with it. You can hide or show your Favorites List in the Navigation pane.

  To show or hide the Favorites in the Navigation tree, on the **View** tab in the **Panes** group, select the **Navigation** pane down arrow. Then, select **Show Favorites** to toggle the appearance of the Favorites on and off.

- **Showing/hiding all folders**—There are a few objects in the Navigation pane that are a bit different than files, folders, drives, or libraries. The Control Panel, Recycle Bin, and Desktop are actually special folders. Control Panel contains small programs used to configure Windows 8. Recycle Bin stores files and folders you have deleted. Desktop is a special folder that holds anything you see on the main Desktop screen. You can hide these folders if you like; though the author sees no good reason to do so.

  To show or hide these special folders in the Navigation tree, on the **View** tab in the **Panes** group, select the **Navigation** pane down arrow. Then, **Show All Folders** to toggle the appearance of the Control Panel, Desktop, and Recycle Bin on and off.

- **Automatically expand to current folder**—This option is near the top of the list of the coolest features in Windows 8. You learn later in this chapter how to navigate to any folder. You probably noticed that these methods do not use the Navigation pane. If you open a folder without using the Navigation pane, you can configure the folder tree in the Navigation pane to expand automatically to that folder. You can also turn this feature off.

  To update the folder tree in the Navigation pane when the address is entered, on the **View** tab in the **Panes** group, select the **Navigation** pane down arrow. Then, select **Expand to Open Folder** to toggle this feature on or off.

Customizing the Content Pane

The Content pane is the main attraction of Windows Explorer. The Content pane shows you the contents of the folder, drive, branch, or computer selected in the

Navigation pane (see Figure 15.8). Think of the Content pane as your workbench. It's the place where you maintain and organize your computer's folder and files, such as copying, renaming, moving, deleting, burning, and so on.

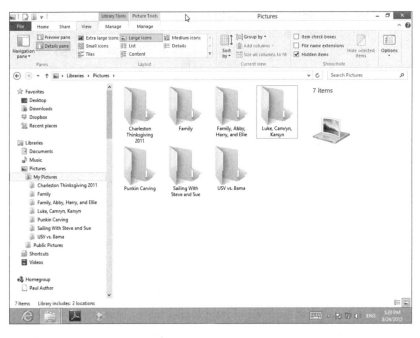

FIGURE 15.8

The Content Pane shows the contents of the folder selected in the Navigation pane.

Selecting items in the Content pane is important because the commands you run, such as Copy, Share, Delete, and all the others, affect the items selected in the Content pane. Refer to "Selecting Files Folders" later in this chapter to review how to select.

You can change the appearance of the icons listed on the Contents pane by choosing the size or layout you want from the Ribbon on the **View** tab in the **Layout** group. The **Current view** group contains commands to change the order in which objects appear.

- **The choice of icon size: small, medium, large, and extra large** is a matter of personal choice and the size of your display. If you have a large display (perhaps greater than 20") and a high resolution (greater than 1024x768), you can fit more of the large icons on the screen.

- The **List** view is helpful when you must select items, especially when you need to make a noncontiguous selection, as shown in Figure 15.9.

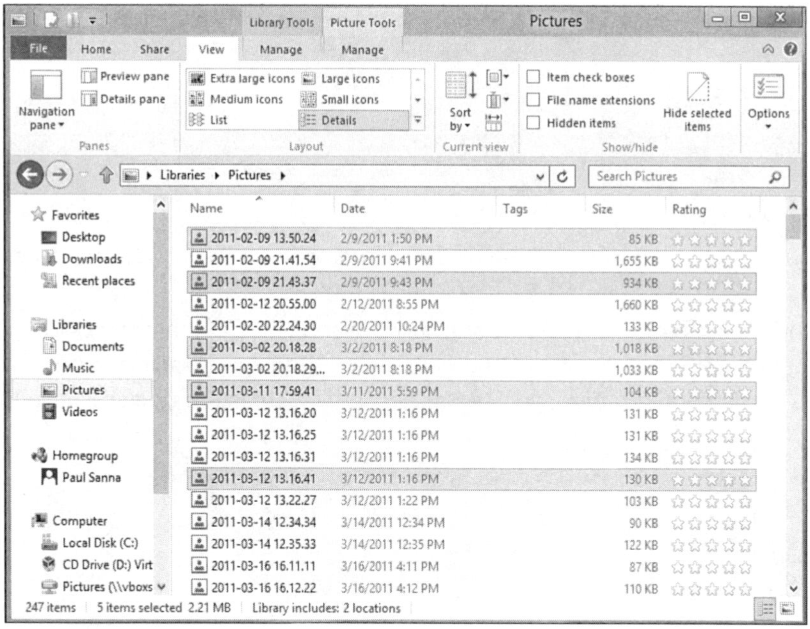

FIGURE 15.9

The List view is extremely helpful when you need to select items that do not appear next to one another.

- The Content and Details views are useful if you need to see (and sort by) the size, type, and the date the items was last modified. Click the name of the column to sort by that field. Click it again to change the sort order. Select **Add Columns** in the Current view group on the View tab to add more information in columns to the view.

- Experiment with the various options on the View tab. As the name of the tab indicates, the commands change only the appearance of the icons on the screen. It is impossible to mistakenly delete anything by making a selection from the View tab.

Exploring the Preview and Details Pane

The rightmost area of Windows Explorer displays one of two panes: the **Preview** pane and the **Details** pane. Only one of these panes is visible at one time. Select the view you want from the Ribbon, as shown in Figure 15.10.

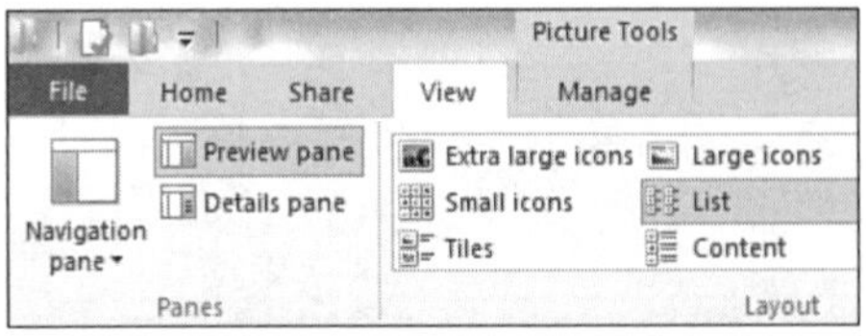

FIGURE 15.10

You can select one of two different views to show in the Preview/Details pane.

Where possible, the Preview pane shows a snapshot of the object selected in the Content pane. If the software used to create the file is installed in Windows 8 or if the file is of a common type, you see a snapshot, such as the one shown in Figure 15.11.

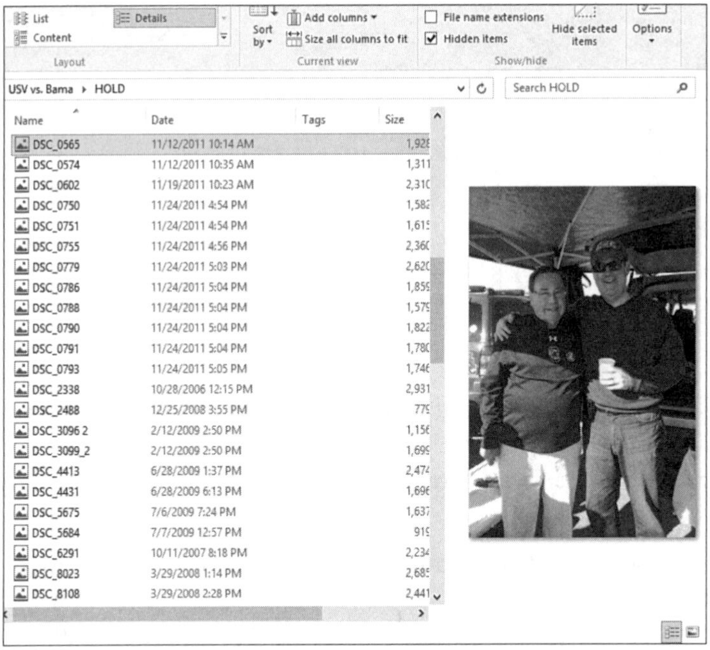

FIGURE 15.11

The Preview pane gives you a look at the file selected in the Contents pane.

The Details pane shows information about the file. Some of the information has been provided by the people who have worked with the file, and some of the information is generated when the file is created. The two images shown in Figure 15.12 shows how the Detail pane can show different information for different file types.

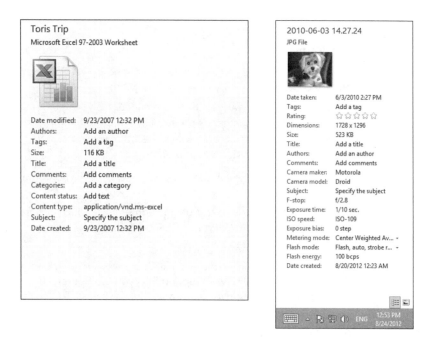

FIGURE 15.12

The Details pane displays information about the item selected in the Content pane. The left example is of a Microsoft Excel file, and the right example comes from a photograph file.

 NOTE   If you want to see a preview of how the Preview pane will appear using any of the icon views shown in the Layout section under the View tab, just pass the mouse cursor over each choice without clicking. The Preview pane changes to the view you hover over.

Folder Options

There are a number of options available that affect how folders work and appear. You can review the most useful of these options in Table 15.1; then follow the instructions to adjust these options after the table.

TABLE 15.1   Folder Options

Option	Description
Always show icons, never thumbnails.	Displaying thumbnails requires extra computing power. You can help Windows run faster by clearing this option.
Always show menus.	The Ribbon provides much of the same functionality as provided by the menus and the commands on them in Windows Explorer. This option ensures the menus are always available as certain processes in Windows hide the Windows Explorer menus.
Display the full path in the title bar.	This option displays the full path to the content displayed in the Explorer pane.
Hidden file and folders.	Show hidden files, folders, and drives. Some files and folders are hidden automatically in Windows. This option displays these hidden files and folders.
Hide empty drives in the Computer folder.	In addition to the main hard drive installed into your computer, you might have additional drives plugged into your computer, such as small, removable USB drives (known as thumb drives). This option hides these drives if no device is plugged in.
Hide extensions for known file types.	As you learned earlier in this chapter, some file extensions are associated with a software program. For example, files with an XLS extension are almost always associated with Microsoft Excel. This option save a little space by hiding the extension for a file when the filename displays and when the file's extension has an association with a program.
Restore previous folder windows at logon.	When you sign on to Windows and start Windows Explorer, this option automatically opens folders just as you left them when you signed off. This is a useful option if you routinely work with the same set of folders or you are working on a special project that requires you to work with several folders.
Show status bar.	This option displays the status bar at the bottom of the Windows Explorer window.
Use check boxes to select items.	If awards were given out for Windows features, this option would win year after year. This option creates a small check box with each file's icon, making it simple to select the file. Read the section "Selecting Files and Folder" to learn more about this option.

To change one or more of these settings, follow these steps:

1. From the Ribbon, on the **View** tab in the last group on the right, select Options and then **Change Folder and Search Options** (see Figure 15.13). The Folder Options dialog box appears, as shown in Figure 15.14.

2. Select the **View** tab.

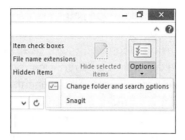

FIGURE 15.13

The command to show folder options is at the end of the View tab.

FIGURE 15.14

There are almost 20 options that help you control exactly how folders work in Windows Explorer.

3. Adjust the options you're interested in.

4. Select **OK.**

Navigating Through Your Folders

Although Windows makes it easy to do most of your work from the shiny Windows 8 interface described in Chapter 3, "Learning Windows 8 Basics," occasionally you must get your hands dirty and work directly with your folders and files. That's why you're reading this chapter, right?

There are many potential reasons for you to work hands-on with your folders and files. You may need to move to a folder to copy a file to another folder. There might be an occasion when you must locate a file on your system; though you are not sure of its exact name or even location. You might need to move a folder from a removable hard drive to your machine's hard drive or vice versa. And as described earlier, you might need to organize some of the folders in your collection to store information for a new project. For these reasons and others, you must know how to move through your file system.

 TIP In several places in this chapter, you can read instructions to reach certain locations in Windows 8, particularly files and folders. What might not always be clear is where you are starting from or what folder you happen to be in. The Windows Explorer title bar always shows the current folder.

This section of the chapter doesn't show every possible way to navigate through your files and folders because there are several, but you do see the simplest ways to get around.

Here are some direct tips for navigating in some special cases:

- To navigate to a folder by typing its name, tap or click once in any empty spot in the address bar. This highlights the contents of the address bar (see Figure 15.15). Enter the name of the folder and press **Enter**.

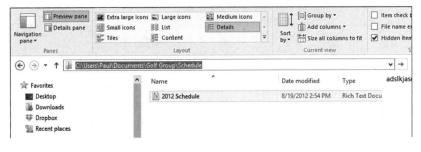

FIGURE 15.15

Clicking anywhere in the address bar highlights the entire field. You can type the name of a folder to navigate to, which replaces the highlighted text.

- To navigate to a folder you recently opened, on the right end of the address bar, tap or click the down arrow, and then select the folder from the list (see Figure 15.16).

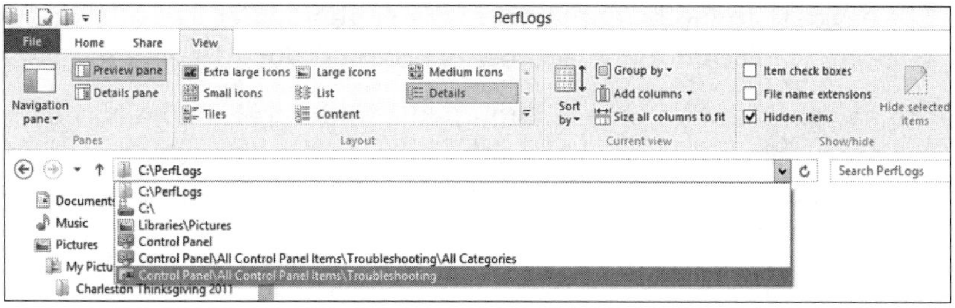

FIGURE 15.16

You can quickly navigate to a folder you visited by selecting the folder from a list of recently visited folders.

- To navigate to the folder you most recently opened, select the back arrow button (see Figure 15.17), or select the Recent Locations button next to the Back and Forward buttons (see Figure 15.17) and select the first item in the list.

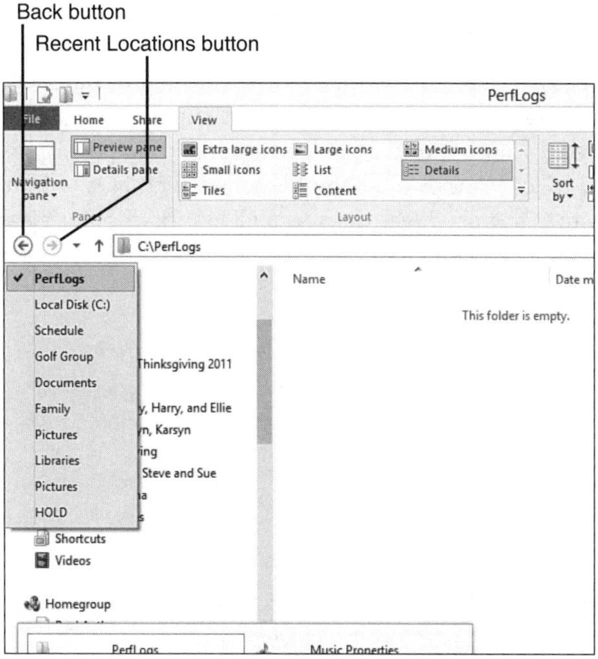

FIGURE 15.17

Choose the Recent Locations button or the Back button to move to the previous location you visited.

- To navigate to the parent folder of the current folder, tap or click the **Navigate Up** arrow adjacent to the address bar or press **Alt+Up** on the keyboard.

- To navigate down a branch through the folder tree, in the Navigation pane, click any folder that you believe is higher in the hierarchy than the folder you're looking for. In the Content pane, double-click/tap a folder to reveals its content, and so on.

Here are a few other useful tips:

- Double-clicking a folder in the Navigation pane expands the folders and reveals what's in the folder

- Selecting a folder name in the address bar displays its children folders in the Content pane.

- Selecting a small arrow in the address bar pops open a list of children folders of the folder to the left of the arrow

Selecting Files and Folders

One of the most important Windows 8 skills to learn, particularly for use with Windows Explorer, is how to select files. As sophisticated as Windows 8 is, it cannot yet read your mind (though developers may be working on this feature), so you need to let Windows 8 know directly which files you may want to delete, copy, move to a thumb drive, burn to a CD, and so on. It's easy to select just one file and only slightly complicated to select multiple files, but there's no doubt you can learn to select files like an expert.

 NOTE Before you read ahead, although, the author refers specifically to files in this instructions, you can use the same techniques to select folders as well, including if you must select files together with folders.

Selecting a Single File at a Time

To select one file, first navigate to the folder where the file is located. Then, do one of the following based on the device you use:

 Tap once on the file.

 Press the arrow keys to move the cursor to the file. If the cursor doesn't seem to be moving, press the **Tab** key repeatedly until the cursor appears in the Content pane, as shown in Figure 15.18.

Click once on the file.

Cursor

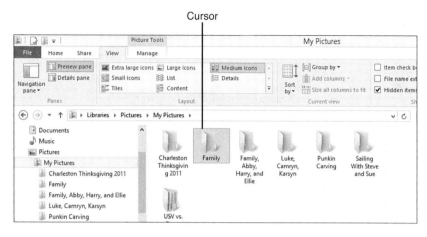

FIGURE 15.18

The cursor may be on a different part of the Windows Explorer window. Press the Tab key to move the cursor to the list.

Selecting Multiple Contiguous Files

To select multiple contiguous (next to one another) files, first navigate to the folder where the files are located. Then, do one of the following based on the device you use:

- Swipe over the list of files. Be careful not to strike the screen when you start to pan or Windows will interpret the start of the pan as a tap.

- Press the arrow keys to move the cursor to the first file in the list of those to select. If the cursor doesn't seem to be moving, press **Tab** repeatedly until the cursor appears in the Explorer pane. With the cursor over the first file, press and hold down the **Shift** key while you use the arrow keys to highlight the files.

- Click and drag the mouse pointer over all the files and folders to select. To do so, point to a spot slightly above and to the left of the group of files, and then drag until all are highlighted, as shown in Figure 15.19. This process is easier if you use the Medium Icons view.

 TIP   It is easier to select multiple files when the contents of the Preview pane display in List or Details view. Read the previous section "Exploring the Preview and Details Pane" to learn about changing the view.

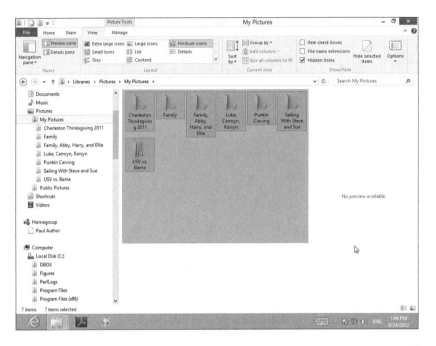

FIGURE 15.19

Select the files with your mouse by dragging over the entire group.

Selecting Multiple Noncontiguous Files

To select multiple noncontiguous (not next to one another) files, first navigate to the folder where the files are located. Then, do one of the following based on the device you use:

- Select the **Use** check box to select the option described earlier in Table 15.1, Folder Options. Tap the check box for each file to select, as shown in Figure 15.20.

- Press the arrow keys to move the cursor to each file in the list. If the cursor doesn't seem to be moving, press **Tab** repeatedly until the cursor appears in the Explorer pane (refer to Figure 15.18). With the cursor over the first file in the list, press and hold the **Ctrl** key while using the arrow keys to move the cursor to other files you want to select. When you reach a file to select, press the **spacebar**. Repeat this process for each file, remembering to hold the **Ctrl** key down.

- Click once on the first file. Next, press and hold **Ctrl** while you click each of the remaining files. Do not release Ctrl until you have clicked each of the files you intend to select.

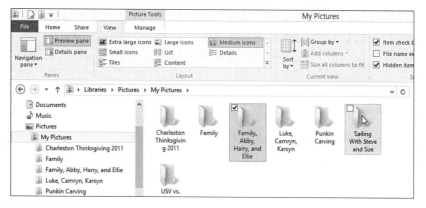

FIGURE 15.20

The Use check box option makes it easy to select files.

 TIP   Selecting multiple files not adjacent to one another can be tricky. If you accidentally release the Ctrl key before you have selected all the files you are interested in, you must start over. An alternative to using the Ctrl+Click technique is to use the Use Check Boxes to Select Items option in Table 15.1.

Common Files and Folders Tasks

If you have been reading straight through this chapter, you've read about navigating and selecting. At this point, put together the skills you read about to finish some basic tasks in Windows.

Each of these tasks are completed with Windows Explorer, which was covered earlier in the section, "Exploring Your Files and Folders with Windows Explorer."

If you are copying or moving several files, or if the files you are copying or moving are large, a message might appear on the screen showing the progress (see Figure 15.21). The message displays a chart illustrating the task. You can see more information about the task by selecting the **More Details** button.

FIGURE 15.21

A dialog box appears when you copy or move files, helping you monitor progress, as well as giving you the opportunity to pause or cancel the process.

If you start another copy or move a task while an earlier one is running, the new task is added to the status screen.

 TIP In each of the following instructions you can also use simple keyboard combinations to cut (Ctrl+X), copy (Ctrl+C), or paste (Ctrl+Y).

To Copy One or More Files or Folders

1. Navigate to the folder where the files and/or folders to be copied are located.

2. Select the files and/or folders to be copied.

3. From the Ribbon, on the Home tab and in the Clipboard group, select **Copy**.

4. Navigate to the folder to which the file and/or folder will be copied. Be sure not to select a folder or file in the Explorer pane.

5. From the Ribbon, on the Home tab and in the Clipboard group, select **Paste**.

To Move One or More Files or Folders

1. Navigate to the folder where the files and/or folders to be copied are located.

2. Select the files and/or folders to be copied.

3. With your mouse, right-click, or with your finger or stylus, press-and-hold on top of one of the items being moved. Select **Cut** from the menu that appears.

4. Navigate to the folder to which the file and/or folder will be moved. Be sure not to select a folder or file in the Explorer pane.

5. With your mouse, right-click or with your finger or stylus, press-and-hold any blank spot on the Explorer pane. Select **Paste** from the menu that appears.

To Rename a File or Folder

1. Navigate to the folder where the file or folder to be renamed is located.

2. From the Ribbon, on the Home tab and in the Organize group, select **Rename**. A small border around the existing name of the file or folder appears, enabling you to edit the text.

3. Type the new name and press **Enter**.

To Create a Folder

1. Navigate to the folder where the new folder is to be created.

2. Right-click with your mouse, or press-and-hold with your finger, on an empty spot in the Explorer pane.

3. Select **New** and then **Folder** from the menu that appears. A new folder appears with its label highlighted.

4. Type the name for the new folder and press **Enter**.

To Delete File or Folder

1. Navigate to the folder where the file or folder to be deleted is located.

2. Select the file(s) and/or folder(s).

3. From the Ribbon, on the Home tab in the Organize group, click the arrow below the Delete icon.

4. Select **Recycle** to delete the file(s) and/or folder(s) with the chance to recover them if you find you made a mistake. To delete the file(s) and/or folder(s) with no chance to recover them, select **Permanently Delete**.

THE ABSOLUTE MINIMUM

Here are the key points to remember from this chapter:

- The raw materials of your Windows 8 system are files and the folders that store and organize them. Files are categorized as either system files, which are used by Windows 8 and the programs that run in Windows 8, or user files, which are the files you work with every day. You normally do not directly interact with system files.

- Windows Explorer, which runs in the Desktop app, is the tool used to manage your user files. You can start Windows Explorer from a tile on the Start screen. You should locate the tile and then pin it to the Start screen if you anticipate using Windows Explorer often.

- If you work with photos or music files or with work files on a regular basis, you'll work with Windows Explorer.

- The organization of the folders in Windows, plus the location of your files in your system, is known as your file system. You use specific techniques with your mouse, style, finger, or keyboard to navigate through your file system.

- You need to select those files that you need to interact with, such as to copy or move. There are specific techniques you use to select files.

IN THIS CHAPTER

- Working with External Hard Drives
- Learning About the New Microsoft SkyDrive
- Burning DVDs
- Learning Some Backup Strategies
- Using the New File History Backup Program

16

STORING FILES ON DRIVES, DISKS, AND THE CLOUD

It's amazing how much content, files, and data users have access to today. It's not a big deal for beginning users to add a 1TB drive to their computer to store photos. These users sleep soundly at night because all their data is backed up to the Cloud, as well as to another drive with 5TB of storage to back up a few other computers in the home. With all this potential data and storage, it's important to understand your options for storing files, as well as how to work with the options you choose. This chapter helps you understand how to manage a new external drive, how to create a solid backup strategy, how to leverage Microsoft's new Cloud storage offering named SkyDrive, and lots more.

Working with External Drives

Chances are you use Windows 8 on a new computer, in which case you probably have lots of empty storage space. The time will come soon when that drive you thought you would never fill up starts to run short of space. That's the time when you might consider acquiring a new external drive. Even if you have a huge amount of free space, you might choose to store certain types of data exclusively on an external drive, such as your backup files or perhaps all your photos or music. Fortunately, it's easy to find an external drive for sale with the space you need and at a price you can afford. And it's just as easy to set up one of these drives.

You can add storage to your computer in a snap as long as you have an open USB port. Figure 16.1 shows you what a USB port looks like on your computer. (Although there are other variations on this plug type pending what device it's intended to connect to.) No other computer plugs can fit into a USB slot, so there is no chance of confusing a USB port for anything else. USB plugs do have a top and bottom, so you may have to flip over the plug for it to fit into the slot.

FIGURE 16.1

The USB port is thin and a bit wide. No other port on your computer looks like a USB port.

To add storage space to your computer, you can acquire an external drive. These drives are usually the same size as a large hardbound novel. As such, they are considered portable, but hardly convenient for on-the-go storage needs. Sure, you can disconnect and move the drive elsewhere, but it's not nearly as convenient to do so as transferring data to a USB key that fits in your pocket.

If price is not an issue, you should buy as much storage as you can afford. A more specific guideline is to buy a drive whose capacity matches or exceeds the capacity of your primary computer. If your computer has a 500GB drive, consider buying another 500GB drive or even move up to a 1TB drive. Finally, if you know exactly the amount of data you need to accommodate, such as the size of all the photos you want to store on the drive, smart advice is to acquire twice that.

Connecting Your Drive the First Time

When you connect your new drive to the computer for the first time, Windows 8 assigns to it a drive letter. The letter distinguishes one drive from another. Your main drive normally is assigned the letter C, whereas new drives typically start after the letter F. In Figure 16.2, you can see that the author has four hard drives connected to his PC, along with a DVD drive and several flash memory ports (listed as Removable Disk).

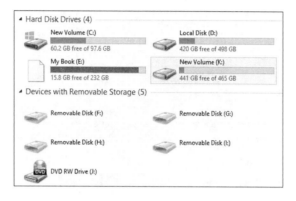

FIGURE 16.2

The existing drives on this computer take up letters C through K.

When the author adds a new drive, as in Figure 16.3, it appears as the next available drive letter, L in this case. You can see your own drives by opening Windows Explorer on your Windows desktop.

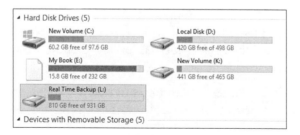

FIGURE 16.3

The new drive picks up the next available letter.

Naming Your New Drive

You'll notice in Figures 16.2 and 16.3 that the hard drives have different names associated with them. If you have a number of external drives, it may make sense to assign names to the drives rather than remember the use of each based on a drive letter. To assign a name to an external hard drive, open Windows Explorer and locate the drive in the Navigation Pane. Right-click or tap-and-hold with your finger on the drive. Select Rename from the menu that appears, as shown in Figure 16.4. Type the new name and press **Enter**.

```
◢ 💻 Computer
    ▷ 🖴 New Volume (C:)
    ▷ 💾 Local Disk (D:)
    ▷ ⬜ My Book (E:)
    ▷ 💾 New Volume
    ▷ 💾 Real Time Backup (L:)
    ▷ 📇 pasanna@live.com (fusionoffice_1)

  ▷ 🖧 Network
```

FIGURE 16.4

*Either right-click with your mouse or tap-and-hold on the drive until a small menu appears. Then, select **Rename** from menu to enter a friendly label for the drive.*

Storing and Sharing in the Cloud

SkyDrive is a personal area to store files such as pictures and documents. What makes SkyDrive unique is that it is located in the Cloud. Although technology folks might give you a more direct definition of the Cloud, as well as of related technologies, such as the Internet, server, software-as-services (SaaS), and more, you don't need to think of the Cloud as anything more than a useful technology that makes it easy for you to share, save, and consume information anywhere you're located and with just about any device.

Also, if you're not used to accepting things or you are skeptical about "free stuff," SkyDrive is the real thing. You get 7GB of free Cloud-based storage, and you can pay a fee to add storage to your SkyDrive.

There is a SkyDrive tile on the Start screen that provides access to the contents of your SkyDrive. To open SkyDrive, select the **SkyDrive** tile, as shown in Figure 16.5.

FIGURE 16.5

The SkyDrive app is available from the Start screen.

As you can tell from Figure 16.6, SkyDrive is organized by three folders: Documents, Pictures, and Public. The picture also shows the App bar, which gives you access to a few tools for working with your SkyDrive. If you were looking for a Music folder, you can stop searching. Music files are not yet supported in SkyDrive. For now, you need to leverage these three starting folder to accomplish tasks and benefits, such as the following:

- If you work with the same document on a number of different computers, such as your work computer and your home computer, or if you also work on tablet, use the SkyDrive account to store the documents. This saves you from emailing the document to yourself.

- SkyDrive enables you to easily share with other folks. You can specify by email address those people who have access to one or more of your SkyDrive folders.

- If you work with a small team, all the documents can be stored in the Public folder of a SkyDrive account. Instead of emailing files around the group, the SkyDrive folders can be the source for all team or project documents.

FIGURE 16.6

The default view in SkyDrive shows your primary folders.

The process to load your files to SkyDrive is easy. There is, though, one important caveat to that statement: As much as Microsoft brags that the mouse interface and touch interfaces are equal to one another, it is equal parts difficult and frustrating to add files to SkyDrive using only your keyboard. You'll be much more efficient if you use the mouse or touch interface. Also, if you have not navigated through the new File Picker tool in Windows 8, take a look at Chapter 3, "Learning Windows 8 Basics," so that you can become comfortable with navigating through folders and drives.

To load files and folders to SkyDrive, follow these steps:

1. Open the SkyDrive app.

2. To upload to a folder on your SkyDrive, open that folder. To open the folder, click or tap the folder.

3. Open the App bar and select **Upload**.

4. Navigate through your file system to select files to upload. For help using the File Picker, refer to Chapter 3.

5. When you have selected all the files to upload, select **Add to Skydrive**. Your files will be uploaded.

You have as many options for managing your SkyDrive as you do for your local drives. You can create folders and subfolders, select multiple files, delete files, and see thumbnails of each. Here are a few of the options:

- To add a folder to your SkyDrive, including adding a subfolder to a folder on SkyDrive, start by opening the SkyDrive app. Open the folder on SkyDrive where the folder will be created. Open the App bar and select New Folder. The screen shown in Figure 16.7 appears. Enter the name of the folder and select **Create folder**.

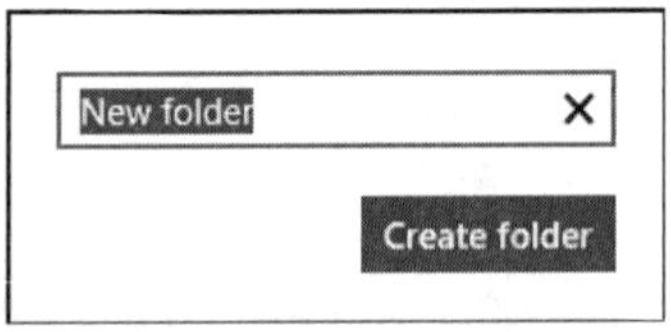

FIGURE 16.7

You can create folders on your SkyDrive.

- If you are moving or copying all of the files in a SkyDrive folder, you can easily select all of the files. Open the folder where the files are located. Next, open the App bar and select **Select all**.

- To delete one or more files on your SkyDrive, start by opening the SkyDrive and then opening the folder where the files are located. Select the files to be deleted. To do so, right-click on the file or, if you are using a touch interface, tap-and-hold on the file. Next, open the App bar and select **Delete**.

- If you need to work with a file on your device that is stored on your SkyDrive, you need to download it. To do so, open the folder where the file to be deleted is located. Select the file(s) and then open the App bar. Select **Download**, and then select the folder on your device where the file should be copied.

As you can tell, you have lots of flexibility with SkyDrive. As you use SkyDrive, you might find you need more space on your SkyDrive. To see how much free space you have, open the Charms bar and select **Settings**. Next, select **Options,** and the screen shown in Figure 16.8 appears. Select **Manage Storage** to reach the Microsoft web page where you can add storage to your SkyDrive.

FIGURE 16.8

From the Settings charm, you can open the Options screen to check the amount of free space available on your SkyDrive.

Saving Data to DVDs

A simple, fast, and convenient way to store data is to save file and folders to a DVD. Saving information to a CD or DVD has the best alternative name in all technology: *burning.* You can burn about 4.5GB of content onto a DVD, which is great for storing documents and a limited amount of music or pictures, but not so great for a large image, music, or video collection. Many people use DVDs as the storage component in their off-site backup strategy. As you will read in the "Data Back Up

Strategies," later in this chapter, keeping an additional copy of your backups at a location separate from other backups is a good idea. There are many applications to burning files and folders to DVD besides creating backups—there's little doubt that you'll come up with your own. Here is what you need to burn DVDs:

- Of course, you need blank DVDs. Look for the type specifically compatible with your computer's drive. Most drives today are compatible with all formats— –R, –RW, +R, and +RW—but some may be compatible only with either the – or + format, rather than both. The RW format enables you to rewrite information onto a DVD, whereas with R you can write data only to a disc once.

- Disc labels or a permanent marker to record the contents.

- Although Windows comes with software that enables you burn data to a disc, if you burn a lot of discs for a variety of purposes, you may want to purchase dedicated software for the task. Plenty of software companies provide these tools—Bing or Google your way to a free trial to see what application you like best.

Here's how to burn DVDs from Windows 8 without any additional software:

1. The first time you insert a DVD into a Windows 8 computer, you will be asked what Windows should do with it. Select **burn Files to the Disc**. This doesn't bind you permanently to this action.

2. Next, a dialog box like the one shown in Figure 16.9 appears. You may enter a name for the DVD and specify how the DVD should be used, as an open-ended disc storage device that you can write to multiple times or as a DVD whose contents are frozen after you finish specifying the files to burn to it.

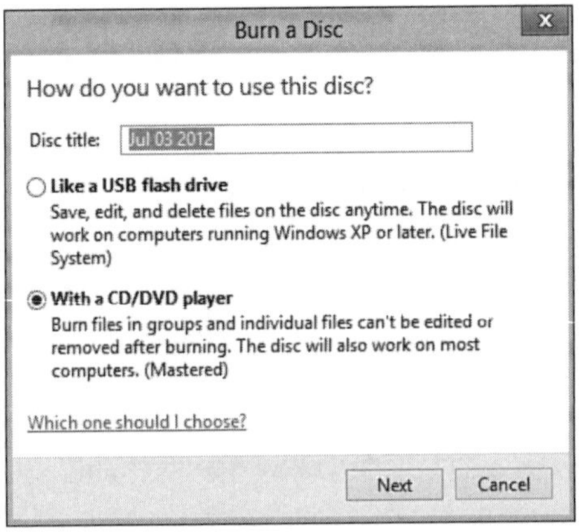

FIGURE 16.9

After you insert a DVD, you are prompted for the use of the disc after files have been burned to it.

3. You land at a Windows Explorer window with the DVD drive selected. The Drive Tools tab is available on the Ribbon. Note the drive letter assigned to the DVD. This appears in the title bar of the Windows Explorer window.

4. Drag the files and folders you want to burn to the Content pane as long as the drive is selected, as shown in Figure 16.10. If another drive or folder is selected in the Navigation pane, select the DVD drive again. For help navigating and selecting in Windows Explorer, refer to Chapter 15.

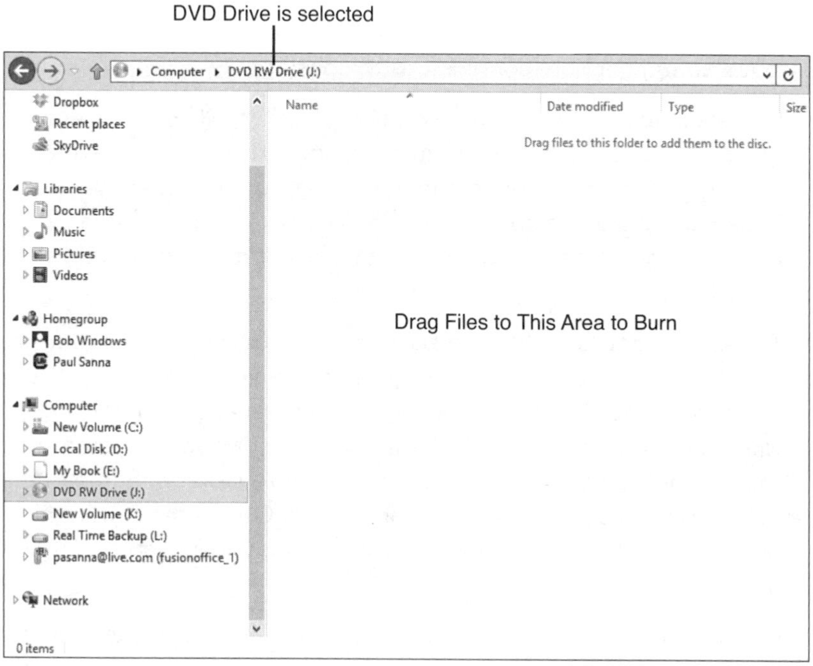

FIGURE 16.10

You can select files and folders to burn simply by dragging them to the DVD drive in Windows Explorer.

5. When you have completed dragging files and folders to the DVD drive, on the Manage tab on the Ribbon, select **Finish Burning**.

6. Enter a label for the DVD. Also, select the check box to close the wizard after the files are written. Select **Next** to start the burn process.

7. The DVD drive opens when the burn process completes successfully.

Data Backup Strategies

With all this talk about data and files all over your machine, external hard drives, and in the Cloud, it is vital to consider a strategy to back up your work and your valuable personal files. There is nothing that compares to the lost feeling in your soul when you realize your treasured photos or critical documents have been lost forever because of carelessness, a mistake, or a hardware problem.

There are innumerable choices for backup technology. Although it is impossible to recommend a particular product without knowing your exact situation and computer setup, here are some issues to consider:

- It's reasonable to use a multiple backup strategy. Having a second backup gives you even more piece of mind. Also, certain backup technologies may be more appropriate for certain files to backup. For example, if you have a large music library, a solution that quickly backs up these files to a local drive is better than an online solution, with which it might take weeks to do the initial backup.

- There are many Cloud-based backup solutions. For a fee, the files and folder you specify are backed up to a dedicated server operated by the vendor you chose. The benefit is obvious: You can back up your key files, usually with no software to install, to a safe location, one where you don't need to worry about replacing a drive or getting more storage. Some offerings do not support backup of external hard drives. Others have reputations of slow performance. Doing lots of prep work before you select a Cloud solution is a good idea.

- Whatever backup software you choose, be sure to consider how easy it is to restore files. This is an area you should focus on when researching Cloud backup solutions. The ease of file restoration usually is the source of the strongest negative feedback to backup programs.

- Create an off-location backup. Create one backup of all your files, including photos, music, and so on, and including files on external drives; then move the backup to another location. This way, if there is a catastrophic loss where your computer is located (fire, flood, power surge, and so on), your backup is not harmed. Update this backup every month or whatever feels comfortable. Remember, this is a last resort backup should your other backups get destroyed or become unusable or unavailable.

Backing Up with File History

File History is a backup solution built into Windows 8. Some of the guts of File History come from a utility in previous versions of Windows known as Shadow Copy, but for this review, assume you know nothing of either File History or Shadow Copy.

File History is focused on files only. Some backup tools can back up your entire Windows 8 system, enabling you to restore everything should you suffer a catastrophic failure. File History, though, is concerned with these files only:

- Files in all your libraries
- Files on your Desktop
- The list of your favorites, including both website favorites and the favorite local drives and folders you've specified in Windows Explorer
- Your contacts

You can set up File History to create a backup of your files. File History does not retain just one version of files it backs up. Rather, it keeps prior versions of files for as long as you tell it to. This way, if you have made several changes to a document over time, but you ultimately want to use the first version you wrote, you can always go back to retrieve it.

Here is an important point: Be sure all files you want to back up are stored in a library or the Desktop. Only files stored in these locations are saved with File History. If someone provides you a removable hard drive with a document on it that they want you to work on, you can certainly double-click the document on the drive to edit it and then save it, but File History is not enabled because it is not stored in one of your libraries or the Desktop. You can find help with libraries and the Desktop in Chapter 15.

Setting Up File History

To start File History, open the **Charms** bar and select **Search**. Enter **File History** in the search box and select **Settings**. Select **File History** from the results on the left side of the screen. The File History window appears, as shown in Figure 16.11.

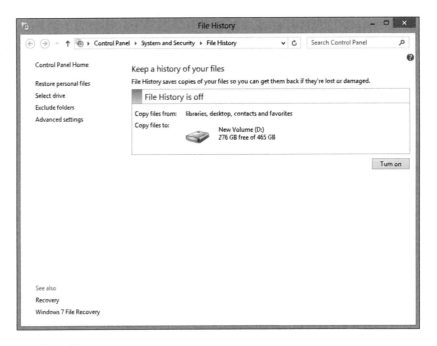

FIGURE 16.11

The File History window show the types of files to be backed up and the drive to which the backup will be created.

There are few easy steps you must take to set up File History for use. After it's configured, there is usually little that must be changed. If you start work on a key project, you might increase the cycle in which backups are created. If your computer is a laptop, you can allocate more space for the backups created on your main drive while away from your primary backup drive.

Select and Set Up the Backup Drive

You need to specify the drive to store your backup files. This drive should not be your main drive. You may need to purchase a new external drive to serve as the backup drive. Follow the advice provided in the first section of this chapter to select a drive:

1. Connect your backup drive to your Windows 8 computer. This can mean simply attaching the drive to your computer or being sure you can reach a network location if you use a network folder as a backup store.

2. To specify the drive to use as a backup, select **Select Drive** (refer to Figure 16.12). A window appears with a list of drives attached to your computer.

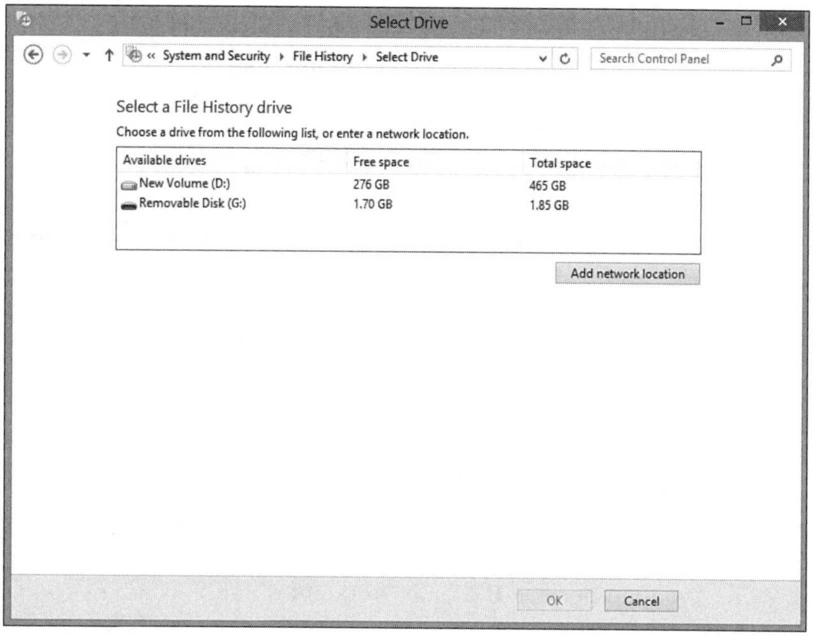

FIGURE 16.12

You can select or confirm the drive to use as the File History backup.

3. Select the drive from the list and then select OK. To back up to a network drive, select **Add Network Location**. Browse through the folders to which you have access. Either create a new folder or select one that has been set up for you. Select **Select Folder** when you have chosen the correct folder.

4. The selected drive appears on the screen.

Specify Which Folders to Exclude

Although File History can back up all the files and folders in your libraries, you may select individual folders to exclude. Many users employ a different backup strategy for certain types of files, such as music. The folder containing music files, in this example, would be one to exclude from the backup.

NOTE Some people, especially those with extremely large music collections, prefer not to back up their music folder. Why? Because you can restore music from the CDs from which you originally imported your music. And if you purchased music online, you can restore your lost music from the service where you purchased the music (sometimes for a small fee per song). It's time-consuming work, but if backup storage space is at a premium, it's a reasonable way to cut a corner.

To exclude folders from File History backup, follow these steps:

1. From the File History window, select **Exclude Folders**.

2. A list of folders that already have been excluded appears. To exclude another folder or perhaps the first folder, select **Add**.

3. Navigate through the file system to the folder you need to exclude. Select the folder and then select **Select Folder**. Doing so adds the folder to the list of excluded folders.

4. Repeat these steps for other folders you want to exclude from backup.

Specify How Often to Back Up

You can specify how often File History should create a backup copy of your file. If you are in the middle of a critical project, you can specify a short duration. This choice creates many more backup files, which impacts the amount of storage claimed on the backup drive. You can always use a more modest setting, perhaps every day and then engage the more frequent duration when needed.

To specify how often File History should back up your files, follow these steps:

1. From the File History window, select **Advanced Settings**.

2. Select the pace at which files are backed up from the list labeled **Save Copies of Files**, as shown in Figure 16.13.

Advanced settings

Choose how often you want to save copies of your files, and how long to keep saved versions.

Versions

Save copies of files: Every hour (default)

| Every 10 minutes |
| Every 15 minutes |
| Every 20 minutes |
| Every 30 minutes |
| Every hour (default) |
| Every 3 hours |
| Every 6 hours |
| Every 12 hours |
| Daily |

Size of offline cache:

Keep saved versions:

HomeGroup

If this PC is part of a homegroup, you can recommend this drive to

☐ Recommend this drive

Event logs

Open File History event logs to view recent events or errors

FIGURE 16.13

Select how often back up versions are created.

 NOTE The File History window is a Control Panel program. You can also access File History by opening Control Panel. You can find a link to File History in the System and Security group.

Backing Up

With the File History options set up, as described in the previous section, you are ready to start backing up your files. To do so, select **Turn On** from the File History window (refer to Figure 16.12). After doing so, the main box around the backup drive changes colors, indicating the backup is running.

Restoring Files

If you need to restore one or more files, open File History and select **Restore Personal Files**. A window appears showing icons for each of the main libraries plus the Desktop, Contacts, and Favorites, as shown in Figure 16.14. Follow these steps as a guide to restore files you backed up.

FIGURE 16.14

Select the library storing files and folders you want to restore.

1. Navigate to the file you want to restore.

2. When you reach the file, select it. To restore a specific version, select it using the version button at the bottom of the screen.

3. Right-click or tap-and-hold on the file to be restored. You can Preview the file to be restored, restore the file to the location from which it was backed up, or restore it to a folder you specify.

4. Repeat these steps to restore other files. Also, you may select a folder to restore by selecting one in step 2.

THE ABSOLUTE MINIMUM

Keep the following points in mind after you read this chapter:

- You don't need to purchase a backup application. The File History tool in Windows 8 provides adequate backup capabilities.

- All Windows 8 users can access their own SkyDrive account, which is an online storage space. You can manage the online drive as easily as you can a drive attached to your device.

- Burning files to a DVD is extremely easy. You shouldn't be intimidated or scared of the idea to create a DVD. Adding a new external drive to your computer also is easy to do. Both of these solutions can address a need to move files off your main drive for any reason.

17

SETTING UP HARDWARE THE EASY WAY

Although hardware setup might not seem like a beginner topic, you'll find success in this chapter. Windows 8 makes it easy to tweak some of the most important settings of the hardware connected to your computer. Setting up some aspects of your hardware might require help from someone with more experience in Windows 8, or you might acquire another book from Que covering more advanced topics, but the tasks covered in this chapter are doable. In this chapter, you learn about setting up your display, mouse, keyboard, sound, and power.

Setting Up Your Display

The computer component you work with the most is the display. The display interfaces with one of the most delicate parts of your body: your eyes. For this reason, you must set up the display the right way. Resolution is the key setting for a comfortable but efficient set up with your computer and Windows 8. In addition, Windows 8 makes it easy to work with a second monitor, another option to make your work (and play) experience a productive one. In this section, you learn how to set your resolution and how to set up a second monitor.

Adjusting the Resolution (Making the Screen Bigger or Smaller)

Resolution is one of the most important *and* one of the most misunderstood aspects of computer use. The resolution determines the level of detail of the image you see on a computer screen. Don't confuse detail with quality. Other hardware on your computer contributes to the quality of the images, such as the richness of colors.

Here is what you need to know about resolution:

- Displays on the screen are of pixels. Each pixel has exactly the same size and shape (usually square or rectangular, but can be any shape). If you are of a certain age, you might remember a toy called Lite-Brite from Hasbro. The toy is a small version of the concept of resolution. Go ahead and Google it!

- Resolution is specified by a size. The size is the amount of pixels used to create images on the screen. This size is expressed as row and column counts, such as 1024x768, which specifies that the grid pattern is 1,024 pixels across and 768 top to bottom.

- The greater the resolution, the more detailed images on the screen will be. Just think of connect-the-dots. Your drawing can be much more detailed if you use 500 number dots rather than 50. If you are unfamiliar with connect-the-dots, you can Google it, too!

- There is a trade-off when choosing a high resolution. Most monitors are not large enough to display higher resolutions at a normal size. So, images appear smaller at high resolution to accommodate all the detail. You trade away some usability because some print and text might be too small to see for the sharpness of a high resolution.

- An LCD monitor has a native resolution, that is, a resolution at which it's designed to operate. Although LCD monitors can operate at difference resolutions, using a non-native setting incurs a considerable hit to image quality, so if you're planning to buy a new LCD monitor, you should note the resolution you prefer to work with and make sure the one you pick is designed to operate at that resolution. A typical HD LCD monitor operates at 1920×1080.

Follow these steps to adjust resolution:

1. To open the Screen Resolution dialog box, start the Desktop app. From the Desktop, right-click any blank spot on the screen, and choose **Screen Resolution**. The window shown in Figure 17.1 appears.

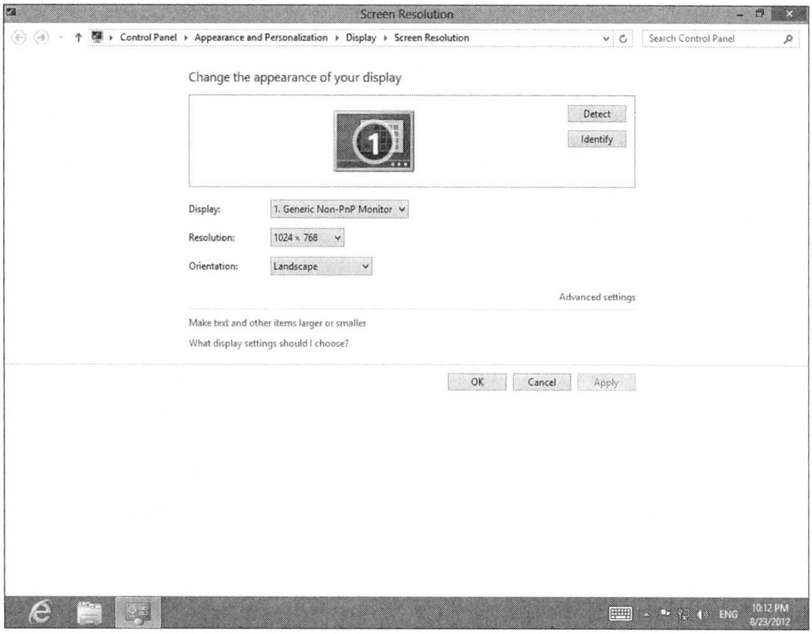

FIGURE 17.1

The Screen resolution dialog box is accessed from the Desktop.

2. The first thing to do is check the Display list. If you have more than one screen attached to your computer, you see each of them represented. Be sure to select the monitor you want to work with in the Display field (or by clicking its representation on this screen). If you aren't sure which monitor is identified in the list, select **Identify**. A number flashes on your screen identifying each monitor.

3. Select the resolution you want from the Resolution drop-down list. Tap or click the box to display the resolutions your hardware can use.

4. Select **Apply** to see immediately the resolution you chose at work. The screen updates to the resolution you selected.

5. If you are happy with the new resolution, select **Keep Changes**. If you want to select another resolution or stick with the original resolution, select **Revert**.

 TIP You can select a resolution your display doesn't support, resulting in a blank screen when you attempt to change it. If this happens, just sit tight for a few seconds. If you don't click Keep Changes on the confirmation dialog, Windows reverts back to the previous resolution.

6. To select a different resolution, repeat steps 3–5. Otherwise, select **OK** to close the Screen Resolution box.

 NOTE To snap two Windows 8 apps to the screen at the same time or to snap an app to one side of the screen, the screen resolution must be set to 1366x768 or higher.

Setting Up Multiple Monitors

You can set up a second monitor if your computer has the capability. Look at the back of your computer near where your monitor is plugged in. If you see a second plug like the one the first monitor uses, you are in good shape. If you are not sure, it makes sense to ask someone because there are a few different plugs for monitors. Most laptops manufactured in the last few years have an external monitor port that can work at the same time as your laptop's built-in display. So, you can take advantage of the extra screen real estate a second monitor provides even if your everyday machine is a laptop.

 NOTE Every computer has a piece of hardware known as a video adapter. The video adapter has a number of capabilities, the most important one being to generate an image for display on the monitor. Your monitor connects to the computer by being plugged into the port on the video adapter.

There are a number of advantages to having a second monitor. You can extend Windows 8 to the additional screen. You can extend your screen horizontally, so you have more room across Windows 8 . You can also extend your screen vertically to have more room top-to-bottom in Windows 8. Using the Desktop app, you can open several programs at the same time and arrange them on your extended display. You can also have the same image generated on both displays, something that can come in handy for presentation purposes.

When you add a second screen to your computer set up (having done so according to its supplied documentation), you can configure it for use with Windows 8 by following these steps:

1. Open the **Charms** bar and select **Devices**. The Devices screen appears, as shown in Figure 17.2.

FIGURE 17.2

Your second monitor appears as a device under the Devices charm.

2. Select **Second screen**. The list of options shown in Figure 17.3 appears.

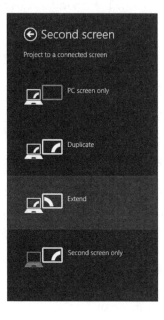

FIGURE 17.3

Select how the two monitors work together.

3. Select how you would like the two monitors to work. You can select whether the computer screen appears on both monitors, perhaps giving you the capability to present the same images in different places in a room. You can also select just one monitor on which the image appears. But the most interesting option is *Extend*, which creates a double-sized screen. You can even set the extended screen to show the Start screen on one side and your conventional Desktop on the other.

Setting Up Your Mouse

A number of settings are available for you to customize exactly how your mouse operates. Some of these settings control basic functions, such as determining which of the two buttons on the mouse is the primary button, and some permit you to express your personality with your mouse, such as replacing the mouse pointer with custom, unique pointers.

Here is a list of the settings you can change for your mouse:

- **Primary button**—Mice are shipped typically with the left button configured as the primary button. You can change this configuration to make the right button the primary button.

- **Double-click speed**—Just a few commands in Windows 8 require you to double-click. You can slow the double-click speed to give you more time to make the second-click.

- **Click for drag**—If you have difficulty dragging items in Windows 8, the ClickLock option possibly can help you. This option enables you to drag an item without holding the mouse button down while you drag the item. Instead, you click the item to be moved, hold the mouse button down over the item for a few seconds, and then release the button. To drop the object you're dragging, you click once where you want the item to be moved to.

- **Pointer speed**—You can configure your mouse pointer to keep pace with you, moving swiftly across the screen as you work. This setting is known as **pointer speed**. However, if when you move the mouse, you find that the pointer tends to fly across the screen out-of-control, forcing you to search for the pointer after you stopped moving the mouse, you may want to slow the pointer down.

- **Snap to default button**—Windows does a good job to ask you to confirm your actions when your actions could cause distress, such as deleting a file or saving a document with the same name as an existing file. Windows confirms your actions with a small window, usually with some text (Are You Sure?) and two buttons (OK and Cancel). Windows can move the pointer to the button it expects you to answer with, making it easy to either click it or select the other button.

- **Display pointer trails**—You can add some excitement to your screen by using pointer trails. This option resembles a snake trailing behind the mouse pointer as you move it across the screen. This option enhances the visibility of the pointer for some people. Figure 17.4 shows you an example of pointer trails in use.

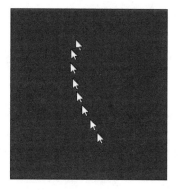

FIGURE 17.4

Mouse pointer trails help you locate the mouse pointer on the screen, plus they add some fun to the display.

- **Hide pointer while typing**—You might find you are distracted by the mouse pointer when you stop scrolling to type into your computer.. Windows provides an option to hide the pointer while you type..

- **Reveal location of pointer**—Some users describe difficulty in locating the mouse pointer on the screen, especially when they use large monitors.. By turning on the Reveal Location of Pointer option on, you can flash an easy-to-spot signal locating the pointer by pressing the Ctrl key, as shown in Figure 17.5.

- **Scroll wheel**—Some mice today come with a scroll wheel. The scroll is positioned near the front of the mouse, enabling you to access it as easily as you can the mouse buttons. You turn the wheel when you need to scroll up or scroll down. The vertical scrolling setting controls the sensitivity of the wheel. The setting is measured in the number of lines scrolled for every notch you spin in the wheel. Some mice even provide a horizontal wheel, enabling you to move left to right and vice versa without moving the mouse.

To change any of the preceding settings, follow these steps:

1. Open Control Panel. Select the **Devices and Printers** category and select **Mouse**. This opens the Mouse Properties window, as shown in Figure 17.6.

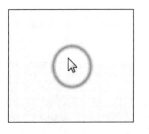

FIGURE 17.5

The Reveal location of pointer option helps you locate the pointer simply by pressing the Ctrl key.

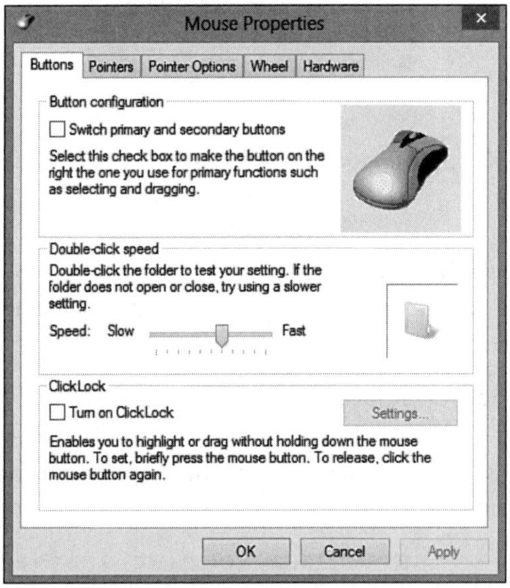

FIGURE 17.6

Change many of settings controlling how your mouse works in the Mouse Properties dialog box.

2. To change the primary mouse button, on the Buttons tab, select **Switch Primary and Secondary Buttons**.. Click or tap the **Switch Primary and Secondary Buttons** setting to clear the check box, making the left button the primary button. The option takes effect immediately. You need to use the right mouse button to select **OK** to close this dialog box if **Switch Primary and Secondary Buttons** is selected.

3. To adjust the double-click speed, select the **Buttons** tab. Then, adjust the **Speed** slider to the wanted speed. This setting takes effect immediately, even before you select **OK** to close the dialog box.

4. On the Buttons tab, select **Turn on ClickLock** to enable the Click for Drag setting.

5. To set the pointer speed, select the **Pointer Options** tab, as shown in Figure 17.7. Then, move the **Pointer Speed** slider to set the speed of the pointer as you move it across the screen.

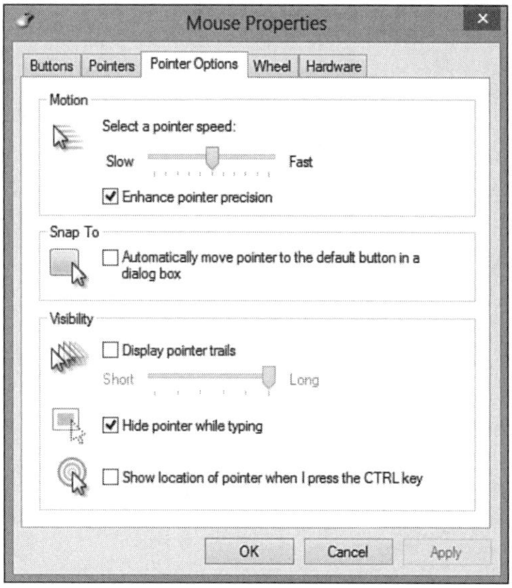

FIGURE 17.7

Many of the mouse options are set on the Properties tab.

6. Select **Enhance Pointer Precision** if you need tight precision with your mouse, such as click and dragging small objects on the screen, or drawing images on the screen. This setting is on the Pointer Options tab.

7. To snap the pointer to the default button, in a pop-up dialog box (when one appears), select **Automatically Move Pointer to the Default Button in a Dialog Box**. This option is on the Pointer Options tab.

8. On the Pointer Options tab, select **Display Pointer Trails**, and then move the slider between Short and Long to create the effect.

9. On the Pointer Options tab, select **Hide Pointer While Typing** and/or **Show Location of Pointer When I Press the CTRL Key** to enable these options previously described.

10. From the Wheel tab, as shown in Figure 17.8, select the up or down buttons on the Vertical Scrolling box to determine how much vertical space is covered by one click of the wheel on your mouse. You may also enter the value by hand.

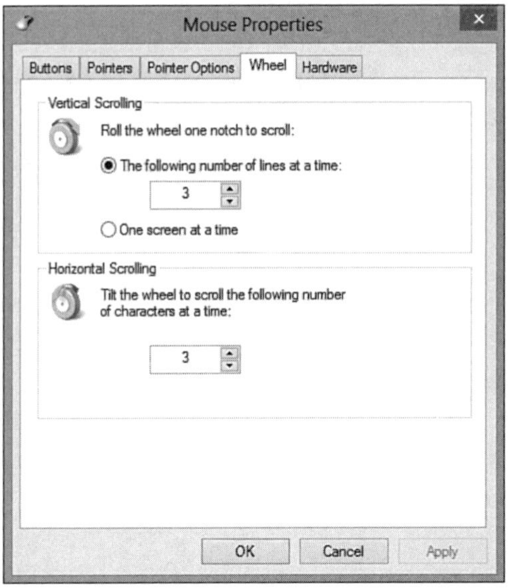

FIGURE 17.8

If your mouse has a scroll button, you can set a number of scroll wheel options on the Wheel tab.

11. Select **OK** to close the dialog box, and save the various changes you made to the mouse settings. Select **Cancel** to discard the changes. Select **Apply** to save the changes without closing the dialog box.

Changing the Mouse Pointers Used on the Desktop

You might want to customize the mouse pointers you use in Windows. You can adjust the pointers to reflect your personality and taste, or you might need to switch to pointers that are larger than normal to make it easier to see them. There are ten different pointers you can customize, such as the selection pointer and the double-arrow head pointer. You can customize one or more of the pointers individually, or you can switch to a full set of ten pointers.

To change mouse pointers, follow these steps:

1. Open the Mouse Properties window. To do so, first search for a setting named **mouse**. Select the Mouse tile from the list of results on the left side of the screen.

   If you have the Desktop app open, right-click/press-and-tap a clear spot on the Desktop, and then click **Personalize**. Next, click **Change Mouse Pointers** near the top-left corner of the window.

2. To use a predefined set of pointers, scroll through the schemes at the top of the dialog box. Select a scheme to inspect the pointers. If you find a scheme you like, select **OK**. Select **OK** again to close the Personalization window.

3. To choose a specific mouse pointer without committing to a set, select the pointer in the list

4. Click or tap **Browse**. A window appears displaying the mouse pointers available to you.

    NOTE You can change the appearance of the mouse pointers in the dialog box used to select a new pointer. Select the View Menu button from the toolbar, and then select the view you want. The Medium Icons view presents the most useful arrangement of icons.

5. Select the pointer you want to use from the list, and then click **Open**. You should be at the Mouse Properties dialog box.

6. Select the next pointer you want to customize, and then repeat steps 5 and 6.

7. Click or tap **OK**.

8. Click the **Close** button to close the Personalization window.

Setting Up Your Keyboard

Though the keyboard is an important part of your computer, there are just a few settings you can change:

- Setting how rapidly characters repeat across the screen
- Setting when a character starts repeating across the screen
- Setting the cursor blink rate
- Using the keyboard in place of a mouse

Note that language and keyboard input settings are discussed in Chapter 4, "Personalizing Windows 8."

There are two settings that control what occurs when you depress a key on the keyboard to repeat the key's character on the page. These settings might not be useful for your everyday work unless you design a form or a document that includes underlines to enter information or characters to create a border.

- **How long a key is depressed before the character begins repeating**—If this setting is too short, the slightest delay in moving your finger off of a key causes the character to begin repeating across the screen (depending on the program you use).

- **How rapidly the character repeats**—This rate can span from a steady pulse to a staccato spray of the character across the screen.

To access the screens where the repeating character rates are set, do the following:

1. Open the Keyboard Properties dialog box. To do so, search for a setting by the name "keyboard." Select the keyboard tile from the list of results on the left side of the screen. The Keyboard Properties should appear, as shown in Figure 17.9.

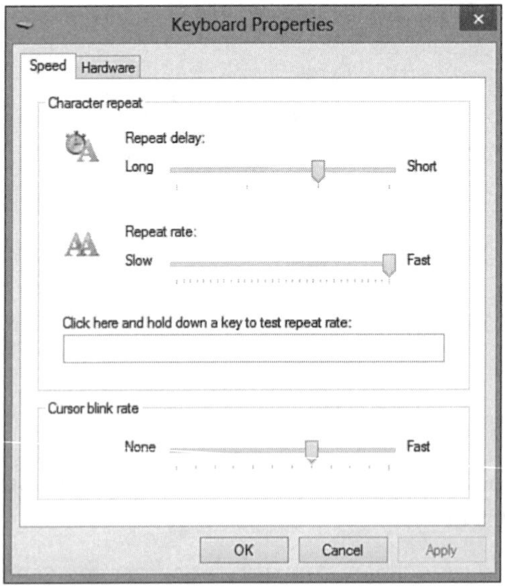

FIGURE 17.9

Set the character repeating rate in the Keyboard Properties dialog box.

2. Drag the pointer on each of the two sliders to the wanted speed. Try your settings in the box in the middle of the dialog box.

3. You may also adjust the rate the cursor blinks across all Windows 8 in the Keyboard Properties dialog box. Drag the pointer along the Cursor blink rate slider to the wanted speed.

4. Select **OK** to save your settings.

Setting Up Sound

Setting up how sound works in Windows 8 might seem like a task that should not be required. Shouldn't your computer play your music and ding and chime at all the appropriate occasions without you having to do anything? The answer, of course, is yes. In this section, though, you learn a few things that are not quite obvious, such as how to get the best sound from the speakers you just purchased how to specify what sounds you hear when certain events occur.

Setting Up Your Speakers

If you play videos or music on your computer, having a set of speakers, or at least headphones, is a requirement. Most computers today can take advantage of a set of surround speakers configured for movies and games—all the way down to two little desktop speakers.

These days, plugging-in speakers is easy. Each of the plugs from your speakers are colored, and the jacks in the back of your computer also are colored. Just match the colors and you're good to go. Follow the instructions provided with your hardware to be sure your speakers are set up correctly. After everything is plugged in correctly, follow these steps to set up the sound quality and configuration:

1. Open the Sound dialog box. To do so, open the **Charms** bar and select **Search**. Select **Settings** and enter "sound" in the search box. Select **Sound** when it appears in the results on the left side of the screen. The Sounds dialog box appears.

2. Select the **Playback** tab.

3. Select the Speakers device and then select **Configure**. The Speaker Setup dialog box appears, as shown in Figure 17.10.

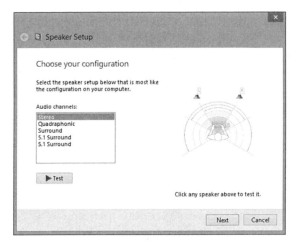

FIGURE 17.10

You must indicate to Windows 8 how to configure your speaker setup.

4. Select your speaker setup from the list. The diagram shows you the configuration. Select **Test** to hear a test sound rotate through each of the speakers. Or click a speaker to hear just one. Select **Next.**

5. On the next screen, you can add or remove speakers from the configuration you just picked (see Figure 17.11). Select **Next**.

FIGURE 17.11

You can add speakers to the configuration matching the real setup.

6. Select the relative size of your speakers, whether small satellites or larger speakers. Select **Next**.

7. Select **Finish**.

8. Try out your configuration with music, videos, and DVDs. Feel free to run through the steps again to fine-tune the setup. Finally, don't be scared to select a configuration that sounds great even if it doesn't match your real setup. You're the boss!

Selecting Sounds for Windows Events

Windows 8 is set up to play certain sounds when various events occur, such as when Windows 8 needs your attention, when an email message arrives, when your battery reaches a low level, and many more. You can change the settings that are set up with Windows 8, such as using the Windows 8 start up sound when email arrives. Or you can use your own sounds, such as gag sounds or short excerpts of music, with Windows 8 events.

Individual sounds are stored in small files that end in .WAV or .MP3. If you have sound files stored elsewhere on your computer, such as if you downloaded sounds from the Internet (certain websites enable you to download famous quotes and sounds from popular movies), you can use them in place of the sounds provided to you by Windows 8.

To set up your own sounds for Windows events, follow these steps:

1. Open the Sound dialog box. To do so, open the **Charms** bar and select **Search**. Select **Settings** and enter **sound** in the search box. Select **Sound** when it appears in the results on the left side of the screen. The Sounds dialog box appears, as shown in Figure 17.12.

2. To use a prebuilt list of sounds already assigned to Windows 8 events, select the scheme from the Sound Scheme list, as shown in Figure 17.13.

3. Select the event in the Program Events list.

4. Select the sound to associate with the event you select from the **Sounds** drop-down list. To use a custom sound, select **Browse**, and navigate through your file system to find the sound file you want to use. Refer to Chapter 15, "Organizing Files and Folders with Windows Explorer," for assistance in navigating the file system.

5. To hear the sound, select the **Test** button.

6. If you are happy with the sound, continue selecting sounds for other events as instructed, starting with step 4. When you finish selecting sounds, continue with the next step.

FIGURE 17.12

You set up a custom sound scheme in the Sounds dialog box.

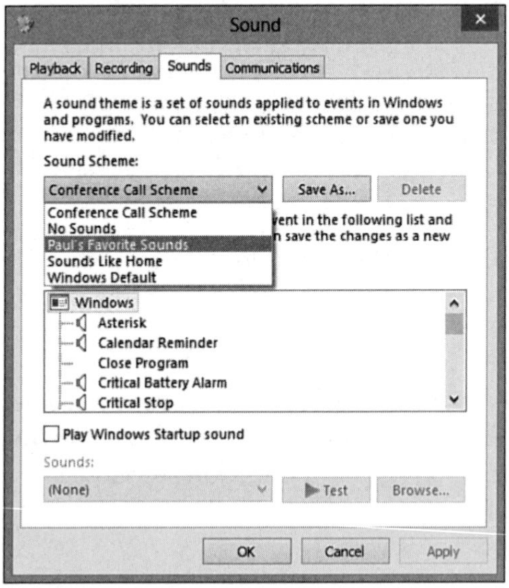

FIGURE 17.13

You can select a Sound Scheme, which is a prebuilt list of sounds assigned to specific system events.

7. To save these new sound settings as a scheme, select **Save As**. Then, enter a name for the scheme, such as **Paul's Favorite Sounds**, and select **OK**. If you want to save your new sounds without committing them to a scheme, select **OK**.

Your new sound set up should be ready to go.

Setting Up Power Use

Windows 8 was released at a time when more people than ever before were aware of the cost and effect of power consumption. Windows 8 is loaded with options enabling you to minimize or simply control power consumption, but these options are helpful beyond wanting to be a good citizen of the environment. If you tend to keep your computer running continually, you may want to consider options to automatically reduce the brightness of your screen after a period of nonuse, as well as other options to reduce wear on your computer. If you travel with Windows 8 installed on a laptop, you may be interested in putting the computer to sleep when you close the laptop to pass security, which makes it easy and quick to restart your computer when on board.

Windows enables you to customize how power is managed on your computer in extreme detail. There are more than 20 different settings you can tweak. One can divide the various methods for setting power options in three groups:

- Easy Method
- Really Easy Method
- Hard Method

You learn the Easy Method and the Really Easy Method here. Before getting into the details, there are a couple terms you should know:

- **Sleep mode**—If you have a problem falling asleep, you might be extremely jealous of Windows 8 your computer. When your computer goes to sleep, which happens in a second, rather than in an hour (like the author's situation), Windows 8 saves any unsaved work and reduces power to the monitor, hard drives, fan, and network connections. Windows takes notice of your system when it goes to sleep, and it retains those settings in a memory where the settings can be accessed and applied quickly. This mode protects your work while the computer sleeps but returns the computer to full power in the same state that you left it in just a few seconds.

- **Hibernate Mode**—Hibernate mode is much like Sleep mode. Hibernate mode also captures the state of your computer so that it can restore it on request, but in Hibernate mode, your computer is powered down. This means restoring a computer from hibernate takes longer. And to be honest, Windows 8 sometimes struggles with the order in which some systems and hardware are restarted, making the restoration fail sometimes.

The Easy Method to Set Up Power Use

The most useful Windows 8 power use settings are the following:

- Specify whether a password is required to unlock your computer after it has been awakened.

- Choose what happens when you press the Power button on your computer.

- Specify the length of time at which you're not at your computer before the display turns off.

- Specify the length of time at which you're not at your computer before the computer goes to sleep.

These options probably give you all the control you need over power use in Windows 8. Here is how to set these up:

1. Open the Power Options dialog box. To do so, search for a setting named **power**, and then select **Power Options** from the list of results on the left side of the screen, as shown in Figure 17.14.

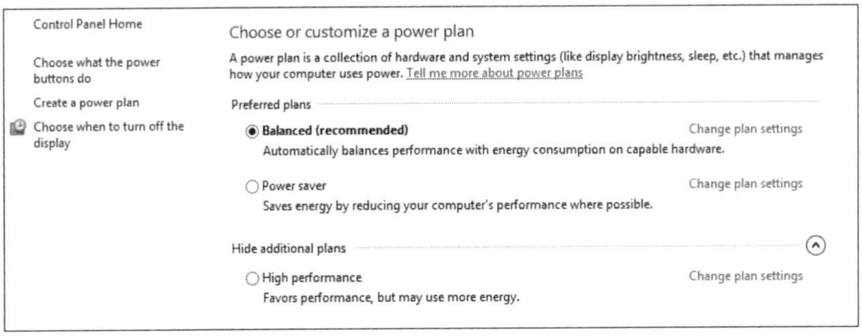

FIGURE 17.14

You can select a predefined power scheme, or create a power scheme of your own design.

2. Select the option you are interested in from the frame on the left. The options are self-explanatory.

The Really Easy Method to Set Up Power Use

The Really Easy method requires you to choose one of a group of *power plans*. A power plan is a prebuilt set of approximately 15 options, each of which manages some aspect of power or energy consumption, such as preventing a slide show from running when the computer is low on battery life. Windows 8 includes one or more power plans, and the company that built your computer might have loaded a plan on the computer. You can create a plan from scratch, change one and give it a new name, or delete one.

Here are some sample power plans:

- **Balanced**—Conserves energy when the computer is not used but uses full power when you are actively working at the computer, such as using multiple applications.

- **High Performance**—Uses full power all the time and will drain power quickly for laptop computers running on a battery.

- **Power Saver**—Reduces power consumption as much as possible, which causes applications to run a bit more slowly, reduces the display's brightness setting, and more.

Follow these steps to select a power plan:

1. Open the Power Options dialog box. To do so, search for a setting named **power**, and then select Power Options from the list of results on the left side of the screen.

2. Select the plan you want to use from the list of plans under preferred, as shown in Figure 17.15. To review the settings for a plan, select the corresponding Change plan settings. Select **Cancel** when you have finished reviewing the plan's settings.

FIGURE 17.15

Select a power plan to engage 15 different power settings.

3. Close the Power Options dialog box. The power settings in the plan you selected should be active.

The Manual Method to Set Up Power Use

The manual method calls for you to specify a value for each of the 20 or so settings. It takes time to do so, but the payoff is a power plan configured to your exact requirements. To do so, select a plan, as previously described in step 2 under "The Really Easy Method to Set Up Power Use." Before you close the Power Options dialog box, as instructed in step 3, select **Change Plan Settings** and then **Change Advanced Power Settings**. Change settings as needed, select **OK**, then **Save Changes**. This updates the plan you select.

THE ABSOLUTE MINIMUM

-   To change the resolution of your display, you must access the Display settings through the Desktop app. Right-click or tap-and-hold on the Desktop (that's right, click the Desktop inside the Desktop app) and select Screen resolution.

-   Windows 8 enables you to position two apps side-by-side on the screen. Positioning these apps is known as snapping the app into place. To snap two Windows 8 apps to the screen at the same time or to snap an app to one side of the screen, the screen resolution must be set to 1366×768 or higher.

-   Windows 8 can accommodate multiple monitors if your computer has the capability. You can specify whether the image from the computer appears on one screen, appears on both screens, or extends across the screens, in effect doubling your screen real estate

-   You can apply a few built-in, ready-to-use power schemes. You can also build your own power scheme that leverages up to 50 different settings.

-   An important component of the power scheme defines what occurs when you press the Power button on your computer. You can specify that pressing the Power button puts the computer to sleep, or you might specify that pressing the Power button actually powers down.

IN THIS CHAPTER

- Setting Up Your Printer and Scanner
- Configuring Your Fax Software and Your Modem
- Sending and Receiving Faxes
- Printing from the Desktop and from the Start Screen

18

PRINTING, SCANNING, AND FAXING IN WINDOWS 8

Many beginning Windows 8 users struggle with scanning pictures and documents and with faxing. And because so many people take advantage of the incredible pricing to get all-in-one devices that include a printer, scanner, and fax machine, printing can be a struggle for some, too. In this chapter, you learn how to set up each of the three devices and how make one of the all-in-one devices work. You also learn how to easily print from Windows 8, how to scan and receive faxes, and how to scan whatever you need to.

Before diving into the meat of the chapter, there's one more introductory topic to discuss. To setup and run your printer, scanner, and fax devices, you may need to work through the Desktop app, as well as with some of the new Windows 8 functions. It may be worth your time to refresh your skills on Windows 8 basics by reviewing Chapter 3, "Learning Windows 8 Basics." In particular, review the information related to the Charms bar.

Printing in Windows 8

There's no mystery or confusion in printing with Windows 8. You need to set up the printer, which could take a few more steps if Windows 8 doesn't automatically recognize it. With your printer set up, printing is just one or two clicks away. First, though, take a look at setting up your printer in Windows 8.

Setting Up a New Printer

Most printers you acquire have specific instructions about how to set up the device. The instructions will be detailed, such as indicating in what order you should insert the CD/DVD into the computer, connect the printer to the computer, and so on. If you make a mistake, you may have to uninstall everything and start from the beginning again, so follow the manufacturer's instructions.

After you follow the printer manufacturer's instructions, open **Control Panel**, and then select **Devices and Printers** to verify your new printer appears in the list of printers, as shown in Figure 18.1.

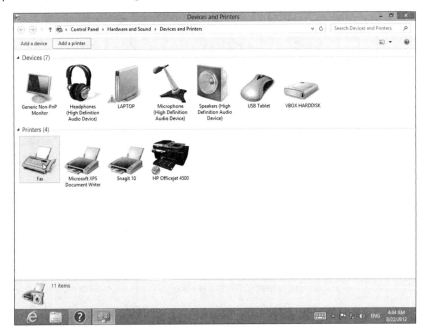

FIGURE 18.1

If you installed your printer correctly, it should appear in the Devices and Printers catalog.

If you come into possession of a printer and you do not have the instructions or CD/DVD, you can visit the manufacturers' website to investigate whether you can review the instructions and possibly download the software. Another option is to simply connect the printer to your computer with the hope that Windows 8 recognizes it. Unless you have an obscure printer, there's a good chance Windows 8 can pick it up automatically.

 NOTE If you had a wireless network in place when you installed Windows 8 AND there was a printer also installed in that network, Windows 8 adds that printer to its list of devices automatically.

Printing in Windows 8

Printing is simple in Windows 8, although you might not consider a task *simple* when you must go to two places to accomplish it. Whether you print from a Desktop program or a new Windows 8 app determines how you print:

- If you use a program that runs in the Desktop environment, you can print using the program's print mechanism. Usually that means you should open the **File** menu in the program you use, and select **Print**. If you do not see a Print command, right-click and check the menu that appears to see if it contains a Print command. Because you use a Desktop program, there will be little consistency to printing—your mileage will vary! Figures 18.2 show an example of the print dialog box in a Desktop program.

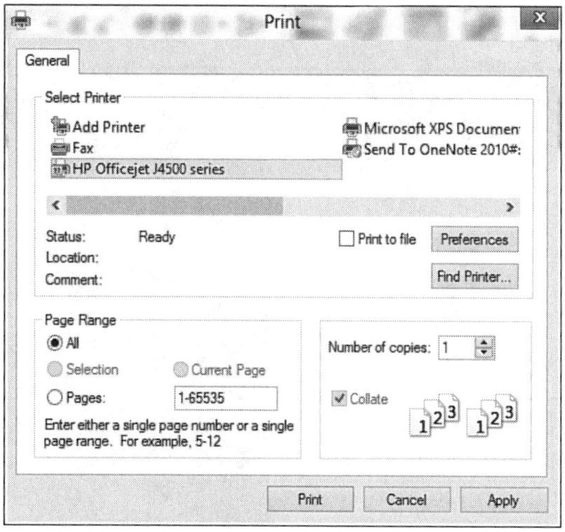

FIGURE 18.2

Desktop programs such as WordPad do not use the centralized printing offered to Windows 8 apps.

- To print from a printer-enabled Windows 8 app, open the **Charms** bar and select **Devices**. Figure 18.3 shows the Devices screen with one printer installed. Select the printer you want to use from the list. You then see a screen like the one shown in Figure 18.4. If you need to access more printing options, select **More Settings**. Make your selections; then go back to the main printing page. When you're ready to print, select **Print**.

FIGURE 18.3

The Devices screen shows all devices, including printers, that you can use with the Windows 8 app.

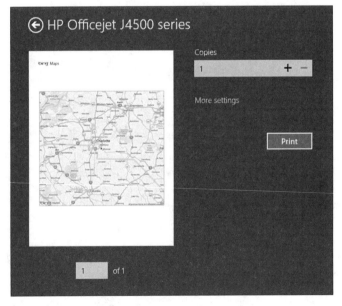

FIGURE 18.4

You can use all of the capabilities and features of your printer in Windows 8.

NOTE You may need to print while your printer is not working properly (maybe it's out of ink), perhaps not even installed, or if, for example, you're on the road. Windows enables you to create a file called an XPS file that is formatted exactly how the paper would have been formatted had you printed using a device.

Later, when your printer is available, you can print the file without opening the app that generated it. This is useful when you absolutely need to capture information as it is presented in an application at a specific time and when you can't bring the application to that state.

To print to an XPS file, simply choose the XPS file device when you select the Devices charm or from the Print dialog box if you use a desktop app (refer to Figure 18.2).

Faxing in Windows 8

You can send and receive faxes in Windows 8 without the need for a fax machine. Here are the absolute minimum items you need to send and receive faxes in Windows 8:

- **Dial-up Modem**—A dial-up modem is a device that connects your computer to other devices by piggybacking information on the telephone. You need a modem to both send and receive fax documents. You can purchase a modem that connects to your computer via USB. You cannot use the connection or hardware that connects your computer to the Internet, like your cable modem or DSL.

- **Telephone cord**—You need a cord long enough to run between the modem connected to your computer and the wall jack.

- **Working analog phone line**—Standard analog phone service is needed. This is the phone service you may still have, although many people now use an alternative phone service, such as an Internet phone (using your broadband connection to the Internet to carry your telephone service) provided by a company such as Vonage or via your cable provider.

- **Windows Fax and Scan**—You need software you use to set up your fax, such as specifying the phone number, cover letter, document to fax, and so on. Windows 8 comes with an application that manages both faxing and scanning. To open it, open the **Charms** bar and select **Search**. Type **fax** and then select **Windows Fax and Scan** from the results on the left.

NOTE If you are at a larger office preparing to fax from Windows 8, you might have access to a fax server. A fax server is a computer that provides modem-like services for the computers and devices in the office from which people send and receive faxes.

Sending a Fax

Follow these steps to send a fax:

1. Be sure the telephone line is connected to the modem, and be sure the modem is powered on if it has a power control.

2. Open the Windows Fax and Scan application described in the previous section.

3. Select **File**, **New, Fax**. With that, the New Fax window appears, as shown in Figure 18.5.

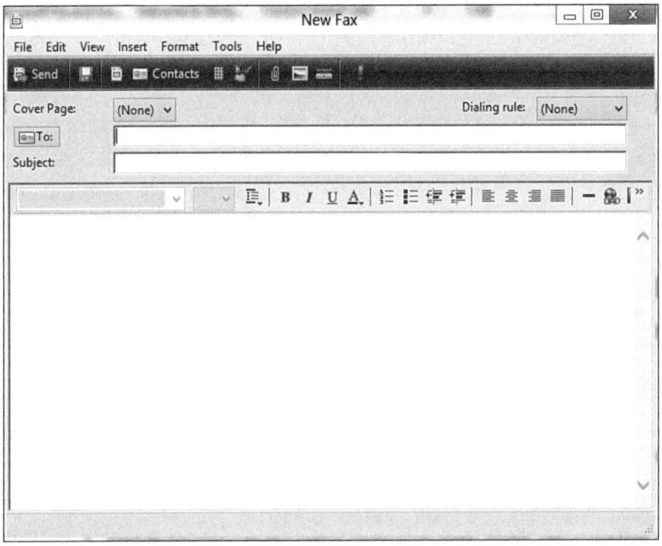

FIGURE 18.5

You are ready to enter the recipient fax number and message as soon as you select New, Fax.

4. Select **Tools**, **Sender Information**. Enter the information that you want to appear in the fax cover page, as shown in Figure 18.6.

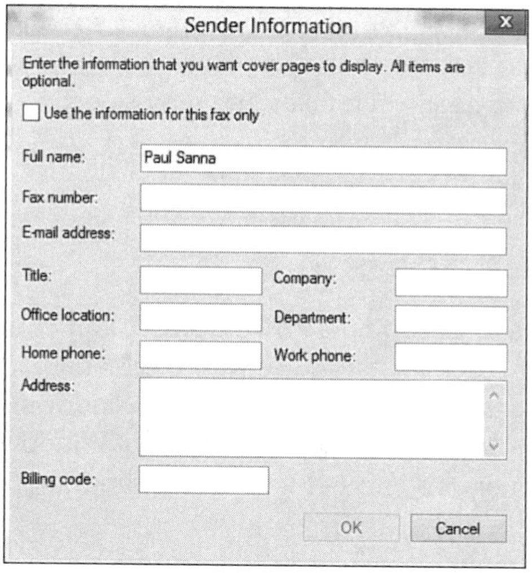

FIGURE 18.6

You can set up your fax cover page simply by filling out this form.

5.   Enter the phone number to fax to. If the fax recipient is in your Windows address book, select **To** and then select the name from the list of contacts.

6.   To fax a document saved on your computer, select **Insert** and then **File Attachment**. Browse for your file. When you locate it, select it and select the **Attach** button at the bottom of the Insert Attachment dialog box.

7.   To fax an image you scanned, select **Insert** and then **Pages from Your Scanner**. Windows attempts to connect to your scanner. Follow the instructions below under Scanning Pictures and Documents for help in scanning.

8.   Enter any information you choose in the Subject box and in the middle empty pane. The empty pane can include a greeting or a short note. There is no need to enter your name or contact info because you supplied this information earlier.

9.   Select **Send**. The fax process should start. Depending on the options you set for tracking and notifications, you see updates and hear sounds as your fax moves through the system to your recipient.

Receiving a Fax

To ensure your system is prepared to receive a fax, select **Tools** and then **Fax Settings**. Under the General tab, be sure your fax device is selected, and you have selected the option to allow the device to receive faxes. You may also set how fax calls are answered, either manually or after a specific number of rings. Finally, under the Tracking tab, select the notifications you want to receive, and set the sounds you want to hear when faxes arrive by selecting Sound options.

Your faxes appear in the Inbox folder on the main Windows Fax and Scan page.

Scanning in Windows 8

To scan pictures and documents in Windows 8, you need a scanner connected to your computer. Look for a scanner with the Made for Windows 8 logo. You can also use a scanner that states support for Windows 7 because there are a few scanners that can work with Windows 7, but not Windows 8. It's a good idea to do some research on the Internet first before shopping and purchasing a scanner.

Setting Up Your Scanner

If your scanner is part of an all-in-one device, it should be installed if you have run through the set up process. If not, you should carefully follow the instructions provided with your scanner. The instructions are detailed, such as indicating exactly when you should insert the CD/DVD into the computer, when you should connect the scanner to the computer, and so on.

After you follow the manufacturer's instructions, open Control Panel, and then select **Devices and Printers** to verify your scanner appears in the list.

 NOTE If you come into possession of a scanner and you do not have the instructions or CD/DVD, you can visit the manufacturers' website to investigate whether you can review the instructions and possibly download the software. Another option is to simply connect the scanner to your computer with the hope that Windows recognizes it.

Scanning in Windows 8

Scanning a document in Windows 8 is a snap. Follow these steps:

1. Be sure the scanner is connected to your computer and is powered on.

2. Place the document or picture on the scanner glass or feeder, as required by the device.

3. Open the Windows Fax and Scan tool. To do so, open the **Search** charm and enter **Windows Fax**.

4. Select **Windows Fax and Scan** from the results that appear on the left.

5. Select the **Fax** button at the bottom-left corner of the Windows Fax and Scan window.

6. Select the **New Scan** button on the toolbar.

7. Your scan device should begin feeding in your document, and the scanning should start. If this does not occur, you may need to initiate the scanning on the device. Check the documentation for instructions on starting a scan from the device.

8. When the scan is complete, it appears on the screen.

9. Select **File, Save as** from the menu, and then enter a name for the scanned file. The document will be saved to a folder named Scanned Documents in your home folder. Refer to Chapter 15, "Organizing Files and Folders with File Explorer," for assistance to navigate files and folders on your computer.

THE ABSOLUTE MINIMUM

If you remember just a few points from this chapter, let them be these three tips:

- Follow the manufacturer's instructions carefully if you purchased or acquired a new printer, scanner, or all-in-one-device.

- To print from the Desktop app, use the program's printing features.

- To print from a Windows 8 app, open the **Charms** bar and select **Devices**. This puts you in contact with your printer.

SAFE AND PRIVATE INTERNET COMPUTING

For something so exciting, enormously helpful, always entertaining, and extremely valuable, the Internet can be a dangerous place. There's risk at every corner of having your personal information stolen, of viruses spreading to your computer, of fake versions of your favorite websites appearing, designed to fool you into entering private information, and of software secretly loading itself on your computer to track your every Internet move. It's certainly sad that individuals try to take what's yours, but after you accept the reality of the situation, you must address the threat and prepare your defenses. This chapter reviews all the important tools available to a beginning Windows 8 user to ensure safe and private Internet computing.

WINDOWS 8 APPS VERSUS DESKTOP APPS

You learned in Chapter 6, "Surfing the Web in Windows 8," that there are two versions of Internet Explorer installed with Windows 8: a Windows 8 app version and a Desktop version. The Windows 8 version generally offers fewer opportunities for malicious software to find its way onto your computer through the browser. The instructions in this chapter refer to the Desktop version of Internet Explorer unless noted otherwise. This means, for example, if you are instructed to select **Tools** and then **Safety** from the menu, you should do so with the Desktop browser. Any settings you change in the Desktop browser automatically apply to the Windows 8 version, too, where appropriate. This means you don't need to switch between both browsers to adjust the same setting.

Understanding Internet Threats and Risks

You might be surprised at the large number and wide variety of risks and threats in the Internet world. Despite the increasing proliferation of all these threats and risks, there's just two parts to the strategy needed to protect you: 1) Learn the threats and 2) Raise the defense. The first part of the strategy is the goal of this chapter. You learn about the myriad ways you can find trouble browsing the web, emailing friends and family, and just plain staying connected to the web.

Web Browsing Risks

The web browser is your doorway to information, news, fun stuff, art, science, and everything in between. The browser can also be a doorway to your personal information, as well as to a launchpad for viruses and other malware. The following is a list of risks that exist while you simply and innocently browse the web:

- Most websites use small files known as *cookies* to help keep track of your preferences as you move from page to page, as well as to remind the site who you are when you return to the site. These cookies are created and then stored on your computer. Cookies can contain whatever information a website needs to provide to a pleasant browsing experience, including personal information. You have probably figured out by now that cookies would be attractive to people interested in you and your personal details. Although cookies are not a risk on their own, a risk is created when access to them is not controlled.

There is some wisdom to never allowing cookies onto your computer. You can direct Internet Explorer to reject all cookies. Doing so, however, prevents some sites from working with your browser. Instead you can use a feature of Internet Explorer called InPrivate Browsing, which enables cookies to be temporarily stored only in a secured area of your computer and then removes them when you leave the site. You can read about InPrivate Browsing later in the chapter.

- Web pages cannot on their own run programs on your computer except to show pages in your browser. Websites with bad intentions have been known to display a pop-up message in which the buttons trigger a program that *can* run on your computer. These programs can do anything, including installing a virus, spreading the virus through your contacts, accessing the network you're attached to, and so on. Not only are pop-up messages annoying, but they represent a potential strong safety risk. Never activate a pop-up message if you don't know what it is.

- If you download software from the web either to try out or for purchase, you are introducing risk to your system. Most of these software downloads are safe, particularly if they come from a known publisher or developer. The installation program does nothing more than load the software onto your computer. Some of these installation programs, especially for smaller try-before-you buy programs, secretly install spyware when they install the program you selected. Spyware is software that secretly tracks your clicks and web browsing, creating a profile of your interests. Worse though, spyware can capture your keystrokes, making it easy to determine your passwords, as well as credit card and banking information.

There are other less significant risks associated with simply browsing the web, but the preceding list represents the most significant threats. To summarize, viruses can land on your computer from pop-ups and other malicious sites (see phishing threats later), cookies can expose personal information, and downloads from the web potentially can contain dangerous, hidden spyware.

Understanding threats exposed by browsing the web is just half of the story. Up next is a review of threats exposed through email.

Learning About Risky Attachments and Other Email-Related Threats

If you have ever opened an attachment in an email sent by someone you didn't know or barely knew, or you opened an attachment not quite sure of the contents, congratulations, you dropped yourself in the middle of a minefield.

Attachments represent more risk than just about any other email or even computer practice. A party looking to ruin your day can package anything they like in an otherwise friendly attachment, including viruses. What might appear like a file filled with jokes or as a larger file containing a cute movie (maybe the file is called "funny_kitty_video") can contain a program that sends a virus in an attachment to every address in your contact list.

Be suspicious of an email with an attachment. If your suspicions outweigh your confidence, see if you can figure out the email address of the sender. Maybe you already have it. Ask them if they sent the email. If so, you should be in good shape. If they don't recall sending it, delete it immediately; as it's likely a piece of malware automatically sent the email from your associate's email account.

Consider the following questions. If you answer no to even one of the questions, you should not open the attachment.

- Do you know the sender?

- Have you received email from the sender before? Have you received an email with an attachment before?

- Were you expecting an email with attachments? Can you guess what's in the attachment?

There is one more feature to worry about when it comes to preventing Internet monkey business while reading email. Your email program might have a feature in which email is automatically displayed in a small window as soon as you scroll over the message in a list, as shown in Figure 19.1. This feature is known as the Preview Pane in Microsoft Outlook. Without specifically intending to, you are opening an email when it appears in your Preview Pane, and some malware is programmed to run or spread the moment the email containing it is read.

Learning Phishing Threats

You may have come across the term *phishing* as something you should be concerned about. This term has nothing to do with pulling creatures out of the sea nor does it refer to the popular improvisation band formed at the University of Vermont. Rather, phishing refers to the practice of trying to gain access to personal information by posing in email (or Twitter, or instant messaging, and so on) as a reputable or official organization, like your bank, credit card company, or another online company that you respect.

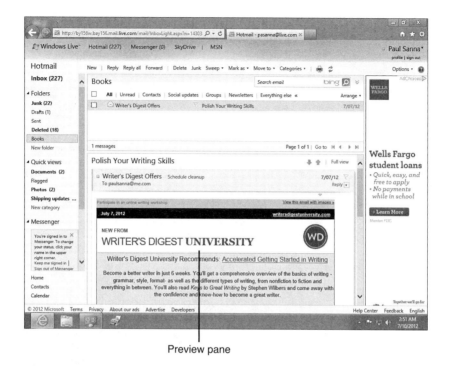

Preview pane

FIGURE 19.1

Scrolling an email through the Preview Pane of your email application can sometimes trigger the loading of a virus.

Phishing scams usually come in the form of an email informing you of some situation that requires confidential information from you. The email appears official, possibly incorporating the organization's colors or logo. You may be told that your account has been upgraded; though your account number or some other form of ID is needed to complete the process. Phishing scams also involve a request for your help in claiming millions of dollars for a cousin or friend (which would require use of your personal account to hold the funds) or even yourself (see Figure 19.2).

A typical phishing practice is to use a website address that resembles that of a real organization. For example, the website address of one of the largest banks in North America is www.bankofamerica.com. You might find yourself directed to a website with the address www.bankamericacom.net that has absolutely no relation to the actual Bank of America website whatsoever.

```
RUGBY2011 LOC AWARD TEAM
Johannesburg
South Africa
0001

Dear Sir/Madam

We wish to notify you that your email address was automatically selected during the RUGBY 2011 world
cup finals kick off in New-Zealand and has won you Cash (Cheque) of £3000.000.00 GBP (Three Million
Great Britain Pounds) Payable through our Paying Bank.

Kindly note that you're Ref: RUGBY2011/00453/NL/11 falls within our Afro booklet Regional
Headquarters representative office in Johannesburg, South Africa as indicated in the play coupon.
All participants were selected automatically World Wide through a computer draw system and emails
were generated from over 1 0, 000.00 internet email service providers. For security reasons, you are
advised to keep your winning information confidential until your claim is processed.

You are hereby advised to Contact Mr. Harry A. Dominic the appointed agent for the immediate release
of your winnings fund:

Your winning prize has been insured and Deposited in our Paying bank an Escrow Account Pending your
Claim with this Payment Reference File Number of Deposit"PPC/ZA5622/2011
```

FIGURE 19.2

Scams can arrive at your desktop in many forms, including news about rugby winnings.

The best and only advice is to ignore and delete these emails if you have even the smallest bit of suspicion. Here are some other thoughts about phishing emails:

- Ignore the urgency of the request. Just because the request claims action must be taken in some period of time or something terrible will occur doesn't mean you should trust the claim.

- A bank would never request your account information or Social Security number over email—wouldn't your bank have this information already?

- Ask the question, "Why Me?" Why would you be singled out to help a needy individual get the fortune of money due to them?

- Do not click a link. A link could launch a program or collect information you didn't plan to provide.

- Resist the urge to reply with some sort of message saying they didn't fool you. That just tells them your email address is current and active and should be targeted in the future.

One more useful strategy to defend against phishing attempts is to use a SPAM blocker. *SPAM* is the term used for unwanted email or advertisements or junk email. A SPAM blocker monitors your inbound email and traps SPAM as it travels to your inbox. With most SPAM blockers, you can configure whether SPAM is immediately deleted, filed to a Junk email folder, or left for you to deal with. A SPAM blocker can sometime capture phishing scam emails. Your Internet service provider (ISP) probably provides a SPAM blocker. You should also search the web for a highly rated option, free or otherwise.

Avoiding Virus Threats

If you have heard anything about Internet risks, it's probably about viruses. A *computer virus* is a piece of software introduced to a computer that can reproduce itself. Usually, a virus doesn't simply reproduce itself and then go dormant. Viruses can make unwanted changes to your computer's setup, sometimes significantly damaging your system. And because a virus replicates itself, a virus usually is concerned with finding its way to other computers, such as by leveraging a contact list or by attempting to infiltrate computers if you connect to a network.

A virus can get onto to your computer in a number of different ways:

- On a CD/DVD you acquire
- Attached to an email
- On a removable drive you attach to your computer
- From a network you connect to

A good antivirus program defends against a virus accessing your system in each of these methods. In addition, all the safe computing guidance presented throughout this chapter also can help protect you. Follow the advice later in the "Absolute Minimum" section.

 It's worth overstating that your antivirus program can do its job only if it's kept up to date. You should regularly confirm that your antivirus program is updated with the latest virus definitions available to it.

Defending Yourself

Unfortunately, Windows 8 does not have a single big button that, by clicking it, defends you from all browsing and email threats. You need to maintain a number of defenses to ensure your data, equipment, reputation, privacy, personal information, and finance are protected.

Each of the following sections describes a component of your Internet defense strategy. The last section of the chapter describes how to bring the various pieces together to create a whole strategy.

Reviewing All-in-One Internet Defense Suites

Many beginners ask the same question about protecting themselves and their computers from Internet threats: Should they buy one of those all-in-one Internet defense suites. The answer to the question is yes, as long as one of the top suites is selected. Here's why:

- Internet threats are constantly evolving and growing. It makes sense to rely on a larger organization that can keep pace with new threats.

- Protecting yourself requires a wide strategy of defense. Although you are capable to raise this defense using the tools available in Windows, a commercial suite can guarantee there are no holes in your defense.

- Many of the solutions also provide coverage for more than one computer.

You should expect to pay approximately $100 and then a nominal fee to update every year. There are plenty of unbiased reviews available on the Internet to help you select a suite.

Defending with Windows Defender

Windows 8 has a built-in antivirus/spyware application known as Windows Defender. Although free software sometimes is viewed skeptically, Windows Defender is quite good. There is no reason not to use it.

Some of the most important Windows Defender features and options you should know about include

- **Updated Definitions**—Windows automatically and regularly updates both virus and spyware definitions. You can also force an update if you like. As soon as the Microsoft security engineers detect the introduction of a new virus into the Internet, a definition of the virus is created and downloaded to all Windows Defender users.

- **Choose How to Deal With Potential Problems**—Windows Defender enables you to review past situations in which the software identified content that had the potential to be a problem. You can see the list of everything suspected as being malicious, see the list of those that you identified as known and okay, and you can see the list of programs that indeed were found to be malicious and have been quarantined.

- **Real-Time Protection**—This option determines whether Windows Defender continually scans your system activity, assessing programs and files your computer comes in contact with. The alternative is to set up Windows Defender to review for malicious files during a regularly scheduled scan. Real-Time Protection should be enabled at all times.

- **Exclude File Types, Names, Locations**—You can specify that certain files be excluded from scanning. You can identify these files by their name, location, or their type. Many people exclude their photos library and their music library if they know for sure that they were the provider of the songs and pictures.

- **Scan or Exclude Removable Drives**—This option determines whether external drives connected to your computer also should be scanned for viruses, and so on.

Setting up Windows Defender

Follow these steps to set up Windows Defender:

1. Open the **Charms** bar and select **Search**.

2. Enter **Defender** and select **Apps**.

3. Select **Windows Defender** from the results on the left. You should see a screen like the one shown in Figure 19.3.

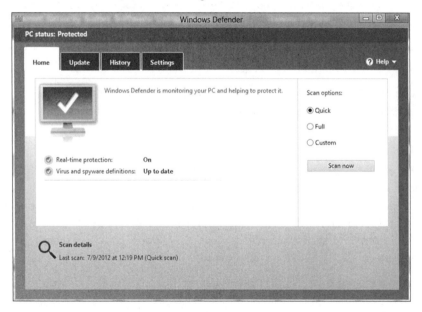

FIGURE 19.3

Windows Defender is built into Windows 8.

4. Select **Settings**.

5. Select **Real-Time Protection** from the list of settings, and be sure the Real-Time Protection setting is selected. This way, dangerous or malicious programs are identified instantly as soon as they approach your computer.

6. Select **Excluded Files and Locations** from the list of settings. Unless you have been told to exclude certain files, folders, or drives from protection by Windows Defender, the lower of the two lists on the screen should be empty. To remove an entry from the list, select it and then select **Remove**. You would not want a key folder, such as Documents, or a key drive, such as C, excluded.

7. Select **Excluded File Types** from the list of settings. Unless you have been told to exclude certain types of files from protection by Windows Defender, the lower of the two lists on the screen should be empty. If there is an entry in the bottom of the two lists that you do not recognize, such as EXE files, select the entry and then select **Remove**.

8. Select **Advanced** from the list of settings. You should accept the default choice under **Remove Quarantined File after of 3 Months**. Otherwise, leave all settings as you found them. The only exception is if you find yourself exchanging removable drives often, perhaps as a way to share photos, and then select **Scan Removable Drives**.

9. If you made any changes in steps 5–8, select **Save Changes**. Otherwise, select **Cancel**.

With the steps completed, Windows Defender is set up to provide you solid protection against viruses and spyware.

Using Windows Defender

There is little for you to do when Windows Defender runs, especially if you have set up the program to automatically receive updated definitions. The only occasion in which you need to take action is when Windows Defender detects a threat, and even then, the only action to take is to look at the offending perp file. Figure 19.4 shows the message you see when Windows Defender detects malware.

For this example, the author used a stream of text characters that resemble a virus saved to a file on the Desktop. Figure 19.5 shows the file in quarantine. At this point, Defender has already removed the file from the Desktop. This is exactly how the program would react to a real virus introduced to your computer.

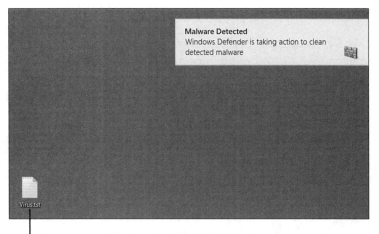

Test "infected" file placed on the desktop

FIGURE 19.4

Windows Defender displays a simple, small message when it believes it has detected a virus.

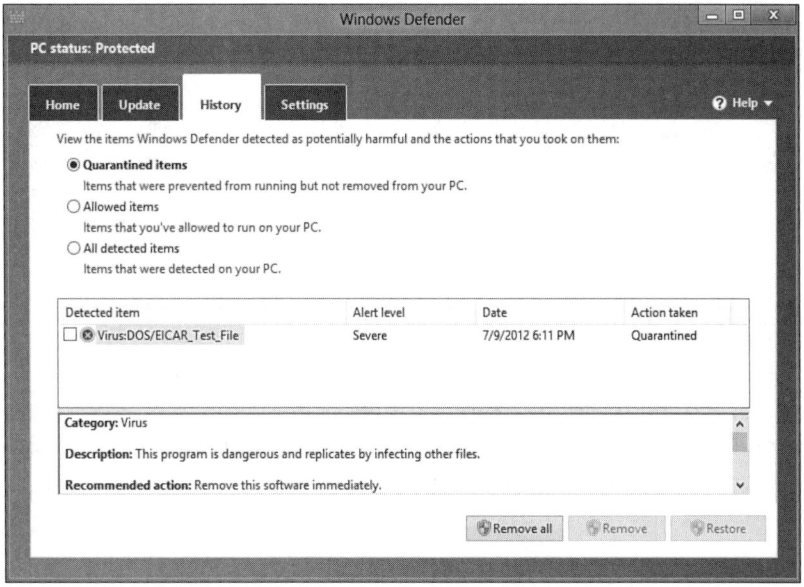

FIGURE 19.5

You can view files quarantined in Windows Defender.

Checking Your Security Status at the Action Center

Windows 8 provides a screen that shows the status of all the settings and controls for protecting your privacy and important personal information. To access the Action Center, search for a setting named Action Center. When the Action Center appears, open the Security section by selecting the down arrow to the right of the label, as shown in Figure 19.6.

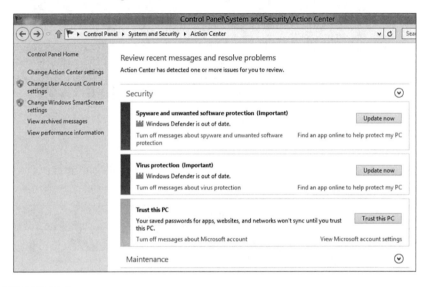

FIGURE 19.6

The Action Center shows you a status of your security options and settings.

Using SmartScreen to Avoid Dangerous Websites

All this discussion about bad people and dangerous sites is made worse by not knowing the good from the bad sites. The SmartScreen feature in Internet Explorer is designed to stop you before visiting bad sites, plus it assists you in a few other areas related to malicious websites.

SmartScreen is a feature in Internet Explorer that monitors the sites you browse to and the files you download for both suspicious files and sites, as well as for sites that are confirmed dangerous and malicious. SmartScreen is passive and unobtrusive, which means you can usually do your thing and not be bothered unless it notices you are doing something that it considers dangerous. There is no reason to turn off SmartScreen filtering except if advised to by a knowledgeable, reputable technical support professional.

Figure 19.7 shows a typical warning when you try to browse to an unsafe site.

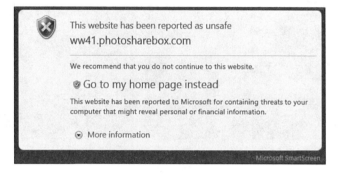

FIGURE 19.7

This is how SmartScreen reports an unsafe website.

If you come across a site that you believe is suspicious, you can easily report it. Even the most innocent-seeming sites, even showing puppies on its home page, can be a phishing site. If you do not want to report a site but would rather check it against Microsoft's list of dangerous sites, you can do so with just a few clicks:

- To report a site you think is dangerous, select **Tools**, **Safety**, and then **Report Unsafe Website** (see Figure 19.8). A page displays asking a few questions about the site you are concerned with.

- To simply check a website, select **Tools**, **Safety**, and then **Check This Website**. You are prompted to continue checking the website. Select **OK**. If the site checks out to be safe, the message in Figure 19.9 appears.

FIGURE 19.8

Although Benji looks lovable, you can report the site where his picture appears as unsafe with just a few menu commands.

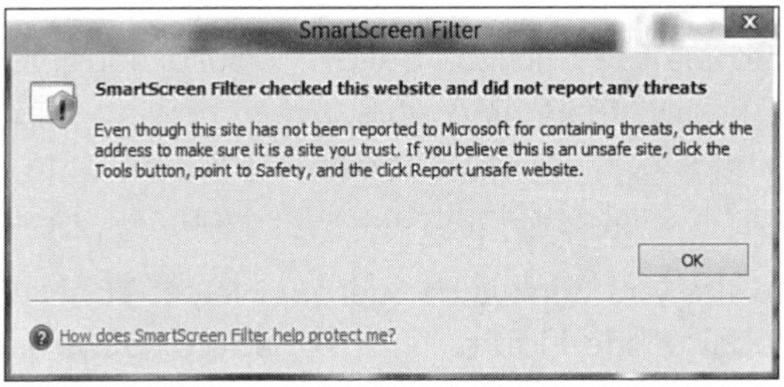

FIGURE 19.9

This is the message you receive when SmartScreen detects no threats with the site you reported.

Covering Your Internet Tracks

Internet Explorer keeps a record of the sites you have visited recently. It keeps this record to help speed up your browsing experience the next time you visit those sites, as well as to make it easy to select a site from a list of those you know the next time you want to visit. This browsing record presents a clear picture of the sites you visit and the pages you browse to. If the computer you use also is used by others, you should consider deleting your browsing history when you are done with Internet Explorer.

- To delete your browsing history, select **Tools**, **Safety**, and then **Delete Browsing History** appears. You can select certain pieces of information not to be deleted, but it makes sense to delete all the fields selected. Select **Delete**.

- To always delete your browsing history when you close the Internet Explorer, select **Tools** and then **Internet Options**. From the Internet Options dialog box that appears, under the General tab, select **Delete Browsing History on Exit**. Select **OK**.

 TIP   If you use the Windows 8 browser, deleting browsing history clears the sites listed in the Frequent sites section, not sites collected in the Tabbed sites.

Browsing Quietly and Invisibly with InPrivate Browsing

Internet Explorer provides a mode of browsing that leaves no trail, evidence, or history of your browsing. It is virtually impossible for anyone using your computer to determine the sites you visited using InPrivate browsing. There are a number of features and tools Windows uses to make your browsing experience a good one, including recording information about your activity at a website, plus using different technologies to show different content (such as movies or animation) on websites. With InPrivate browsing, Windows engages these tools only as needed and quickly erases any evidence that they were used. Although InPrivate browsing might seem similar to the Delete Browsing History explained earlier, InPrivate browsing actively maintains anonymity while you browse.

To switch to InPrivate browsing, select **Tools**, **Safety**, and then **InPrivate Browser**. Using the Windows 8 browser, right-click with your mouse or tap-and-hold with your finger or stylus. Select the Tab Tools button, as shown in Figure 19.10, and then select the **InPrivate** Tab.

FIGURE 19.10

The Tab Tools button gives you access to the InPrivate browsing option.

Using Windows Firewall

A software firewall is a barrier between the computer and the network outside of the computer, the Internet being the network firewalls are most concerned with. Like a physical firewall, a software firewall blocks traffic at the most critical point. A firewall running on a computer like yours usually works with a policy. The policy mandates what information can come through and reach the computer and what can't. The Windows Firewall is aware of most of the mainstream and popular software programs, services, and sites, and it permits traffic out and back between these known sources and your computer.

When the firewall detects communication from an unknown source, it prompts you for action. You can decide whether to permit or deny access. When you acquire new software, there is a chance that the firewall might not recognize it, and you will be asked to create a policy that determines how the firewall should handle communication with the program in the future.

There are dozens of rules that control the firewall's behavior, and each rule has at least one dozen settings. The only setting covered here is the on-off setting. It makes sense to keep the firewall running. When the firewall detects a new application/service/site and alerts you to it, you can determine whether to allow it. If you recognize the application/service/site, allow it. If you don't recognize it, you should deny and then note the source of the warning. You can look into the source, perhaps by searching the Internet, and you can later change the rule of the firewall to either deny always or allow connections for this application/service/site.

Managing All Your IDs and Passwords

If you've used the Internet for any length of time, you know that most sites these days allow (and want) you to register with them, providing at least your email address and asking you to create a password. It can be frustrating, but unless you want to be a web hermit and visit only sites that enable you to use all their features anonymously, you must comply...and that's how the trouble starts. Just how do you maintain all those user IDs and passwords?

You are certain to have read advice that says not to use the same user ID and password at every site that requires credentials. The thinking is that if somehow your user ID and password is disclosed from one site, then you have put at risk your information at all the other sites where you must sign in. But if you follow that advice, how do you possible remember all those IDs and passwords? Here's some advice you can put to good use:

- Group the sites you visit as follows: 1) Sites that hold important financial or personal information, such as credit card, bank, and health-related sites, 2) Sites that have your credit or bank information to make purchases or renew a service, 3) Sites that ask you to register simply to save your preferences, and 4) Sites that do not ask you for credentials.

- Use just one user ID/password combination for Group 3. Create unique user ID/password combinations for each site in Group 1 and Group 2.

- There are a number of password generators on the web. Generate a password for each site in Group 1 and 2.

- Avoid any of the following in any part of your password:

  - Your name or any family member's name

  - A pet's name

  - A favorite anything, such as food, car, color, actor, and musical act

  - Any number relevant to you, such as a street address, part of your birthdate, age, number of children, and so on

  - Anything descriptive about you, such as CheerDad, JuneTeen, or JustTurned30

- Here is perhaps the most radical tip: Purchase a small blank notebook, preferably a nice one with a leather cover. You can also consider one of the newer notebooks with the special paper used, purportedly, by William Faulkner. Use this notebook to store all your user IDs and passwords for Group 1 and Group 2 sites.

  You can use one the online password managers, but they are a hassle to download and keep updated, and not every website works well with them. Also, people tend to create passwords that are easy to use if they have to remember. If you commit your passwords to paper, there's no reason not to go with a complex format. There is little chance of losing the book.

  If you need a password outside of the house, write down the password and place it in your wallet. When was the last time you lost your wallet? Besides, if someone found the small piece of paper in your wallet, what would they do with this information: *t^^Gr11m(xA)*?

THE ABSOLUTE MINIMUM

The following is the absolute minimum steps you should take, as well as how often, to protect yourself from Internet threats:

- Consider investing in an all-in-one Internet security suite, such as from Norton. This way, you gain access to all the tools you need in one package, and you benefit from the two layers of defense by leveraging the free defense tools provided by Windows 8.

- Do not deactivate Windows Defender. Let it run all the time. There is no reason to shut it down.

- Set Internet Explorer to delete your browsing history when you leave the browser.

- Exercise extreme caution when you receive an email with attachments. Unless you know the sender and you expect the email with attachments, do not open the attachment.

- Ignore any emails from anyone that asks you for any kind of personal information. Show extreme caution when these emails appear regardless of how official they appear. Just think, would your bank or other financial institution ask you for your account number? Wouldn't they have it already?

IN THIS CHAPTER

- Keeping Current on Windows Update
- Defragmenting a Hard Drive
- Deleting Unused Files
- Keeping Virus and Antimalware Definitions Current

20

PERFORMING ROUTINE MAINTENANCE

If you installed Windows 8 on your own, you probably found the process both thorough and easy to follow. If you didn't do the install, it actually seems as if Windows installs itself after you answer just one or two questions. As easy as it is to install Windows, there is some regular maintenance to perform on a regular basis once you're up and running. This routine maintenance isn't terribly technical or complicated. Even a user at a beginning level can handle each of the chores described in this chapter. This chapter walks you through these tasks, both helping you understand why this maintenance is important, as well as to carry out the work. At the end of the chapter, you'll find a sample maintenance schedule you can use.

Before diving into the chapter, there is one small but important topic to cover. The tools discussed in this chapter are both new Windows 8 apps, as well as Windows 7 Control Panel applets. You'll enjoy the apps more and also understand the content in this chapter with an understanding of how to navigate through these types of apps. It probably makes sense to review Chapter 3, "Learning Windows 8 Basics," to fully take advantage of the tools and features described in this chapter.

Keeping Current on Windows Update

With a system as large and complicated as Windows 8, it's probably not a surprise there are issue and problems with the software that many folks run into every day. These problems get discovered through ongoing internal testing by Microsoft and by customers and partners who report issues. Problems in software programs are known as *bugs*, and corrections to bugs are known as *fixes*.

Microsoft continually makes fixes available to customers over the Internet. It does so for almost all its products and for many versions of each. Although any particularly serious fixes are released as soon as they're ready, less serious bugs are prioritized and addressed over a long span of time. These fixes are bundled into small units that download to your computer and automatically install themselves.

Windows Update is both the name of the service previously described, as well as the software that controls the entire process on your computer. Here is how the Windows Update service and software works:

- The Windows Update software, which installs automatically into Windows 8, can detect which fixes are appropriate for your computer.

- Windows Update also keeps track of what fixes already have been installed on your computer, so you won't be prompted twice to install a fix.

- You can set the Update process to run automatically, or you can set it up for you to approve each fix suggested for your computer.

- When a fix is available, the Windows Update service both downloads the software and installs the fix.

- You choose whether important updates should be installed automatically. Some advanced users apply updates only after the users have had a chance to review the fixes, fearing compatibility issues with software or hardware presently running properly in their system. It is absolutely recommended to automatically install important updates. Some serious problems can put important data at risk.

 NOTE If you tend to leave applications running and documents open in between work sessions, including leaving your computer in this state overnight, perhaps you should not allow updates to install automatically. Often, an update requires your computer to reboot even if you have open documents or running programs on the Desktop. You might lose work in this scenario or, minimally, you'll need to recover your work from a version of the document automatically saved.

- You can specify when automatic updates should be applied. If you work late in the evening, you should schedule updates to run after your work is complete.

To configure Windows Update:

1. Open the Control Panel.

2. Select **System and Security**, and then select **Windows Update**. The Windows Update dialog box appears, as shown in Figure 20.1.

FIGURE 20.1

You access the Windows Update dialog box from the Control Panel.

3. If the Windows Update dialog box already shows that you are set to automatically install updates, you are halfway to your goal. If not, select it from the list. There are other choices available.

4. Select **Change Settings**. The Windows Update Setting dialog box appears, as shown in Figure 20.2.

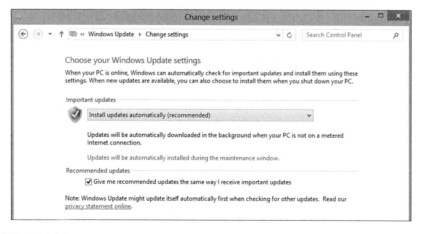

FIGURE 20.2

You can tell easily if you are set to receive updates automatically.

5. From the list in the **Important Updates** section, select **Install Updates Automatically**.

6. Select **Updates Will Be Automatically Installed During the Maintenance Window**. The Automatic Maintenance dialog box appears.

7. You can select the time at which all automated maintenance occurs, including applying Windows 8 updates. If the time shown is acceptable, check the option below the time to be sure Windows 8 wakes up if it is asleep at the time maintenance should run. If the time is not acceptable, select a better time from the list.

8. Select **OK** to save these settings.

9. Select **OK** again to close the Windows Update settings dialog box.

10. Congratulations. You've set up Windows Update to run automatically. Your computer will always be synchronized with Microsoft's most important Windows software updates.

You can always verify that you receive updates correctly. To do so, open the Charms bar and select **Settings**. Select **PC Settings**, and then select **Windows Updates**. The screen shows your update status (see Figure 20.3). To check for recent updates, select **Check for Updates Now**.

FIGURE 20.3

You can easily check whether an update is available.

Delete Unused Files

Over time, you will unknowingly accumulate a large number of unused files of varying sizes. As you browse the web, install programs, download files, enter information into websites, and simply run programs, files are created or downloaded for various purposes onto your computer, but many times they are left on your system when the job is complete. Over time, this can rob you of plenty of system storage. One of the challenges to manage this situation is that these unused files are hidden from view. Fortunately, there is a utility in Windows that shows you these unused files and helps you delete then.

Table 20.1 shows you the types of files that can accumulate without your knowledge. Look at the file types carefully; you can choose from this list of files to be deleted.

TABLE 20.1   Types of Internal Files

File Type	Description
Downloaded Program Files	Some web pages contain content that requires a small program to display in your browser, such as ActiveX controls or a Java applet. These programs are downloaded to your computer when needed. They stay on your hard drive for the next time you open a page that has the same type of content. You can delete these files if you choose. New copies of the programs will be downloaded the next time you need them.
Temporary Internet Files	Certain web pages and images are downloaded to your computer to speed things up the next time you visit one of the sites. You can delete these files without ill effect.
Offline Web Pages	Some websites enable you to continue reading their pages or to continue entering information into their pages even when the site is inaccessible. You can certainly delete this content, saving you some storage space.
Recycle Bin	Most files are not deleted the moment you press Delete. The files are stored in the Recycle Bin until you empty the Recycle Bin. You can empty the Recycle Bin as part of this process.
Setup Log Files	Some installation programs carelessly leave certain files on your computer, even after the program that used the files was installed properly.
Temporary Files	Some programs use a folder on your computer where they store files needed for short-term use. You can delete these files without negative effect.

TABLE 20.1 (continued)

File Type	Description
Thumbnails	Windows 8 creates smaller versions of certain images when needed. You can delete these to free up some space, but the thumbnails will be re-created when they are needed again.
User Windows Error Reports	Windows stores logs of problems and errors. These logs do not get erased.

 NOTE The files noted in Table 20.1 are created per user. This means that each user with a Windows 8 account must sign on and complete the process to be sure all unnecessary files are deleted.

To delete unused internal files, follow these steps:

1. Open the Control Panel, and go to the System and Security group.

2. Select **Administrative Tools**, and then select **Free Up Disk Space**. The Disk Cleanup dialog box appears, as shown in Figure 20.4.

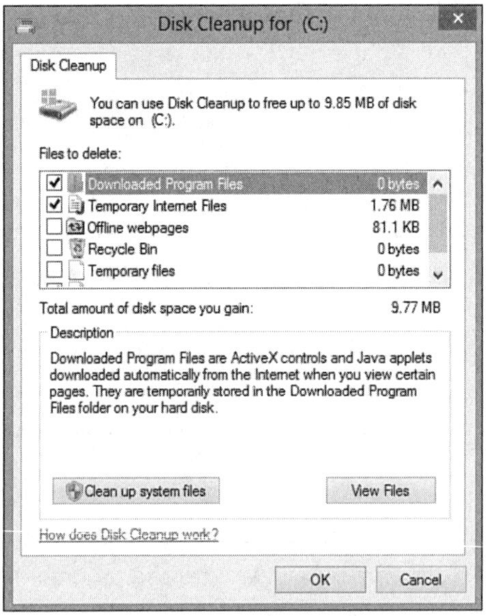

FIGURE 20.4

The Disk Cleanup tool enables you to clean up files left over from different administrative and maintenance processes.

3. Select the files you would like to delete from the list. Take a look at the disk space you would gain back by deleting the files.

4. Select **OK**. You will be asked if you are sure you want to delete the files. If so, select **Delete Files**.

5. Windows deletes the files you specified. Depending on the number of files you chose to delete, this process could take a few minutes. If you like, you may open the Disk Cleanup dialog box again to see the results of your work.

Defragmenting Your Drive

Defragmentation is a condition that occurs over time as a result of heavy use of your computer and its file system. Data on your hard drive is not always stored sequentially on the physical disk. As it is deleted, modified, and added to, the data for even a single large file can end up in multiple places on the disk surface. This is called *fragmentation*, and the more fragmented the data on your hard drive, the more work the hard disk has to do to retrieve it, and the slower your computer acts when accessing it. *Defragmentation* is the process to locate fragmented data and put it back together on the drive to improve efficiency and overall performance.

Windows does a capable job to manage disk defragmentation for you, but you can also do it manually. To defragment your drive, follow these steps. The process starts with determining whether your drive should be defragmented. Most experts believe a drive should be defragmented when the drive is more than 20% fragmented.

1. Open Control Panel.

2. Select **Systems and Security**.

3. Under Administrative Tools, select **Defragment and Optimize Your Drives**. The Optimize Drives dialog box appears, as shown in Figure 20.6.

4. If your computer has multiple hard drives, they all will be listed in the list in the middle of the screen. You may analyze and optimize only one drive at one time. Select one of the drives by clicking or tapping once on it.

5. Select **Analyze**. This process runs for seconds up to minutes, probably not more than 1 hour. If the Analysis reports less than 20% fragmentation, choose **Close**. If the drive is more than 20% fragmented, continue with step 6.

6. Select **Optimize**. The process runs, potentially taking more than 1 hour if you have significant fragmentation of a larger drive. If you need to pause or stop the process, you can certainly do so without harming your hard drive.

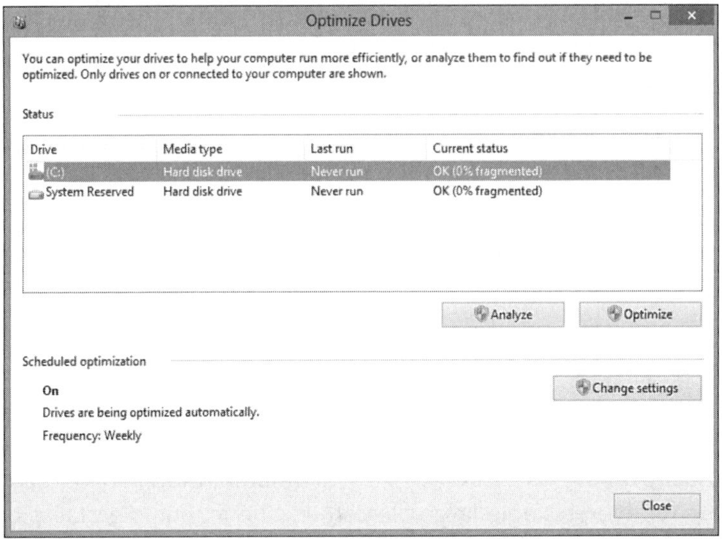

FIGURE 20.5

You select which drives you want to defragment.

7. If disk defragmentation isn't schedule to run automatically (it's usually on by default), you can schedule the Analyze and Optimize process to run automatically. To do so, select **Turn On**. Then, select how often to run the process and for what drives, as shown in Figure 20.6. Select **OK**.

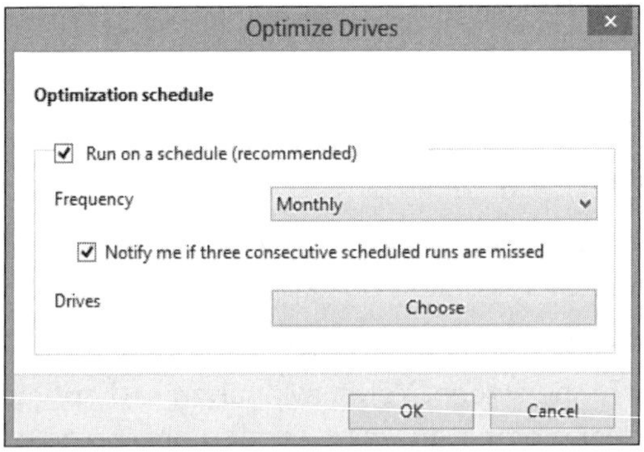

FIGURE 20.6

You can schedule defragmentation to run automatically.

8. Select Close to exit the Optimize Drives screen.

Update Internet Security Definitions

If you use the built-in antivirus and antimalware programs that come with Windows 8, you can skip this step. If you use any other Internet security programs, such as to prevent computer viruses or attacks from malicious software, then you need to ensure those products are up to date.

Any modern Internet security solution routinely updates its list of threats, which is done over the Internet. Be sure those products are up to date and that they receive updates automatically and on a regular basis. These applications usually have an automated system for updates, but this step is important enough that it's worth the effort to double-check.

Refer to the last section of this chapter for advice on how often to verify that Internet threat definitions are up to date. You can also learn more about keeping your system safe and secure in Chapter 19, "Safe and Private Computing."

Sample Maintenance Schedule

Table 20.2 shows a schedule you can use to ensure you maintain your system properly.

TABLE 20.2 Sample Routine Maintenance Schedule

Process	How Often
Windows Update	Automatic
Defragment	Every 3 months
Delete Unused Files	Once each month
Update Internet Threat Definitions	Once each week (if needed)
Update System Information	Once each month

THE ABSOLUTE MINIMUM

Configure Windows Update to run automatically. This way, you do not miss an important software fix that could possible save you from losing important information.

If saving or opening files seems sluggish, defragment your drive first before paying for support.

There may be a significant amount of drive space being wasted with unused or temporary files. It's a good idea to check for unwanted files after you have installed a new software programs, in addition to doing so on the schedule suggested above.

No matter what Internet security system you use, be sure the virus and malware definitions are up to date at all times.

IN THIS CHAPTER

- Knowing How to Find and Use the Troubleshooting Wizards

- Using Task Manager to Halt a Program

- Where to Find Information About the Windows 8 System Installed on a User's Computer

- Learning When and How to Use Refresh and Reset

21

TROUBLESHOOTING AND SOLVING PROBLEMS IN WINDOWS 8

Microsoft has invested tens of thousands of hours of testing to ensure Windows 8 runs properly. But with a system as complex as Windows 8, you can bet some issues snuck out the door. These issues aren't limited to a feature not working. Sometimes a feature or capability is difficult to use, making it easy for a user to set up some aspect of Windows 8 the wrong way. The troubleshooting tools in Windows 8 can help solve some of those problems. In addition, the Task Manager can help shut down a program that gets stuck. And when all else fails and a user wants to start over, the Refresh and Reset functions enable you to do that. These problem solving tools are covered in this chapter.

Using the Troubleshooting Wizards

Windows 8 has almost 30 different tools for dealing with difficulties and trouble you encounter in the software. Each of these troubleshooting wizards focuses on a particular aspect of the software, such as sound problems or connecting to the Internet. Each tool is different, of course, suggesting some basic or some challenging fixes plus lots of suggesting in between.

To use a troubleshooting wizard, follow these steps:

1. Open the **Search** charm.

2. Enter **trouble** and select **Settings**.

3. Select **Troubleshoot** from the list of results on the left side of the screen. A screen that looks the one shown in Figure 21.1 appears.

4. Select **View All**. The entire list of troubleshooting wizards appears, as shown in Figure 21.2. Select the wizard that matches your issue.

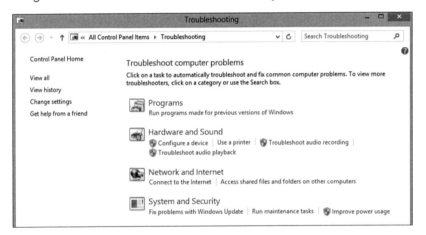

FIGURE 21.1

Windows show troubleshooting wizards for the areas of the system you've been using lately.

Troubleshoot computer problems				
Name	Description	Location	Category	Publisher
Connection to a Workplace Using DirectAccess	Find and fix problems with conne...	Local	Network	Microsoft ...
Hardware and Devices	Find and fix problems with device...	Local	Device	Microsoft ...
HomeGroup	Find and fix problems with viewin...	Local	Network	Microsoft ...
Incoming Connections	Find and fix problems with incom...	Local	Network	Microsoft ...
Internet Connections	Find and fix problems with conne...	Local	Network	Microsoft ...
Internet Explorer Performance	Find and fix problems with Intern...	Local	Web Brow...	Microsoft ...
Internet Explorer Safety	Find and fix problems with securi...	Local	Web Brow...	Microsoft ...
Network Adapter	Find and fix problems with wirele...	Local	Network	Microsoft ...
Playing Audio	Find and fix problems with playin...	Local	Sound	Microsoft ...
Power	Find and fix problems with your c...	Local	Power	Microsoft ...
Printer	Find and fix problems with printi...	Local	Printing	Microsoft ...
Program Compatibility Troubleshooter	Find and fix problems with runni...	Local	Programs	Microsoft ...
Recording Audio	Find and fix problems with record...	Local	Sound	Microsoft ...
Search and Indexing	Find and fix problems with Wind...	Local	Windows	Microsoft ...
Shared Folders	Find and fix problems with access...	Local	Network	Microsoft ...
System Maintenance	Find and clean up unused files an...	Local	System	Microsoft ...
Windows Media Player DVD	Find and fix problems with playin...	Local	Media Pla...	Microsoft ...
Windows Media Player Library	Find and fix problems with the Wi...	Local	Media Pla...	Microsoft ...
Windows Media Player Settings	Find and fix problems with Wind...	Local	Media Pla...	Microsoft ...
Windows Update	Resolve problems that prevent yo...	Local	Windows	Microsoft ...

FIGURE 21.2

You can leverage a number of troubleshooting wizards to solve problems you encounter.

Using Task Manager to Close Unresponsive Programs

The Task Manager is a utility that gives you visibility into the programs running in Windows 8 plus the impact they have on system resources. You can see how much memory a program is gobbling up, whether one program is dominating use of the CPU or other system resources, how much data is transmitted by certain programs, and lots more.

Not everyone will have a deep appreciation for all the information presented in Task Manager. Actually, you would need expert knowledge in computer science and technology to truly understand the significance and meaning of many of the reports shown. However, one item of interest a beginning Windows 8 user might appreciate and learn to leverage is how to shut down a program that might be frozen.

Once in a while a program stops functioning for no apparent reason. You know when this occurs because the program seems to dim on the screen, and the title of the program has the phrase Not Responding tagged on to the end of it. And of course, when the program is unresponsive to your mouse clicks or tap, you know the program has left and is not coming back.

In the past, you may have been forced to shut down your entire computer to bypass an issue with one locked program. Those days are gone. In Windows 8, if a program locks up, you can close it down with help from the Task Manager.

To open the Task Manager, press Ctrl+Alt+Delete. A menu should appear with just a few choices, Task Manager being one of them. Scroll down to Task Manager and press **Enter**. After doing so, the Task Manager should appear, as shown in Figure 21.3.

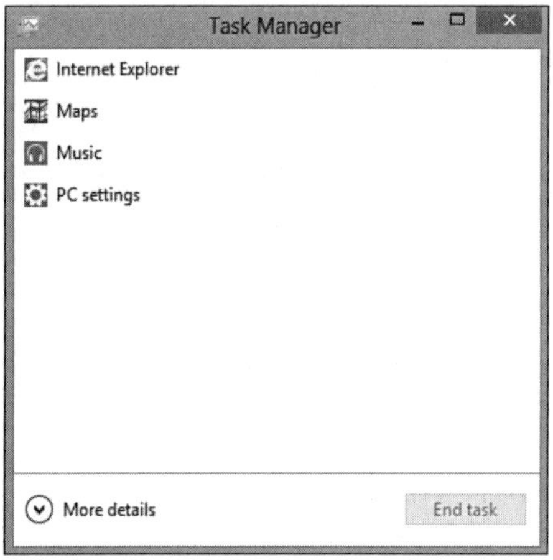

FIGURE 21.3

The Task Manager enables you to review performance and resource use in Windows.

Select **More Details** for every application or program running in your system. Find the entry for the program that seems to be frozen. Right-click or tap-and-hold on the problematic program. Select **End Task**, and then verify your action by selecting **OK** if you are prompted. The program will halt almost immediately.

Understanding Refresh and Restore

Once in a while, no matter how much advice you've received or troubleshooting you have tried, you may need to take a step back and restart your experience with Windows. This doesn't refer to forgetting what you've learned. Rather, it may be wise to reinstall Windows or simply go back to a point before you started customizing Windows 8. Short of backing up everything, deleting everything on your computer, and reinstalling Windows and all your other programs, you have two options to start over. The options are named, simply enough, Refresh and Reset.

Getting a Do-Over with Refresh

Refresh is designed to undo everything that might have been done that has made the computer perform less sharply than before. The refresh does not delete your personal files or any of the settings that affect the appearance of Windows. Rather, the settings that control how Windows 8 operates are set back to their original value. Any non-Microsoft software you installed is removed. Any apps acquired from the Windows store will *not* be affected. Refresh is a great way to restore Windows to a state where it was running properly without investing the time to reload all your files and programs.

To refresh your system, follow these steps:

1. If you installed from a DVD, insert the DVD into your computer but cancel the setup program when it starts, or simply close the AutoPlay dialog box if it appears.

2. Open the **Charms** bar and select **Settings**. Select **PC Settings** and then select **General** from the menu on the left side of the screen.

3. Scroll down the screen on the right until you see the Refresh your PC without affecting your files section. Select **Get Started**.

FIGURE 21.4

The Refresh program enables you to save your files and settings while returning Windows to its just-installed state.

4. Read through the instructions. If you want to continue, select **Next**.

5. At this point, you may be prompted for the Windows 8 DVD. Insert it if required.

6. If you are sure you want to proceed, select **Refresh**.

7. The Refresh program runs, and eventually your computer restarts. This process takes approximately 15 minutes.

Restarting from Scratch with the Reset Option

Reset is designed to restore the computer to its state before you ever touched it. The reset returns the computer to its factory-shipped settings, removing any trace of your or your files from the system. Use the Reset option in these situations:

- You want to rebuild your Windows 8 environment from scratch, installing everything again and setting every option again. Only use the Reset option in this scenario if you have backed up your personal information to an external drive (not to the drive on which Windows 8 is installed).

- You want to give away or sell the computer but you would like Windows 8 running on it when you do.

Before Windows 8 is reinstalled, the Reset program can clean the hard drive of your files. You also have the option to completely erase the drive beforehand. You might have heard that some clever individuals can still access files that have been deleted or were stored on a file that has been formatted. This option specially formats the drive so that it would be extremely unlikely for someone to recover your files from the drive.

To reset your system, follow these steps:

1. Have the original product key handy for when the Reset program reinstalls Windows 8.

2. Open the **Charms** bar and select **Settings**.

3. Select **PC Settings** at the bottom of the screen, and then select **General**.

4. Scroll about halfway down the screen until you see the option to **Remove Everything and Reinstall Windows**.

5. Select **Get Started** to get to the screen shown in Figure 21.5.

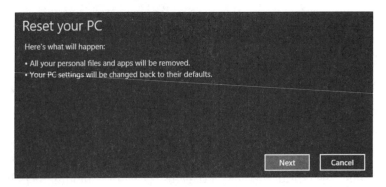

FIGURE 21.5

The Reset program enables you to start from scratch with Windows.

6. Select **Next**. A screen like the one shown in Figure 21.6 appears.

FIGURE 21.6

You can choose whether your entire drive is erased when Windows is reinstalled.

7. To remove your files during the reset, select **Just Remove My Files**. To remove your files and to prepare the entire drive so it is hard to recover them (for example, if you want to sell or donate your PC), select **Fully Clean the Drive**.

8. You will be prompted one more time. Select **Reset** to continue or **Cancel** to return to the Start screen.

9. The reset process runs for approximately 20 minutes if you choose to just remove your files. It can take at least twice as long if you choose to also prepare the drive. When it finishes, you will be prompted for your Windows 8 product key. Enter it and select **Next**.

10. Proceed through a few more guided steps to finish the reset program. When complete, Windows 8 will have been reinstalled to an otherwise empty drive.

Reviewing Your System Core Info

Every once in a while, you may be asked a question that exceeds your technical knowledge about your computer. For example, you may need to supply information to a tech support service to get help solving a problem or replacing a part. Or you might need to know if your computer has the right set up to run a software program. It's OK not to know certain information as long as you know *where* to find the information. Fortunately, Windows provides a single place where you can go.

You can review basic information, as shown in Figure 21.7, by opening the System panel in the Control Panel under System and Security. The basic view shows core information about your processor and memory, plus basic information about your network environment.

FIGURE 21.7

You can review a number of basic Windows 8 settings on one screen; although there are a number of links that enable you to hop to more detailed screens.

THE ABSOLUTE MINIMUM

Keep the following points in mind after you've completed reading this chapter:

- Use the Task Manager to close an unresponsive program rather than restarting Windows 8.

- Use the Refresh program to retain your files while resetting Windows 8 to the default settings.

- Use the Reset program to prepare your computer to be sold or donated or to create a fresh copy of Windows 8 loaded in your computer.

KEEPING CURRENT WITH THE BING APPS

Along with all the new business applications, Internet browsers, Xbox games, and music and video apps in Windows 8, Microsoft introduced a family of apps that bring topical news and information to the Windows 8 Start screen. With just a single-click, tap, or key press, you can check the top headlines from the world of sports, news, weather, finance, and travel. There is also a new Bing Internet browser that clues you in on the hot topics. Even a new Map app is thrown in, too. As you can probably guess, the Bing apps are easy to use. There are just a few options in each app, and the main content in each, such as the current weather conditions or the big news story, fill up the home page of each app. This chapter explains the basics about these apps and explains some of the useful options loaded into each app. Each section covers one of these apps.

Before diving into the chapter, there is one small but important topic to cover. The apps discussed in this chapter are new Windows 8 apps. You'll enjoy the apps more and also understand the content in this chapter with an understanding of how to navigate through these types of apps. It probably makes sense to review Chapter 3, "Learning Windows 8 Basics" to fully take advantage of the tools and features in each Bing app. In particular, review the sections related to snapping apps and opening the App bar.

Introducing the Bing Apps

The new applications are designed to bring you the latest and most important stories from the worlds of news and current events, sports, weather, travel, and finance. There are also new Search and Map apps. These apps are collectively known as Bing apps, named after Microsoft's browser-based search engine. With these new Windows 8 apps, the Bing brand has grown to include Microsoft's entire family of Internet information.

These seven apps appear on the Start screen by default, so all you need is a connection to the Internet to reach this content. Figure 22.1 shows you the tiles for these apps. Your Start screen probably won't be organized like the one shown here because the tiles are arranged so that they can be pictured together.

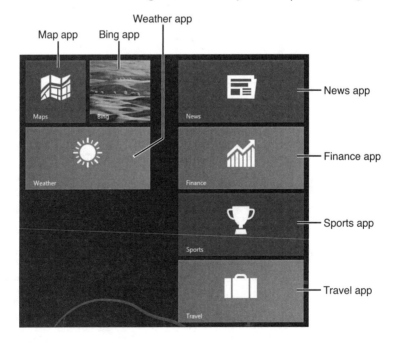

FIGURE 22.1

You can find each of the tiles shown in this picture on the Start screen.

NOTE You probably won't spend long stretches of time with any of these apps, except if you read several stories in one sitting in the News or Sports apps. This isn't to say that these apps are not engaging or interesting. Rather, you might consult the info in an app like Weather or Finance briefly a few times a day. The apps presented in this chapter are perfect candidates to share the screen with apps you work with. If you build a budget, write a document, review other documents, or do other work in Windows, you can snap News, Weather, Sports, or whichever Bing app you like alongside of your work task. For instruction in snapping apps to the screen, check out Chapter 3.

Read the News That's Fit to Bing

The Bing News app brings you the daily top story. The daily story fills up the screen when you start the app, as shown in Figure 22.2. To read the story, click or tap on the headline or any part of the story. Using your keyboard, press **Tab** until the headline on the screen is selected (a thin border appears around the headline), and then press **Enter**. To return to the story's headline page, select the back arrow button or open the App bar (which appears on the top of the screen) and select **Bing Daily**, as shown in Figure 22.3.

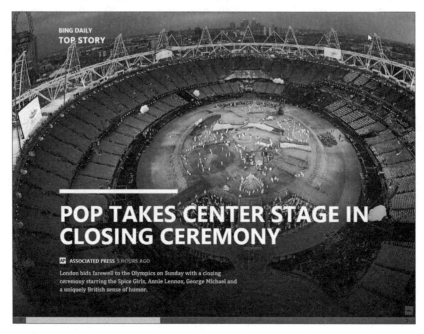

FIGURE 22.2

The News app presents a main story when you start the app.

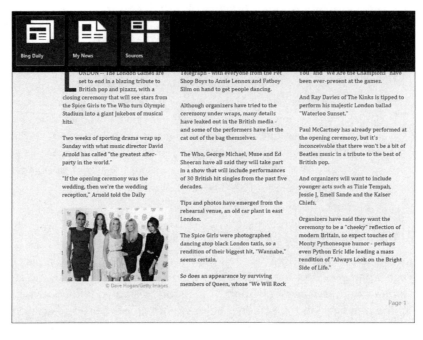

FIGURE 22.3

The App bar appears at the top of the screen. The Bing Daily tile on the App bar brings you back to the News home page.

You can scroll to the right to reveal additional stories, including sections of related stories, such as technology, business, and more. When you see a story that interests you, you can read the story on its own page. To do so, select the story by clicking or tapping the story, headline, or any photos associated with the story.

You are not limited to the sources of news Bing and Microsoft use to deliver the headlines and stories. You can browse through dozens of news sites directly from the News app to read stories produced worldwide. To read from one of these sources, open the App bar and select **Sources**. Select the news source you want to read from and then select a story to read, as shown in Figure 22.4.

FIGURE 22.4

The News app also enables you to read stories from several worldwide sources.

Getting the Bing Weather Report

You might find some news days to be slow, your favorite sports teams taking the day off, the financial markets closed, and you might not have any money to spend travel. For these reasons, the News, Sports, Finance, and Travel Bing apps might not get regular attention. That's not the case with Bing Weather, which provides full-screen weather conditions and forecasts, as shown in Figure 22.5.

Like all Bing apps, you can scroll across to see other views of weather. For Bing Weather, you can see an hourly forecast, maps, and historical weather patterns off to the right of the home page. Use the scroll bars with your mouse, finger, or stylus, to scroll to the right and back again.

The first time you open the Weather app, you are asked whether the app can figure out your home location on its own. Some folks believe use of this location technology is a violation of privacy. If you also believe so, you can select **Block** when this message appears. You'll have to supply your location manually by supplying address information.

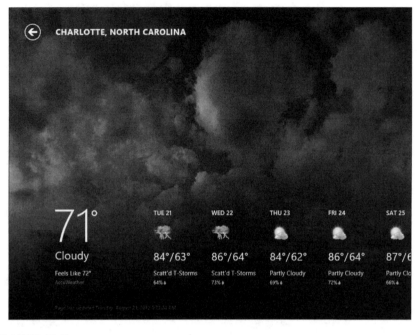

FIGURE 22.5

Bing Weather gives you instant access to your local weather report.

If you're interested in the weather at places besides home, you can add more places to your list of favorites. This way, you can quickly switch to different locations you're interested in, such as places you plan to visit or places where family and friends live. To do so, open the App bar (which appears at the top of the screen in this app), and select **Places**. Select the tile with the plus symbol, and then enter the name of the location whose weather you want to monitor. To see that location's weather, open the App bar, again select **Places**, and then select the tile for the place you want to review, as shown in Figure 22.6.

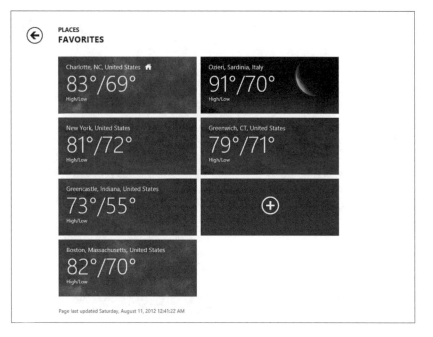

FIGURE 22.6

Using the Places feature you can receive weather reports about multiple locations.

Keeping Score with Bing Sports

The Sports app delivers scores and stories directly to the Start screen in Windows 8. The photos used to illustrate the story are presented full screen and look gorgeous, just as they do for Bing Daily (refer to Figure 22.2). With a headline or photo on the screen, select the headline or the photo to read the supporting story.

You can jump to a section of the app that contains exclusive content for a specific sport or league or even just today's big sport events. To display the list of specialized content, open the App bar (which appears at the top of the screen) and then select the topic in which you are interested. You'll be brought to the top story for the topic you selected. You can read the story and scroll to the right to see other stories and scores related to your chosen content, as shown in Figure 22.7.

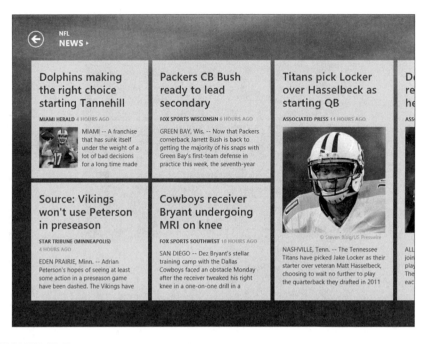

FIGURE 22.7

Bing Sports enables you to get your sporting news from a variety of sources.

Getting the Bing Money Story

The Bing Finance app brings together stories about finance, financial markets results, rates for individual instruments, and more. When you start the app, the top story in Bing Finance appears. To read the entire story, click or tap the headline. To read other current money stories or to review other market data, from the Finance home page, scroll to the right. Again, if a table, chart, or headline interests you, click or tap anywhere on the story or box containing the numbers and words.

Another source of content is the App bar (see Figure 22.8), which opens at the top of the screen. Select from broader news about the financial markets and world economy, mortgage, home equity, and other loan rates, currencies, and more.

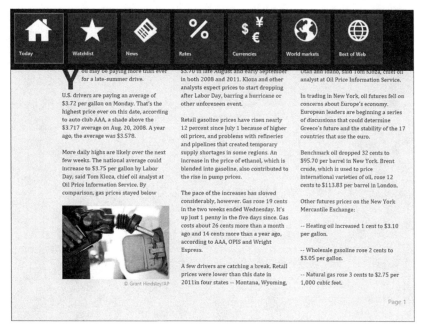

FIGURE 22.8

The App bar provides access to other finance material.

The App bar shown here illustrates a Watchlist tile. Selecting it brings you to a page on which you can create a list of investments to watch, as shown in Figure 22.9. As discussed in the Note in the beginning of this chapter, a page like the Watchlist is a useful page to snap alongside of an app you're working on during the day.

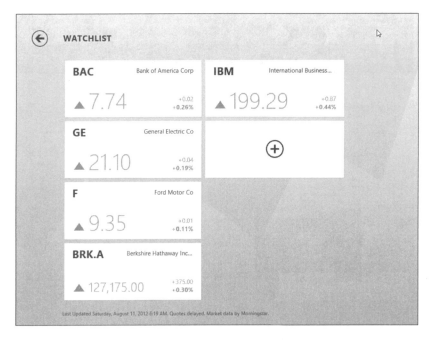

FIGURE 22.9

The App bar provides access to other finance material, including your watch list.

Vacationing with the Bing Travel App

The Bing Travel app is a useful tool for two audiences. For the leisure traveler, the app enables you to select a travel spot from a list of hundreds, as shown in Figure 22.10, including by region. You can also start your destination search from the travel spot or *destination* of the day, which appears when you start the app. Having selected a destination, the leisure traveler can then review several pages of travel content related to their chosen spot by clicking or tapping on the destination's tile (see Figure 22.11).

- Places to visit

- Restaurants

- Nightlife

- Hotels

- Planning a trip

FIGURE 22.10

You can select from hundreds of potential travel destinations.

FIGURE 22.11

With a travel site in mind, you can review details about the destination.

Business travelers also can benefit from the app. On the App bar, you'll find two links—one to hotels and one to flights—that make it simple to get to travel options unencumbered and undistracted by advertisement-loaded pages you would normally see on most travel websites (see Figure 22.12).

FIGURE 22.12

You can use Travel to search for flights (pictured) and hotels.

Trending Topics with Bing

The Bing app is simply a frontend to the Bing search engine. The results are presented in an easy-to-review format, as shown in Figure 22.13. By clicking or tapping the results, you are brought to Internet Explorer with the page open containing the select results.

If you have fallen behind on the interesting and hot topics that people are talking, texting, tweeting, and posting about, the Bing app can help you. When you start the app, you see several words, each representing one of those hit topics. Selecting one of those words launches a Bing search based on the term you select.

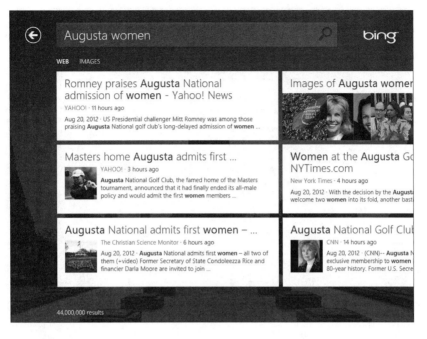

FIGURE 22.13

The Bing app helps you search the Internet, and the results are presented each in a tile.

Finding Your Way with Bing Maps

The Bing Maps app is an easy-to-use tool to locate places on a map and display directions from one location to another (see Figure 22.14). The app includes fairly standard functionality, perhaps easier to use than the other map applications available. If your Windows 8 device is a tablet, you'll probably find the Maps app a useful and convenient tool to get you from one place to another. To use the direction tools, open the App bar (which appears on the right side of the screen) and enter your start and end locations.

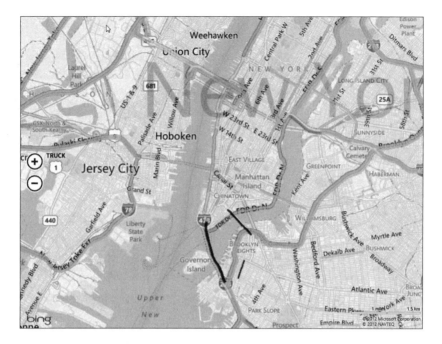

FIGURE 22.14

You can use the Bing Map app to show any location you like, including traffic patterns at your location.

THE ABSOLUTE MINIMUM

Keep these points in mind as you wrap up this chapter:

- The Bing apps are new Windows 8 apps, which means you can snap them alongside of other apps you use in Windows 8.

- Open the App bar to reveal options and features for any of the Bing apps.

- Most of the Bing apps have a Home button, which brings you to the first page of any app. To reveal the button, open the App bar.

- The Maps app is a great choice to provide you directions when you're on the road (do not drive and work with the app at the same time!), especially on a tablet device.

- Use the Travel app to find flights and hotel reservations very quickly, probable faster than you could using one of the popular travel sites on the web.

23

ENJOYING YOUR DIGITAL PHOTOS

It's almost impossible to find regular people who take photos with film, have the photos developed, and then store those photos in albums. Technologies have been steadily emerging for many years that have made it cheaper and easier to store pictures on a computer, make excellent prints on affordable consumer printers, and share photos on the Internet. Fast-forward the tape to Windows 8, where you can not only view pictures you have shot, but also see photos on many of the sites where you have uploaded and shared photos. The toolset for managing your digital photos in Windows 8, known as the Photos app, certainly is not ground-breaking and advanced, but given the app is free, it will be popular and worth exploring. This chapter covers the basics of the app, including how to connect with online sites, to consolidate your photos in one place.

Before diving into this chapter, you should be familiar with the various techniques and gestures you use in Windows 8. In particular, it would be helpful if you understand how to open Charms, as well as the Apps bar. You can find instruction on these topics in Chapter 3, "Windows 8 Basics."

Learning Photos App Basics

Everyone today likes to look at their digital photos and share pictures, too. For many, it's a race home from an event to load photos onto a computer and then to upload them to a website for others to enjoy. Of course, those with smartphones can upload photos right from the event so that the entire world can get instant visual updates of what happens! Although it's not filled to the brim with features, the Photos app in Windows 8 provides an easy-to-use hub for your digital pictures, including, as you'll see, those pictures you've loaded to different social media sites.

The Photos app in Windows 8 is an extremely easy-to-use tool for reviewing your digital photographs. You're not limited to photos you take with your camera and then load into your computer. You can import photos from your accounts on Facebook and Flickr, plus you can mix in photos you have stored on SkyDrive. Figure 23.1 shows the various sources for photos for the Photos app.

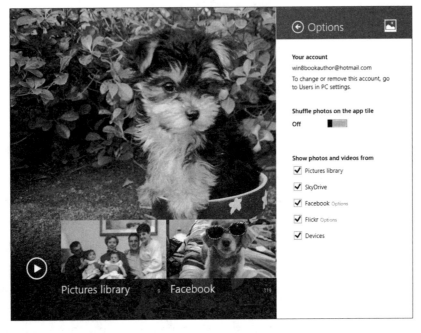

FIGURE 23.1

The Photos app consolidates your favorite pictures from five different sources.

NOTE SkyDrive is an online storage service designed to integrate with Microsoft products. You can read about SkyDrive in Chapter 16, "Storing Files on Drives, Disks, and the Cloud." You can save photos to SkyDrive as easily as you can to the hard drive on your computer, and you can barely tell the difference between browsing through SkyDrive or through a local drive.

The span of capabilities and features in the Photos app might seem limited compared to some of the applications available in the Windows Store, or even in the Windows Media Player program that runs on the Desktop. You can surely find an application that creates much fancier slideshows, and there are dozens of sites that can help you publish a stunning picture book. However, the ease of use of the Windows 8 Photos app can't be challenged. If you're more dedicated to photography and working with photos, perhaps the role the app can play for you is to provide a streamlined, simple central library for your photos, enabling you to leverage other applications to do the interesting work.

To open the Photos app, select the tile shown in Figure 23.2. If you cannot locate that tile, open the **Charms** bar and then select **Search**. When the Search pane opens, enter **photos** into the search box and then select Apps. Select the Photos tile from the list of results on the left side of the screen. Having done so, the Photos app will open, as shown in Figure 23.3. After you link the Photos app to the various sources of photos, your Photos app will look similar to the app shown in Figure 23.4.

FIGURE 23.2

This tile opens the Photos app.

FIGURE 23.3

You see few pictures (if any) in the Photos app until you supply information about where your photos are stored.

FIGURE 23.4

After a few minutes of work, the Photos app fills every corner of the app with your favorite photographs.

If you do not have photos in a particular service, such as Facebook, or at a particular location, such as in your local library, you can hide these portraits in the Photos app. Later in this chapter, in the "Bringing in Your Facebook and Flickr Photos" section, you learn how to include photos from Facebook and Flickr in your Windows 8 photo library.

To hide a photos source, follow these steps:

1. From the Photos app, open the **Settings** charm.

2. Select **Options**. The Photos settings Options screen appears, as shown in Figure 23.5.

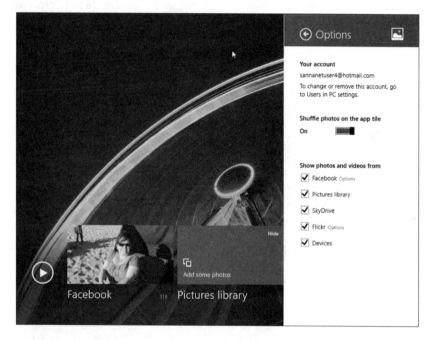

FIGURE 23.5

Use the Photos app Options screen to select which of the photo sources you want to use.

3. Each of the photos sources—picture library, Facebook, Flickr, SkyDrive, and a device attached to your computer—are represented by a check box. Select the check box to clear the check box and hide that source from the Photos app.

4. Just click or tab back on the screen that was open when you opened the Settings charm in step 1 to close the Options screen.

Browsing Through Your Photos

It's extremely easy to browse through your photos in the Photos app. You can move forward and backward through the photo library, and you can also zoom in on one photo. Here are some tips:

- Click an album or folder to open it. You can tell an album or folder because the number of photos it contains appears at the bottom of its picture.

- Select a photo to display the photo in full-screen mode.

- If you have opened a particular photo source in the Photos app and then drilled into one of its folders or albums, just click the **Back** button to navigate back to the main Photos app home screen. If the Back button does not appear on the screen (top-left corner), just click or tap once on the screen.

Figure 23.6 points out the buttons you use to navigate through your library.

FIGURE 23.6

You move back and forth through your photos, as well as zoom in or zoom out.

The easiest way to review your photos is to launch the app's slide show. To do so, open the **Apps** bar and select **Slide Show**. Your screen automatically opens each photo in the library, album, or folder you are looking at. The Photos appears for a few seconds before the show advances to the next photo. The slide show displays the pictures in the same order in which they appear in their folder or album. There are no options to control the slide show, such as transitions or duration.

Working with Your Photos

There are a handful of easy tasks you can complete as you browse through your library in addition to simply admiring the fine photography on the screen. This list provides you the details and simple instructions:

- **Open the photo in Flickr or Facebook**—You can always hop into Facebook or Flickr to see where a photo you see in the Photos app actually lives. With a photo from one of those services on the screen, open the **Apps bar** and select **View on Facebook** or **View on Flickr**. This opens the appropriate site directly on the page where your Photos appears.

- **Share a photo through email**—If you see a photo that you absolutely must share with someone over email, you can do so in just a few steps. You can share any photo except for one on your SkyDrive. Open the **Share** charm and then select **Mail**. Figure 23.7 shows how the email Windows sets up with the photo included.

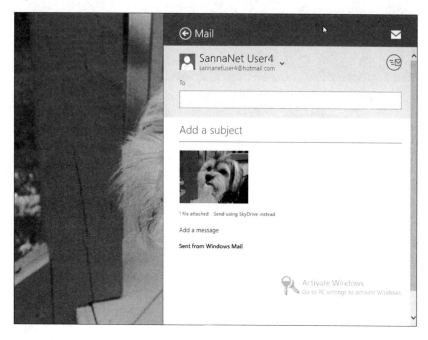

FIGURE 23.7

You can email a photo without leaving your library!

- **Set a photo as the lock screen image**—To replace the image that appears while Windows 8 is locked, including while Window waits for you to sign in after Windows has been restarted, browse to the photo to use. Open the **App bar**. Then, select **Set As** and then **Lock Screen**. You can see the result in Figure 23.8.

FIGURE 23.8

You can choose any photo you like as your lock screen background.

- **Set a photo on the app's tile**—To use a photo as the Photos app's tile image, browse to the photo to use and then open the **Apps bar**. Select **Set as** and then **App Tile**. You can see the result in Figure 23.9.

  To automatically rotate through all the photos displayed in the Photos app as the app tile's image, open the **Settings** charm, select **Options**, and then move the Shuffle slider to the right for On.

- **Set a photo as the app's background**—To use a photo as the Photo app's panoramic background, browse to the photo you want to use, and then open the Apps bar. Select **Set As** and then **App Background**. You can see the result back in Figure 23.1.

FIGURE 23.9

Select a particularly small image to use on the Photos app's Start screen tile.

Bringing In Your Facebook and Flickr Photos

Facebook and Flickr are two of the most popular websites for exchanging and sharing photos. You can view photos directly from those sites, integrating photos stored there with photos stored on your computer and on SkyDrive.

Bringing In Facebook Photos

Facebook is one of the five photo sources in Windows 8. Windows 8 organizes your Facebook photos by the same albums you use in Facebook. You bring your Facebook photos into Windows 8 by establishing a connection between Facebook and Windows 8. You do this by specifying a Facebook account from which to access photos. This can be any Facebook account, but to link, you need to have both the username and password. You can bring in photos from more than one Facebook account.

To bring in your photos from Facebook into the Photos app, follow these steps:

1. Open the **Photos** app.

2. Open the **Settings** charm.

3. From the Settings screen, select **Options**..

4. Find the entry for Facebook. If the check box is clear, select it to turn the Facebook option to **On**.

5. Select the **Options** link for Facebook. A browser page opens where you connect to Facebook, as shown in Figure 23.10. Keep in mind that Microsoft changes the design of web pages frequently, so the page you see today might not be identical to the one shown in Figure 23.10.

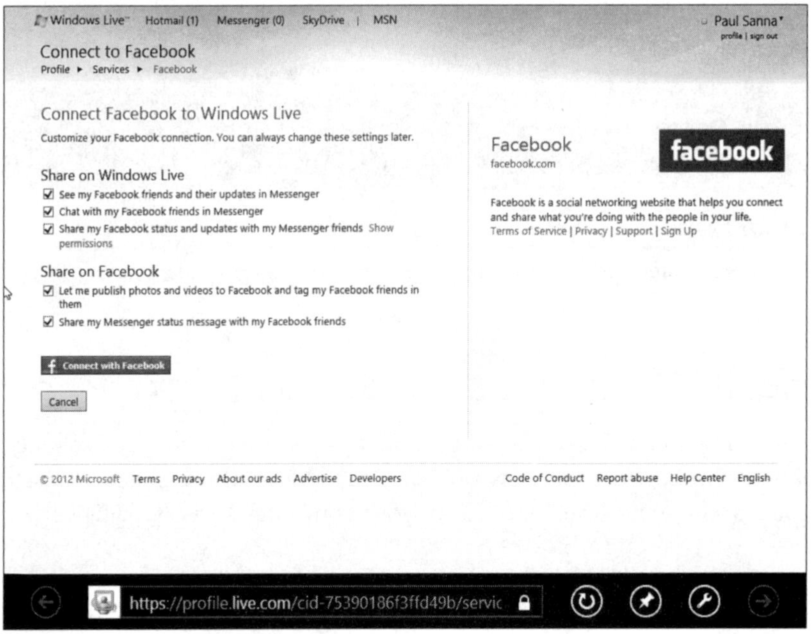

FIGURE 23.10

You set up your link between Windows 8 and Facebook on a web page at Windows Live.com.

6. Although there are a number of options on the screen to connect Facebook with Windows 8, you should be concerned with just the one that enables you to share photos and videos. Be sure that option is selected. Then, select **Next** or **Save**.

7. Enter the email address and password of the account whose photos you want to bring into Windows 8. Then, select **Log In** at the bottom of the screen.

8. You are returned to the Photos app, and soon photos from Facebook appear in your library.

Bringing In Flickr Photos

Flickr is an online photo and video-sharing site and community. It's a great option to share photos and videos if you're not interested in the social media aspects of Facebook. You need to supply your Flickr username and password to bring your Flickr photos into Windows 8. Don't worry. You need to enter that information only once. From then on, your Flickr photos automatically flow into your Windows 8 photo library. Follow these steps to connect Flickr to Windows 8:

1. Open the **Photos** app.

2. Select the Flickr portrait.

3. Enter your Flickr credentials, which is actually a Yahoo account. You needn't select the Keep Me Signed In option. Select **Sign-In**.

4. On the next page, review the text on the page describing how the link works. If you are comfortable with the rules, select **OK, I'll Authorize It**.

   You should be returned to the Photos app. If you land at another browser page, simply return to the Start screen and return to the Photos app.

Bringing In SkyDrive Photos

The process to bring your SkyDrive photos into the Photos app in Windows 8 is easy. Actually, you may already have completed this step without knowing it.

If you had a Windows Live account before you signed into Windows 8 for the first time, and there were photos in your SkyDrive account, and you used the same account to sign into Windows 8, those photos should already be visible.

If you had a Windows Live account before you signed into Windows 8 for the first time, and there were photos in your SkyDrive account, but you used a different account to sign into Windows 8, including creating a new Windows account, you need to move the photos or join the two Windows accounts.

As for maintaining your SkyDrive photo library, there is nothing to it. Just be sure you copy photos to the Pictures subfolder on your SkyDrive. These pictures will show immediately in the Photos app. A real time-saver for uploading your picture to SkyDrive is to add a SkyDrive link to Windows Explorer, as shown in Figure 23.11. You can find information about installing the SkyDrive Desktop app on Live.com.

FIGURE 23.11

The SkyDrive Desktop application makes it easy to load pictures directly to your SkyDrive account.

THE ABSOLUTE MINIMUM

Keep these points in mind after you finish reading this chapter:

- The Photos app consolidates your digital photographs from many, but probably not all, sites. You can include photos you've loaded into your local library, photos shared on Facebook and Flickr, and photos stored in your SkyDrive account.

- You connect to Facebook and Flickr by supplying your username and password to Windows 8.

- The account you use to sign in to Windows 8 must match that of the Live account that stores photos in SkyDrive you want to include.

- You might need to supplement the Photos app with other applications to handle everything you want to do, such as to publish photo books or create custom slide shows.

24

ENJOYING MOVIES AND VIDEOS IN WINDOWS 8

If you watch movies and other videos on your computer, you should begin a friendship with the xbox video app. The app is easy-to-use, yet it has enough features and capabilities to meet just about all of your needs. Certainly some folks with a bit more experience in integrating digital media with personal computers might bellyache at the lack of interesting features in the **xbox video** app, but you cannot argue with the price (free) or the ease of adding in your content to the library. This chapter covers all the basics, from navigating through all the movies and TV shows offered in the marketplace, to renting or purchasing a selection that interests you. In addition, the slightly challenging project to move your collection of videos to your Windows 8 library also is presented.

Getting Started with the xbox video App

The **xbox video** app is an easy-to-use program that enables you to watch videos from both your private collection and from the enormous Xbox LIVE marketplace. If you are bored with your own collection, you can purchase almost any video offered in the marketplace. If you don't want to make a purchase commitment, you can always rent one or more of the videos offered. If you don't have the time to watch a full movie, you can always occupy a few minutes by watching the 10-minute previews available for each movie. You can also occupy yourself reading the artist profiles.

To start the **xbox video** app, select the tile, as shown in Figure 24.1. If you cannot locate the tile, open the **Charms** bar and then select **Search**. When the Search pane opens, enter "videos" and then select **Apps**. Select the **Video** tile from the list of results on the left side of the screen.

FIGURE 24.1

Launch the **xbox video** *app from the tile on the Start screen.*

Setting Up Your Xbox LIVE Account

A few seconds after the apps starts, Windows 8 tries to sign-in to Xbox LIVE with the account you used to sign-in to Windows. Xbox LIVe is Microsoft's online digital media service. It provides videos, music, and games to Windows 8, plus it offers tons of toys and fun to other members. Connecting to Xbox LIVE makes it easy to buy and rent video content, as well as to take advantage of the other services offered by Microsoft.

If you have not created your account yet, open the **Settings** charm and select **Account**. If the screen shown in Figure 24.2 appears, select Try Again. When Windows 8 was released, Microsoft was squashing the last bugs in the video and other apps. After doing so, the screen shown in Figure 24.3 appears. Enter your first name, select the marketing options if you want to receive information in email, and then select **I Accept**.

FIGURE 24.2

You may have to retry your connection with the Xbox LIVE service to create your account.

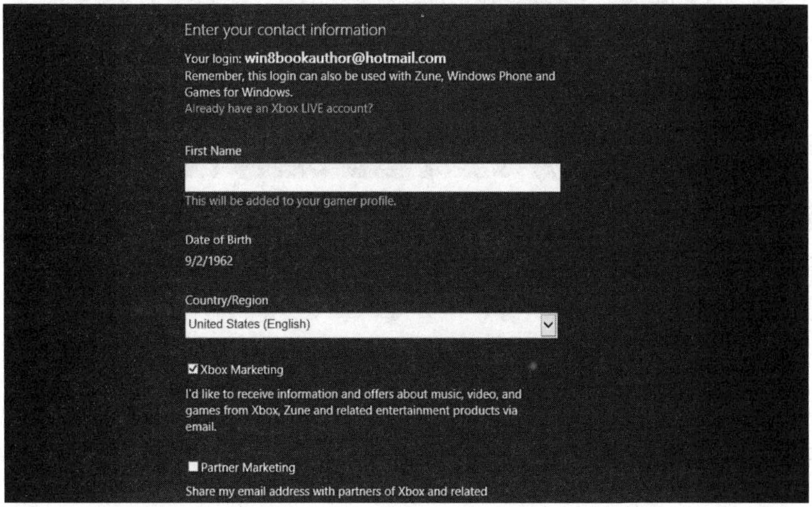

FIGURE 24.3

Your account is initially created after you supply just a few pieces of information.

After accepting the provisions of your account, you're next presented with some information about your account, most notably your gamertag (see Figure 24.4). The gamertag is the ID you use to identify yourself in the Xbox LIVE universe. Select **Account**. At this point, Windows 8 finishes creating your account, and you are returned to the app. You can browse through the videos in the app, including rent a title that interests you. To set up your account for purchases and to perform any kind of account maintenance, open the Settings charm again and select **Account**. A menu of account choices appears, from which you can supply credit card information to pay for videos you rent or purchase, upgrade your Xbox LIVE account, and more. If you have any questions about the Xbox LIVE service, visit www.xbox.com. Microsoft often times make changes to the services, plus promotions are usually available. Visit the site to read the most up-to-date rules and news.

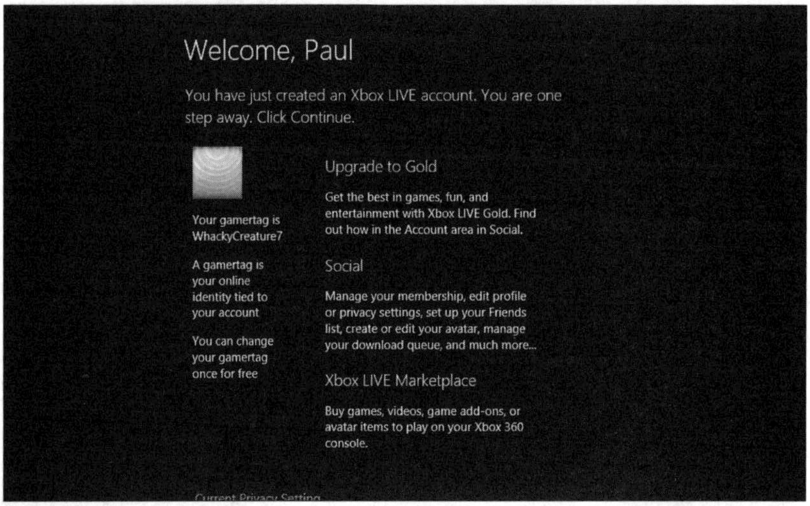

FIGURE 24.4

Your gamertag is your unique identifier in the Xbox LIVE universe.

Adding Your Videos to the Videos Library

If you have acquired digital movies and TV shows in the past, or if you have downloaded and saved lots of the fun and informative videos from the Internet (legally only, please), you'll want to add those movies to this library. You can also load videos you've recorded with a recorder or even your phone into Windows 8. By loading all of your video content into Windows 8, you can access all your on-screen digital content from one place. Until you add your own content to the **xbox video** app, the screen shown in Figure 24.5 appears.

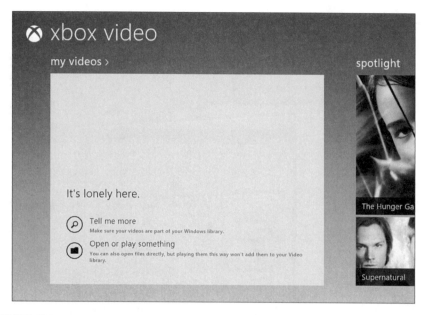

FIGURE 24.5

This message almost begs you to load your videos into the library!

If you have no digital videos—that is, you have never purchased videos online and you have never imported videos into your computer—you can skip this section. If you do own movies, TV shows, home movies, and other videos, you will be linking their location to the Videos library in Windows 8.The xbox video app uses that library as its source for your videos. You can learn as much as needed about libraries in Chapter 15, "Organizing Files and Folders with Windows Explorer."

Keep in mind, though, that you must maintain the link to your videos collection's location, such as across your home network or to a removable hard drive, for your videos to be available. If your Windows 8 computer is a laptop, it's likely you'll move that computer to a location away from the network or drive where those videos are located. If your computer stays in one place, of course, you won't have this problem.

Follow these steps to link your collection of videos to Windows 8 and the **xbox video** app:

1. Open Windows Explorer on the computer where Windows 8 is running.

2. Add the location (a folder) where your videos are stored to the list of folders of your Videos Library, as shown in Figure 24.6. Editing a library is covered in detail in Chapter 15. If you have videos scattered in different locations, either consolidate all of the content to one place, or repeat these steps for each location where videos are stored.

3. Open the **xbox video** app. Check **My Videos** to verify your videos are present.

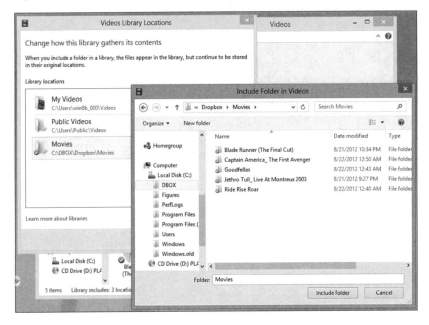

FIGURE 24.6

Add the location of your videos to the Windows 8 Video Library.

Moving Through the xbox video App

The **xbox video** app is organized into four main sections. These sections are organized laterally across the screen. Unlike applications you're probably used to working with, in which you move up or down to reach cool features and content, in the **xbox video** app, like in all Windows 8-style apps, you move across the screen. Here are the main four sections, in order from left to right:

*   **My Videos**—The first section on the left gives you access to videos in your library (see Figure 24.7). There is also a link that enables you play a video anywhere on your drives or network that has not been added to your network.

*   **spotlight/Featured Videos**—This section is the first section showing Xbox LIVE marketplace selections (see Figure 24.8). It shows the current hot videos or those Microsoft and its partners want to make noise about.

FIGURE 24.7

My Videos displays content from your Video library.

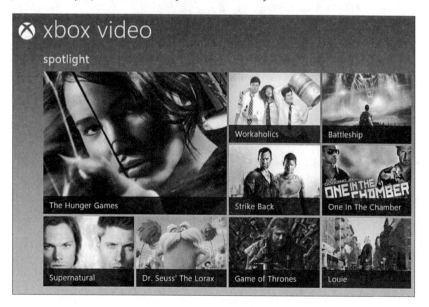

FIGURE 24.8

Review the selection of hot current movies and videos.

- **movies store**—This section enables you to view all movies in the marketplace (see Figure 24.9). You can browse though and play movies, including those recently in the theaters all the way back to black-and-white classics. You can rent movies, or you can purchase selections that become part of your collection forever. You usually can view a 10-minute preview of any video.

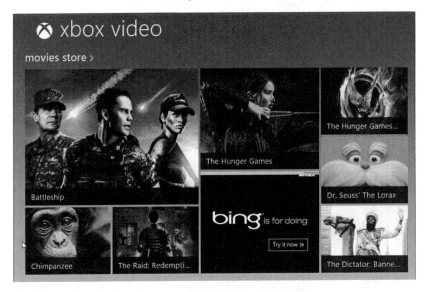

FIGURE 24.9

The movies store offers a huge selection of films, spanning a broad period of time.

- **television store**—This section enables you to shop for and then watch shows that appear and have appeared throughout on TV (see Figure 24.10). You can pay for and then watch selections from the main networks and from the specialty and pay networks. There are free shows offered, as well.

To access the content organized in the four sections, scroll through the sections of the app. With your mouse, point to the scroll bars at the bottom of the screen. With your finger or stylus, swipe left or right to move around. The keyboard-only support in this app seems to be weak. Use the arrow keys on the keyboard to move across the screen.

To drill deeper into one of the sections, select the name of the section. You can do the same with an artist or movie or TV show. Just select the item you're interested in to see more information about it.

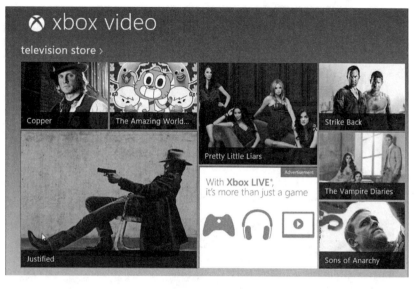

FIGURE 24.10

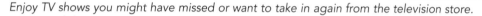

Enjoy TV shows you might have missed or want to take in again from the television store.

Inside a marketplace, you can access a specialty area by selecting the name of the area just below the main title of the section, as shown in Figure 24.11. Figure 24.12 shows the new releases specialty area in the movie marketplace. Some of the specialty areas permit you to sort and select in a few different ways, as shown in Figure 24.13. To back up, select the Back button that appears at the top left of most screens. If you open a small screen, such as to view details about a move, you can simply click anywhere outside of the screen to close it.

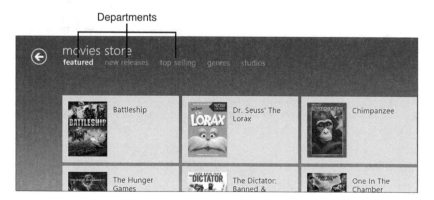

FIGURE 24.11

Each store is organized into departments.

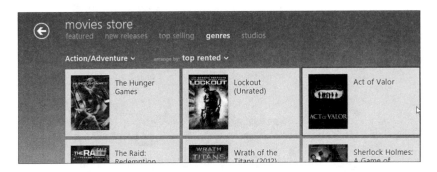

FIGURE 24.12

Inside of a department, you can browse through the many selections.

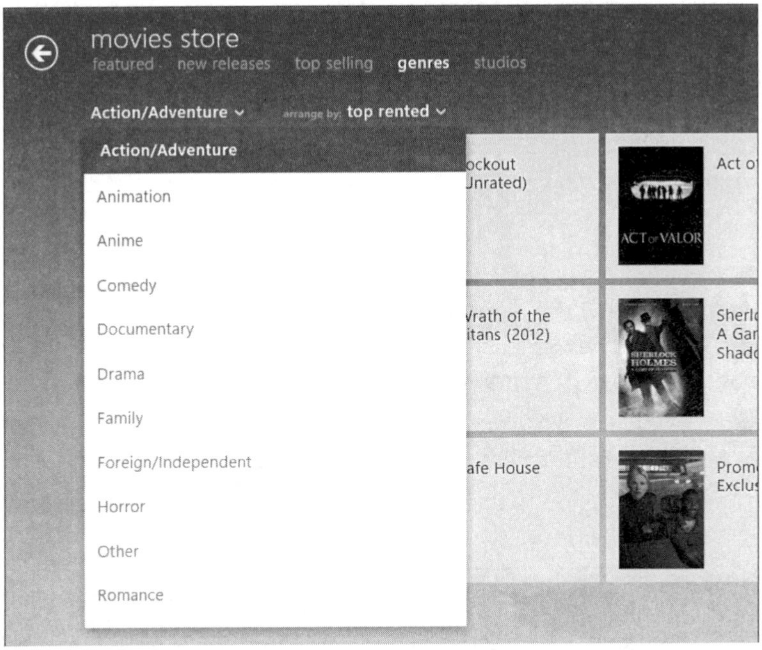

FIGURE 24.13

Some departments also have an option to sort, group, and select a specific video collection.

To return to the previous screen, select the Back button at the top left of each screen, as shown in Figure 24.14.

Back button

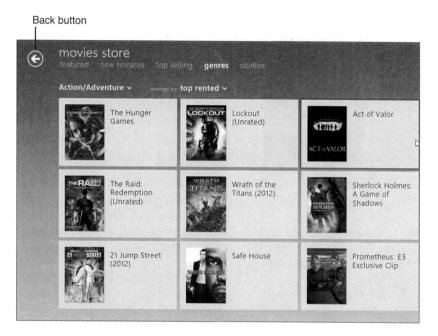

FIGURE 24.14

Select the Back button to return the previous screen.

Shopping for Videos

You can browse through the movies and TV shows presented in each section with an eye toward buying or renting. You usually have a choice between standard edition (SD) and high definition (HD) versions of a video. If you are unfamiliar with the idea of renting or purchasing a digital movie or TV show, especially with Xbox LIVE, this section explains how that works. Just keep in mind that the screens and options used to process your purchase or rental certainly can change, so what you see here may have some variation compared to your own experience.

Making a Purchase

When you decide to make a purchase, select **Buy** or **Rent** on that video's page in the **xbox video** app, as shown in Figure 24.15. First, though, select the movie or TV show you want to take in. You may also purchase a "season pass" for certain TV shows in which you pay upfront to watch new episodes as they air during the season.

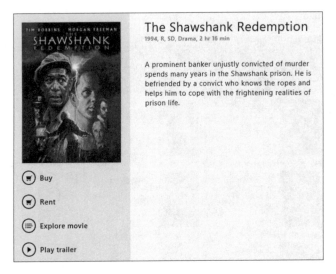

The Shawshank Redemption
1994, R, SD, Drama, 2 hr 16 min

A prominent banker unjustly convicted of murder spends many years in the Shawshank prison. He is befriended by a convict who knows the ropes and helps him to cope with the frightening realities of prison life.

Buy

Rent

Explore movie

Play trailer

FIGURE 24.15

After you select a file or TV video, you'll see choices for watching, including renting and purchasing.

After making your selection to Buy or Rent, a confirmation of your order appears on the screen. The confirmation shows the amount of Microsoft Points your purchase costs and your Microsoft Points balance. If you have questions about your account, how Microsoft Points are accrued and purchases, look at the support information on Microsoft's Xbox LIVE website at www.xboxlive.com.

After you confirm your order, the video downloads to your computer. It appears in the **My Videos** section of the app. To see the physical movie in file form, open File Explorer and navigate to the Videos library. You see a folder for the movie you purchased and the movie file in the folder designated as the Save folder for the library. Refer to Chapter 15 for information about libraries.

Renting a Selection

If you prefer not to make your purchase permanent, you can rent most titles on Xbox LIVE. Terms tend to change on an unannounced basis, so you should certainly check for the most current details about Microsoft's rental policies on www.xboxlive.com. At the time of this book's publish date, here is what is known about video rentals:

- After you start playback of a rental, you must complete watching it in 24 hours before the rental become nonfunctioning.

- During the 24-hour rental period, you can watch the movie as many times as you like.

THE ABSOLUTE MINIMUM

Keep the following points in mind after you've completed reading this chapter:

- If you plan to purchase or rent a video in the Windows 8 **xbox video** app, be sure to create your Xbox account before you start. It can save some work by doing it upfront.

- If the Windows Live ID you use for Xbox is different than the one you use to sign in into Windows 8, look into merging these two accounts. You can find information about merging Windows Live accounts on www.xboxlive.com.

- Move your videos to your Windows 8 computer so that they can be integrated into the library with other selections you might acquire. Doing so also enables you to watch your videos whenever you choose.

- You can also consider linking to the existing location of your videos by adding the physical folder location of your videos to the Video Library accessed through Windows Explorer. This is an easier option than moving your videos, but you can't access this content if you move your computer to a place where it can no longer connect with your video library's location.

25

LISTENING TO THE MUSIC IN WINDOWS 8

The new Music app in Windows 8 is fun to use, attractive to look at, and generally does everything you'd expect it to do. You can play music you've purchased in the past, and you can buy new music. The new Music app isn't full-featured, though. You may want to play music that resides on another computer in the house, or someone else in your home may want to play tunes on your computer. These and a few other features are not available in the Music app; though there are other tools in Windows that can substitute for the Music app for these tasks. In this chapter, you learn the basics—playing music, setting up your library, looking through your library, shopping for music online—plus learn when you must use another tool.

Getting Started with the Music App

The Music app is a new program for playing and managing your music in Windows 8. You can bring in to the Music app the music you've purchased or imported from CDs before Windows 8, and you can purchase new music. As a Windows 8 app, you can play music full screen and enjoy the animated collages that play in the background. Or you can dock the Music app while you do other work in Windows 8. You can play a single song, a playlist of your own design, an entire album, or perhaps all the music you can find for one artist. Some tasks that you might expect to accomplish here in the Music app aren't possible. From using other programs like iTunes from Apple, you might be wondering how you create a music CD or import music from a CD. These capabilities are available from the Windows Media Player program. You can find a brief overview of these tasks in one of the two last sections of this chapter.

To start the Music app, select the tile, as shown in Figure 25.1. If you cannot locate the tile, open the **Charms** bar and then select **Search**. When the Search pane opens, Select **Apps** and then enter **Music** into the search box. Select the Music tile from the list of results on the left side of the screen.

FIGURE 25.1

Select the Music app from the Start screen.

Learning What's Where in the Music App

The Music app is loosely organized into three sections: My Music, New Music, and Popular Music. You pan left or right to access each section:

- **My Music** shows music from your library, as shown in Figure 25.2.

- The latest releases from Microsoft's Xbox LIVE music service are presented in **now playing**, as shown in Figure 25.3.

- Popular Music presents tunes from a huge library of Xbox Music selections.

FIGURE 25.2

The My Music area shows music from your library.

The App bar plays an important role in the Music app, presenting the exact commands you need, no matter what you're doing in the app. For example, as shown in Figure 25.4, when you play music, the App bar presents commands to play the next song, repeat the current song, and more.

- As a reminder, to display the App bar, either right-click or swipe up from the bottom middle of the screen.

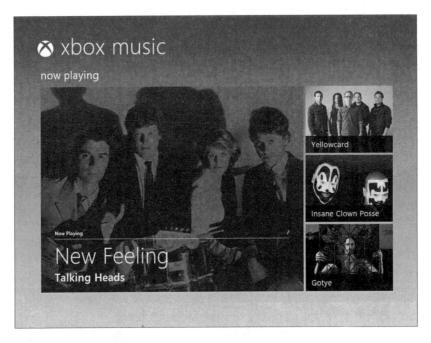

FIGURE 25.3

now playing *places you two clicks or taps away from the most popular music or whatever music you are playing in the Music app.*

FIGURE 25.4

The App bar gives you access to commands you would see on an MP3 player as you play music in the Music app.

Setting Up Your Xbox LIVE Account

A few seconds after the apps starts, Windows 8 tries to sign-in to Xbox LIVE with the account you used to sign-in to Windows. If you have not created your account yet, open the **Settings** charm and select **Account**. If the screen shown in Figure 25.5 appears, select **Try Again**. After doing so, the screen shown in Figure 25.6 appears. Enter your first name, select the Marketing options if you want to receive information in email, and then select **I Accept**.

FIGURE 25.5

You may have to retry your connection with the Xbox LIVE service to create your account.

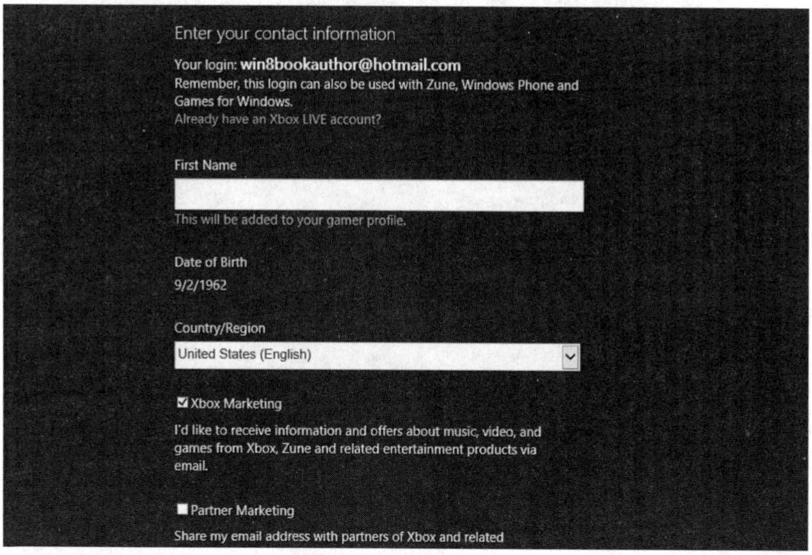

FIGURE 25.6

Your account is initially created after you supply just a few pieces of information.

After accepting the provisions of your account, you're next presented with some information about your account, most notably your gamertag. The gamertag is ID you use to identify yourself in the Xbox LIVE universe. Select Account. At this point, Windows 8 finishes creating your account, and you are returned to the app. You can browse through the videos in the app, including rent a title that interests you. To set up your account for purchases and to perform any kind of account maintenance, open the Settings charm again and select **Account**. A menu of account choices appears, as shown in Figure 25.7, from which you can supply credit card information to pay for music you want to download and own or simply want to listen to with a Xbox Music Pass account. You can also manage other aspects of your account from the same screen. If you have any questions about the Xbox LIVE service, visit www.xbox.com. Microsoft often times make changes to the services, plus promotions are usually available. Visit the site to read the most up-to-date rules and news. Your account details appear in the Music app, as shown in Figure 25.7.

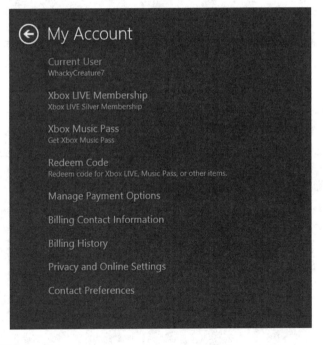

FIGURE 25.7

Once your account is created, you are linked to the Xbox LIVE service.

Loading Your Music into Windows 8

Along with buying new music, the whole point of the app to listen to your music, right? Well, before doing so, you need to bring your music into the Music app. If you have no digital music, that is, you have never purchased music online and you have never imported CD music onto your computer, you can skip this section. However, you should be prepared for your library to grow quickly (and your expenses to rise as quickly) because the Music app makes it incredibly tempting and easy to buy new music.

The Music app does a lot with a little. The app presents an attractive, well-laid-out, informative, and well-organized library of music, simply by moving your music files to the correct spot in your file system. As you read shortly, you can get the same benefits if you simply specify where your music collection is located rather than moving your music. The point is there are a number of benefits to the Windows 8 design that don't commit you to a specific system of storing your music file, as is the case with iTunes.

You have two options to bring your music into the Music app:

- You can simply link to your existing collection of music, even if it's on another computer or is on a removable drive.
- The other option is to either copy or move your entire collection from a different system to the computer running Windows 8.

The following two sections each explain how to connect your music to Windows 8 using these approaches.

How to Link Your Music

Linking to your music takes advantage of the libraries function in Windows Explorer. A library is a special grouping of file that consolidates folders from different locations on your computer to make all of the folders appear to be in the same location. The Music library is a built-in library in Windows 8. The Music app uses the music library to populate the My Music section. You can find information in Chapter 15, "Organizing Files and Folders with Windows Explorer," for instruction on working with libraries. Be sure the Music library points to all of the locations in which music is stored on your computer, as shown in Figure 25.8. These locations can included networked folders and removable drives. Keep in mind if you cannot reach the network or you cannot travel with your removable drive that you will not have access to your entire collection of music.

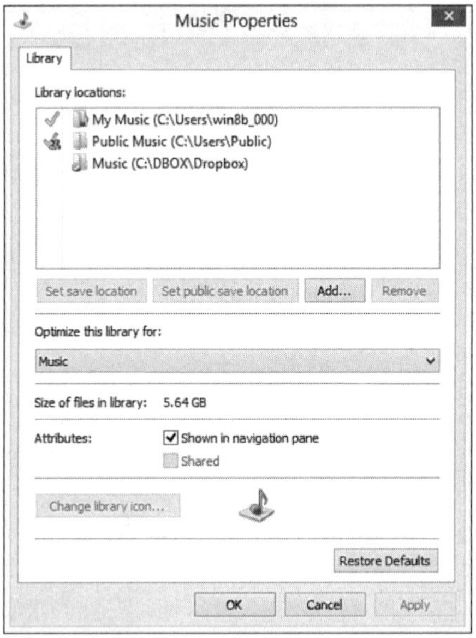

FIGURE 25.8

The Music Library points to all of the music on your computer. The Music app leverages the Music library to present your music in the app.

How to Move Your Music

Follow these steps to move your music to the computer running Windows 8:

1. The first step is to prepare your music. It will be easier, but not required, to move your music if all your music is in a single folder or grouped in subfolders within a single folder.

2. Check that your Windows 8 computer has enough free disk space to accommodate your music. Ensure that you have more than 10% of the total drive capacity available after copying your library.

For example, say that your music takes up 10GB, you have 250GB hard drive, and 50GB is free. When you add your music to your hard drive, you have just 40GB free space remaining, but 40GB is greater than 10%, so in this example, you are clear.

3. Move or copy your music folder to the My Music folder on the Windows 8 computer. You may need to use a removable drive to move the folder, or you can use a homegroup network to complete it.

4. Open the Music app. Check **My Music** to verify your music is present.

Browsing Through Your Music

You can easily review your music library in the Music App. You might review your library to verify you set up your music library in Windows Explorer correctly. More likely, you'll browse through your library looking for something interesting to play.

To look through all your music, pan all the way to the left, and click or tap **My Music**. The screen shown in Figure 25.9 appears. From My Music, you can

- Group and sort your library.

- See all the music for an artist or on an album.

- Create a playlist.

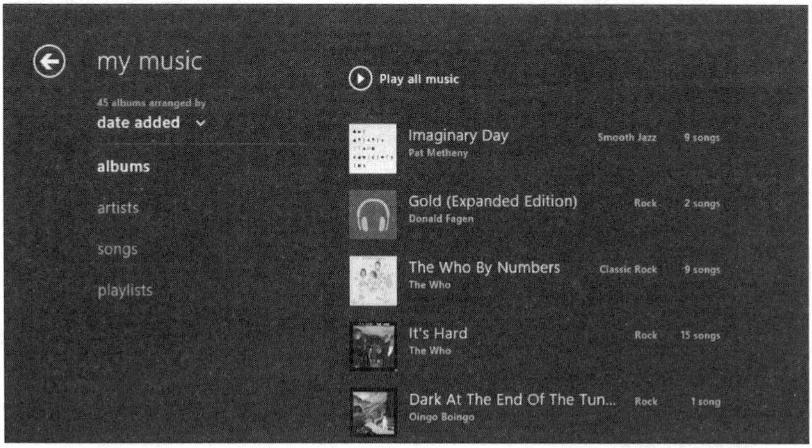

FIGURE 25.9

My Music gives you the opportunity to review your entire library.

Inside of My Music, you can select **albums**, **songs**, **artists**, or **playlists** to see your library grouped by one of those items.

You can also sort your library inside of the group you selected. Your sort order can be by the date the song was added to your library, year the music was released, genre, artist, or alphabetically. Figure 25.10 shows how to select the sort order.

When you have one or more album covers on the screen, such as in My Music, you can click or tap to see the details about an album (see Figure 25.11).

FIGURE 25.10

The sort options appear below the current displayed sort order.

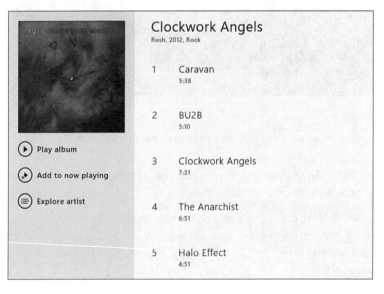

FIGURE 25.11

Select any album cover to play one or more songs from the album or add the album to the Now Playing list.

An album cover also can link you to details about an artist, where you can inspect all the music loaded for that artist. Selecting **Explorer artist** sends you to the Artist Details page, where you can view all the artist's work and buy music, filling in your collection. This is a convenient way to shop for music for an artist.

Playing Music

You can play a song from a number of places in the app. Just look for the Play button, which appears on an artists' album page, as well as in album song list when you have an album selected (see Figure 25.12). To add a song to the queue of music to play, select **Add to now playing**. To play a selection immediately, select **Play.**

FIGURE 25.12

Play a single tune by selecting the song in the album playlist.

As the song plays, the Now Playing panel on the screen shows your song. To see the album cover collage while your music plays, select the **Now Playing** panel.

Purchasing Music

You can purchase music wherever you see the Buy buttons. You can buy one or more individual songs or complete albums, as shown in Figure 25.13. Here's more of what you need to know about purchasing music:

- Music purchased in the Music app is funded from a Microsoft Xbox LIVE account. You can attach a credit card to your Xbox LIVE account.

- Songs you purchase appear in your music library. To see the file, open Windows Explorer and look at the Music library. You can read about libraries in Chapter 15.

- If you have not created an account when you purchase music, you will be prompted for billing information.

 TIP   You can see a song's file without first starting Windows Explorer. Select the song and then open the Apps bar. (Right-click or swipe up from the bottom of the screen.) Select the Open File button.

- To find music in the Xbox LIVE music marketplace, open the Search charm and enter the artist name or song. You should the portrait for the Music app selected, as shown in Figure 25.14.

- To listen to Xbox LIVE music as you like without having to purchase every song you want to hear, purchase an Xbox music pass. This allows you play any music you like.

Alone/But Never Alone	
Larry Carlton, 1985, Jazz, Verve	
1 Smiles And Smiles To Go 5:47	
2 Perfect Peace 4:29	
▶ Preview	
🛒 Buy album	3 Carrying You 4:00
☰ Explore artist	
	4 The Lord's Prayer 5:10
Get unlimited music with Xbox Music Pass!	5 High Steppin' 5:45

FIGURE 25.13

The Buy button can be found on portraits for songs and albums you don't own.

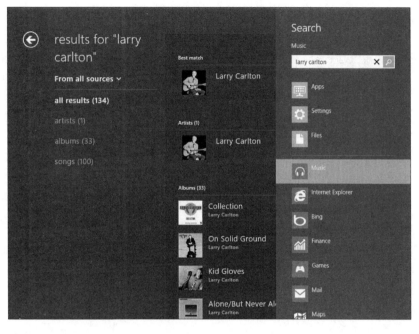

FIGURE 25.14

Use the Windows 8 Search charm to locate music at Xbox LIVE.

Importing and Creating Music CDs

So far in this chapter, you've read about managing music stored on your computers and hard drives, as well as music in the Xbox marketplace. With all the great music in your library, it's a sure bet you'll want to create a music CD of your own design. And it's also a good bet that you'll come across CDs in your home or office whose music you want to add to your library. These two likely scenarios are the focus of this section.

As mentioned in the first paragraph of this chapter, the Music app isn't up to the task to address all your music enjoyment needs. To import a new CD into your library or to create a new CD, use a desktop app called Windows Media Player. Users of past versions probably know the Windows Media Player, which is a handy tool that manages all your digital media, such as photos, movies, videos, and music.

 NOTE If you use your Windows 8 computer as part of a home theater setup, where you control it from the comfort of a couch, you should look into using Windows Media Center, a purchasable add-on for Windows 8 that comes free with Windows 8 Pro.

Importing Music from a CD

You can import songs from music CDs using Windows Media Player. The music you import becomes part of your music library. In almost all cases, Windows can identify the CD, so the name of the artist, the name of the album, and the name of each selection is loaded into the library. If it doesn't, you need to enter that information manually.

TIP If you find that you need to use Windows Media Player often, it's not a bad idea to pin it to your Start screen. Just search for Windows Media Player using the Search charm, right-click (or tap and hold) it in the search results, and select Pin to Start.

Follow these steps to import music from a CD:

1. Open the Windows Media Player. The program opens on the Desktop, as shown in Figure 25.15.

FIGURE 25.15

Windows Media Player runs on the Desktop.

2. Load your CD into the CD drive. Wait while Windows recognizes your CD. Do not press any buttons for a few moments.

3. The CD's tracks plus a snapshot of the cover artwork associated the CD appears, as shown in Figure 25.16.

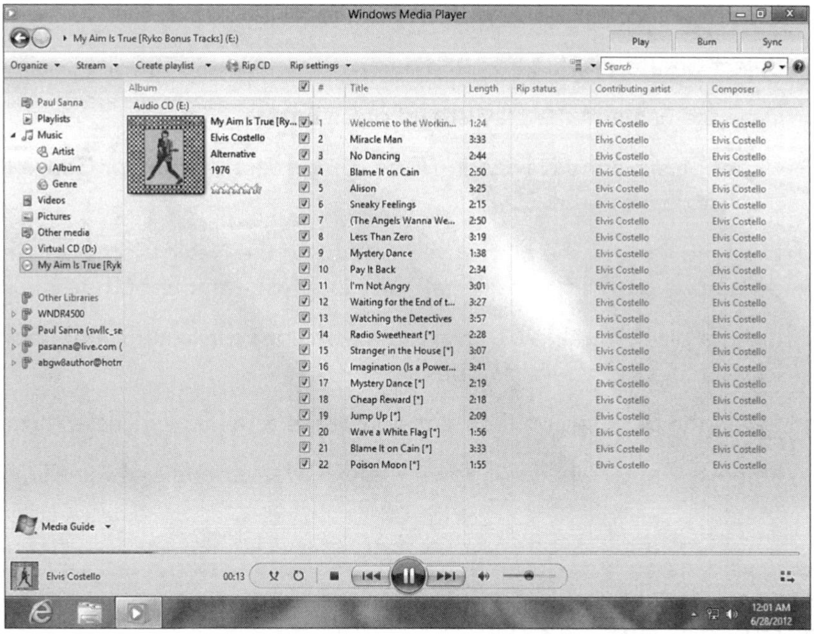

FIGURE 25.16

The CD's contents appear enabling you to deselect songs you do not want to import.

4. Select **Rip Settings** from the menu.

5. Select the first command on the menu: **Rip and the Name of Your CD**.

6. Wait for each track's **Rip Status** to become Ripped to Library. You may eject the CD when complete.

Creating a Playlist and Music CD

If you've used any previous version of iTunes or Windows Media Player, you probably know about creating playlists. Playlists are custom song selections that you pick to play together. Maybe it's a "best of" Tom Petty mix or a selection of your favorite classical music. A playlist can be whatever you want it to be.

Burning a CD using Windows Media Player is just an extension to create a playlist, which is why they are covered together here. To burn a CD, you first need to create a playlist. Follow these steps to create a music CD based on a playlist you've created:

1. Open Windows Media Player. Note the tree structure of your media on your computer on the left side of the screen. This is known as the **Navigation Tree**.

2. If you have a playlist you want to burn to a CD, skip to step 7.

3. Select **Create Playlist** from the menu. Select **Create Playlist** again.

4. Type the name of the playlist and press **Enter**.

5. Under Music in the Navigation Tree, click **Artist**, **Album**, or **Genre** to choose music to burn to the CD.

6. Drag the song to the playlist you created in the Navigation Tree. Repeat steps 5–6 until the playlist contains all the music you want to burn to the CD.

7. Insert a blank writable CD into a drive on your computer capable of burning CDs. Select the playlist to burn.

8. Select the **Burn** tab on the right side of the screen. Next, select **Start Burn**.

9. Remove the CD when Windows Media Player reports that the CD is complete.

THE ABSOLUTE MINIMUM

Keep the following points in mind when you're finished reading this chapter:

- You can play existing music in the Music app either by moving the music directly into your Windows 8 machine or by using the library feature in File Explorer to indicate where the music is located.

- You may also connect to a music source over a home network, but this solution will fail when you move your computer out of range of the network, such as if one of the computers is a laptop you typically travel with.

- Either create an account in the Xbox LIVE marketplace or have a credit card at hand if you plan to purchase music.

- A large number of features are available throughout the Music app. Open the App bar when you listen to music, look at an album list, or read about an artist to see options available.

- You need to use Windows Media Player if you want to import music into your library from a CD or if you want to create a new CD.

26

GAMETIME WITH WINDOWS 8 AND XBOX 360

Microsoft's Xbox LIVE service and the Xbox 360 console together play an important role in Windows 8, and the role is a fun one. Windows 8 leverages the console and its Xbox LIVE online service to bring music, movies, videos, and games to Windows. This digital content is presented and managed in Windows 8 through the new Music, Video, and Games apps. Read Chapter 24 for information about movies and videos in Windows 8 and Chapter 25 for information about playing and purchasing music in Windows 8. With the new Xbox Smartglass app, you can control Xbox from your Windows 8 device, delivering Xbox content right to your tablet, server, laptop, or desktop Windows 8 hardware. In this short chapter, you'll learn how to connect your Windows 8 device to Xbox 360. You'll also get an overview of the Games app. Of course, the prerequisite for this chapter is that you own an Xbox 360 platform. Without one, your read of this chapter should be very short.

Using Xbox LIVE with Windows 8

Xbox LIVE is Microsoft's online gaming and digital media services. The service has evolved since it was introduced around 2002, and it is certain to continue to grow and evolve, especially as the services it provides become more a part of Windows 8. Here are the features that Xbox LIVE offers today to the Xbox 360 console community:

- Enables players to compete online in Xbox games. Members can also try out demos of new games, as well as purchase games.

- Enables members to enjoy music, movies, and TV shows from an enormous library of selections. Content can be rented, played, or purchased; although not every selection can be rented.

- Enables members to share content, chat, issue voice commands, consume content from other providers (such as HBO), find opponents, find people who share the same interests, and much more

 NOTE If you think all this Xbox LIVE stuff sounds like the Microsoft Zune service, you've been paying attention. The Zune brand is being discontinued, and Microsoft is transitioning its digital media content to the Xbox LIVE brand. The videos and music available from Xbox LIVE today are provided by the former Zune services.

A BRIEF HISTORY OF THE XBOX

Before diving into the Xbox LIVE service, it makes sense to go back in time and review the origins of all this cool digital content: the Xbox 360 console. Released in late 2001, the Xbox was Microsoft's first game console. Less than 5 years later, Microsoft launched the Xbox 360, which has gone on to become the most successful game console of its generation.

Few other aspects of a game console contribute more to its success (or demise) than the quality of the games that run it. The Xbox-only game *Halo*, with its three major installments (and a couple spin-offs) is among the most popular console games of all time. The Xbox 360 is also noted for its comfortable, innovative controller design, its sharp high-definition (HD) graphics, plus the online environment it creates for players. It's easy to find friends to compete against online, as well as to download game demos and to experience movies, videos, and music online.

Some of these benefits don't translate exactly to Windows 8. Here's how Windows 8 works with Xbox LIVE's services:

- From the Music app, you can shop the Xbox LIVE music service, also known as **Xbox music**, for both current and past songs and albums. You can audition music you might like, and then purchase and download music you want to keep. You can snap the Music app next to another app you're working with, giving you some entertainment as you toil away.

- From the Video app, you can review the Xbox LIVE library of movies and TV shows, also known as **Xbox videos**, both current and past. You can rent some titles and purchase and download others. You can watch the video content on your device, including project it to a wall or screen to get the movie theater experience.

- From the Xbox LIVE Games app, you can play games against other Xbox LIVE gamers. You can also shop for Xbox games, as well as download game demos and full games. If you were impressed by the *Solitaire* game loaded into many versions of Windows over the years, you will be astounded by the great Xbox games you can run on your computer or tablet.

- With the Windows 8 SmartGlass app, you can control Xbox 360 from your Windows 8 device, as well as review Xbox content on that device. Your Windows 8 device becomes a remote control for Xbox, as well as another display for Xbox.

Access to all this great content on Xbox LIVE does not come automatically. You need to connect your Windows account to Xbox LIVE in order to enable all the cool functionality described above. If you have already set up the Music app or the Video app with an Xbox account, then your job in this chapter is easy. You use the same Xbox LIVE account throughout Windows 8. If not, read the next section to understand how to join your Windows account to Xbox.

Setting Up Your Xbox LIVE Account

Each time you start the Xbox Games or Xbox SmartGlass apps, Windows 8 tries to sign-in to Xbox LIVE. You are sure to notice the "Signing in" message on the top-right corner of the screen. If you have not created your account yet, open the **Settings** charm and select **Account**. If the screen shown in Figure 26.1 appears, select **Try Again**. After doing so, the screen shown in Figure 26.2 should appear. Enter your first name, select the Marketing options if you want to receive information in email; then select **I Accept**.

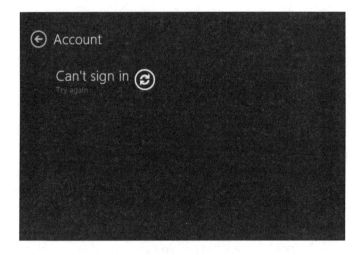

FIGURE 26.1

Depending on demand on the Xbox LIVE servers, as well as maintenance going on, you might see an error message when you try to sign-in.

FIGURE 26.2

The first step in creating your Xbox LIVE account is to provide your name.

After accepting the provisions of your account, you're next presented with some information about your account, most notably your gamertag. The gamertag is ID you use to identify yourself throughout the Xbox universe. To continue, select **Account**.

At this point, Windows 8 finishes creating your account, and you are returned to the app. To set up your account for purchases, such as to buy games and other Xbox LIVE content, as well as to perform any kind of account maintenance, open the Settings charm again and select **Account**. A menu of account choices appears, as shown in Figure 26.3, from which you can supply credit card information to pay for whatever purchases you make.

You can also manage other aspects of your account from the same screen. If you have any questions about the Xbox LIVE service, visit www.xbox.com. Microsoft often times make changes to the services, so you should visit the site often to read the most up-to-date rules and news, as well as to see about promotions. Your account details appear in the Music app, as shown in Figure 26.4.

FIGURE 26.3

There are several options available to maintain your account.

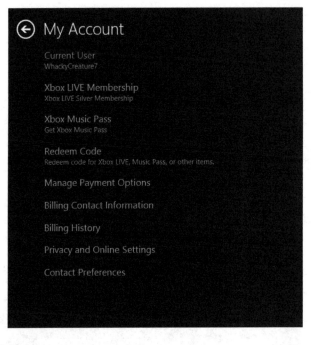

FIGURE 26.4

Once your account is created, you are linked into the Xbox LIVE service.

NOTE If you signed in to Windows 8 with a local account and you want to enjoy the Xbox Games, you have two choices. You can convert your local account to a Windows account or create a Windows Live account if you don't have one. You won't be forced to sign in to Windows 8 with this new account. Rather, you use it only to access Xbox LIVE. You are prompted for this account when you access the Xbox apps. It's clearly much more convenient to sign in to Windows 8 with a Windows account.

Controlling Xbox from Windows 8

Xbox SmartGlass is a Windows 8 app that enables the computer or other Windows 8 device to control an Xbox 360 console. At first thought, perhaps you don't consider this to be all that useful. Why would anyone want to use a computer to control Xbox when the console's own controls are easy to use? Also, why would you want to be tethered to a computer to manage your console? These are reasonable questions. Here are, hopefully, some reasonable answers:

- Its midday and you are already thinking of the evening's activity. There is a movie that you missed at the theater that is now available to download and watch online. Use Xbox SmartGlass to either buy or rent the movie so that the movie is ready to go when you get home.

- A game you have been looking forward to playing on Xbox Live Arcade finally is released. You can't wait to play it, but you have an evening of work in front of you. With Windows 8, you can snap your work to one side of the screen, and snap Xbox SmartGlass to the other side. This way, you can do some work and do some gaming at about the same time!

- You have a new Windows 8 tablet. Use the Xbox SmartGlass installed on that tablet to control everything you see on the screen right from your couch or favorite chair.

- You have an outstanding monitor attached to your computer. Use SmartGlass to use Xbox 360 on the device that can access that monitor.

- You can play your Xbox 360 anywhere you like, as long as your Windows 8 device can reach your console over your home network.

Installing Xbox SmartGlass

The Xbox SmartGlass app is available in the Windows Store. In addition to installing the application from the store, you also need access to your Xbox 360 console to set everything up. Be sure your Xbox 360 is configured to connect to the Internet and has any available software updates.

 NOTE Your Xbox console checks for updates automatically when it's connected to the Internet. When it notifies you that an update is available, all you need to do is give it permission to download and install it.

Follow these steps to install the app from the store:

1. Open the Windows Store. The Store tile is on the Start screen.

2. Open the **Search** charm.

3. Enter "Xbox" into the search box, and then select **Xbox SmartGlass** from the results on the left.

4. Select **Install**.

5. After the installation process finishes, open the app.

6. Do not select Connect. Instead, turn your attention to the Xbox 360 console.

7. Turn on your Xbox 360 console.

8. On the console, select **Settings** and then select **Console Settings**.

9. Locate the Xbox SmartGlass setting.

10. Turn Xbox SmartGlass to **Available**.

11. Go back to Windows 8 and select **Connect**.

12. If everything is connected properly, you see a message confirming the connection.

Using Xbox SmartGlass

The Xbox SmartGlass is an app that enables you to manage some aspects of your Xbox 360 console. You can direct the console to download or purchase content from one of the Xbox LIVE marketplaces, as shown in Figure 26.5 and, depending on the game, you can even control the game while you play it from your Windows 8 device.

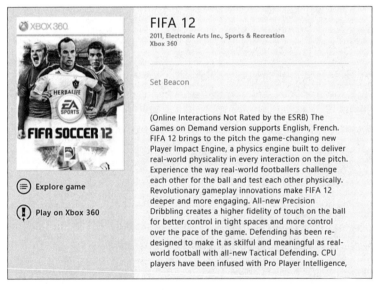

FIGURE 26.5

The SmartGlass app provides access to the Xbox LIVE services as if you were working at the console.

Before commanding Xbox 360 to download great new music or to blow up the bridge separating you from the bad guys in a fun, interactive game, you need of course to start the app. To start the Xbox SmartGlass app, locate the tile on the

Start screen (see Figure 26.6) and then select it. SmartGlass is a new Windows 8 type app, so be sure to review Chapter 3, "Learning Windows 8 Basics," if you need help navigating through the screens and options.

FIGURE 26.6

Start the SmartGlass app from the Start screen.

With the SmartGlass app open, you navigate through menus and screens on your device as if you operating a controller and viewing the monitor to which Xbox is connected. You can use your mouse, finger, or keyboard to navigate through the app. Most of the content you can access is already available through the Music, Video, or Games apps. When you see content you are interested in, just select it to see more detail. Depending on what you selected, you see options like:

- Explore

- Play a game on Xbox 360

- Play a move trailer

- Review information about an artist

You will typically be transferred to the appropriate app when you need to see detail or to review the content without Xbox 360.

When you do need to use the Xbox controller interface, such as to play a game, open the App bar and select **Xbox Controls**, as shown in Figure 26.7.

Figure 26.8 shows how to send commands that simulate your use of the Xbox controller by clicking or touching locations on your computer monitor or tablet screen.

FIGURE 26.7

You engage the Xbox controls from a command on the App bar.

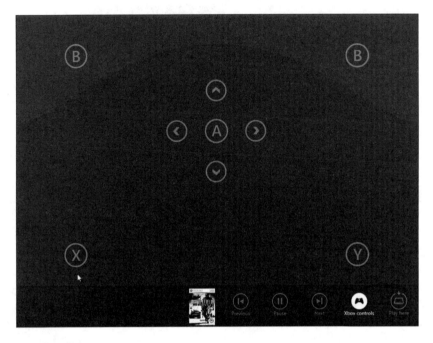

FIGURE 26.8

You tap or click your computer or tablet screen matching the buttons you would press on your Xbox controller.

Learning the Xbox Games App

Perhaps the most fun-filled app in Windows 8 is the Xbox Games app, though it is referred to often simply as Games. To start the app, select it from the Start screen. The Games app is organized in a few sections. As you scroll across the screen, you can review

- Current games Microsoft and its partners are promoting in the Spotlight section

- Windows 8 games you can acquire from the Windows store

- Xbox games you can download and then play from your Windows 8 device with the SmartGlass app

- Review your gamer profile

Fortunately, as is expected, this app is simple to use. Here are some tips for use with the app:

- If you purchase an Xbox 360 game, it can only be used on the console to which it was first downloaded.

- If you issue the command to play a game, you are automatically switched to the SmartGlass app.

- When you install a Windows 8 game from the Windows store, you can also launch it from the Games app.

So that's it for the overview. It would be troublesome if a games application required long instruction. The best advice would be to click where intuition tells you to. The game should do most of the work for you, at least until the competition starts.

THE ABSOLUTE MINIMUM

Keep these points in mind even after you've completed reading this chapter:

- The Xbox movies, videos, and games apps make content available to you (the user) from the Xbox LIVE service.

- You must supply a Windows account to access the Xbox LIVE content that plays through the Xbox-powered apps in Windows 8. You may still sign in to Windows with a local account, but you need to supply your Windows account credentials every time you access one of the apps.

- Xbox LIVE prompts you for information to connect your Windows account to Xbox LIVE when you open one of the Xbox apps. After you answer the prompts, you won't hear from Xbox LIVE again.

- You must supply a credit card to your Xbox LIVE account if you want to purchase music or movies, as well as to rent videos.

- Games you acquire from the Windows store can be played from the Games app.

Index

Q-R

S

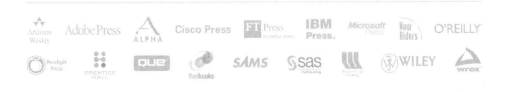

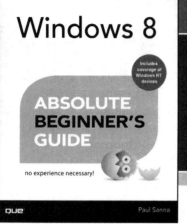

Windows 8

ABSOLUTE BEGINNER'S GUIDE

Includes coverage of Windows RT devices

no experience necessary!

que

Paul Sanna

Safari®
Books Online

FREE
Online Edition

Your purchase of *Windows 8 Absolute Beginner's Guide* includes access to a free online edition for 45 days through the **Safari Books Online** subscription service. Nearly every Que book is available online through **Safari Books Online**, along with thousands of books and videos from publishers such as Addison-Wesley Professional, Cisco Press, Exam Cram, IBM Press, O'Reilly Media, Prentice Hall, Sams, and VMware Press.

Safari Books Online is a digital library providing searchable, on-demand access to thousands of technology, digital media, and professional development books and videos from leading publishers. With one monthly or yearly subscription price, you get unlimited access to learning tools and information on topics including mobile app and software development, tips and tricks on using your favorite gadgets, networking, project management, graphic design, and much more.

Activate your FREE Online Edition at
informit.com/safarifree

STEP 1: Enter the coupon code: DVGHEBI.

STEP 2: New Safari users, complete the brief registration form.
Safari subscribers, just log in.

If you have difficulty registering on Safari or accessing the online edition,
please e-mail customer-service@safaribooksonline.com